W9-BJA-662

WITHDRAWN

EX LIBRIS

SOUTH ORANGE
PUBLIC LIBRARY

POLITICS
FOR BETTER
OR WORSE

Critical Readers

Edmund R. Hanauer, Babson College
Richard D. Humphrey, The Loop College
Ronald F. Lipton, Southhampton College
Michael A. Weinstein, Purdue University
Herbert R. Winter, Rhode Island College
Truman D. Wood, Mankato State College

POLITICS
FOR BETTER
OR WORSE

ALFRED de GRAZIA

Professor of Social Theory in Government

New York University

Scott, Foresman and Company

Glenview, Illinois   Brighton, England

320/
De

Library of Congress Catalog Card Number: 77-188617
ISBN: 0-673-07660-1

Copyright © 1973 Scott, Foresman and Company, Glenview, Illinois.
Philippines Copyright 1973 Scott, Foresman and Company.
All Rights Reserved.
Printed in the United States of America.

Regional offices of Scott, Foresman and Company are located in Dallas,
Texas; Glenview, Illinois; Oakland, New Jersey; Palo Alto, California;
Tucker, Georgia; and Brighton, England.

Acknowledgements

The cover art is based on one of the earliest known caricatures in human
history, from the time of the Egyptian pharaoh, Ramses III

All cartoons in the book, with the exceptions of the ornaments on pages 88,
90, 335, 336, and 343, were completed and executed by Clark Weinreb (El
Clarko) on the basis of the cartoon ideas and scripts of the author, and his
artistic contribution is gratefully acknowledged.

The author and publisher are grateful for permission to reprint the following
material:

Page 127.   Data from the Survey Research Center Study #473 by John Appel.
            Reprinted by permission of the Institute for Social Research (The
            University of Michigan, Ann Arbor).

Pages 155–156.   The charts "Bacchus, Apollo, Hercules" and "Leader-Fol-
            lower Groups" are modified after similar charts in *Elements
            of Political Science* by Alfred de Grazia. Copyright 1952.
            Reprinted by permission of the author.

Page 160.   "The Rest" and the excerpts from "Commission" from Ezra
            Pound, *Personae*. (British Title: *Collected Shorter Poems*) Copy-
            right 1926 by Ezra Pound. Reprinted by permission of New
            Directions Publishing Corporation and Faber and Faber Limited.

Pages 172–173.   Editorial from *The Indianapolis News* (Jan. 8, 1972). Re-
            printed by permission.

Page 176.   Quotation from "The Papers and The Papers" by Samuel Abt from *International Herald Tribune* (May 9, 1972), p. 12. Reprinted by permission of *International Herald Tribune*.

Page 178.   Quotation from an article by Warren Weaver from *The New York Times* (Oct. 25, 1970). Copyright © 1970 by The New York Times Company. Reprinted by permission.

Pages 189–91.   Quotation from "Additions to the Book of Esther" from *The New English Bible*. © the Delegates of the Oxford University Press and the Cambridge University Press 1961, 1970. Reprinted by permission.

Page 199.   Data based on a national representative sample of 1,533 workers in an Institute survey conducted in late 1969. Institute for Social Research *Newsletter* (The University of Michigan, Ann Arbor); Autumn 1971, p. 5. Reprinted by permission.

Pages 229–30.   Quotation from "Salvationist censorship condemned by author" from *The Times* (Sept. 18, 1970). Reproduced from *The Times* by permission.

Page 238.   Catalog entries from the 1969 *General Services Administration Stock Catalog*, Part II.

Page 279.   The article "The Rich Get Richer, etc." by Tom Wicker from *The New York Times* (June 29, 1972). Copyright © 1972 by The New York Times Company. Reprinted by permission.

Page 286.   Editorial from *Chicago Tribune* (Oct. 29, 1971). Reprinted courtesy of the *Chicago Tribune*.

Pages 319–20, 345.   Quotations from *Four Essays on China and World Communism* by Mao Tse-Tung. Copyright © 1972 by Lancer Books, Inc. Reprinted by permission.

Pages 322–23.   Quotation from "Behavioral Study of Obedience" by Stanley Milgram *Journal of Abnormal and Social Psychology* 67. Copyright 1963 by the American Psychological Association, and reproduced by permission.

Page 329.   Quotation from "The Stake at SALT—Survival" by Bernard T. Feld from *The New York Times* (Dec. 9, 1970). Copyright © 1970 by The New York Times Company. Reprinted by permission.

Page 334.   "A Soviet History Omits Big Purges" by Theordore Shabad from *The New York Times* (Jan. 8, 1972). Copyright © 1972 by The New York Times Company. Reprinted by permission.

Page 350–51.   The curriculum in the appendix is from *The Behavioral Sciences: Essays in Honor of George A. Lundberg*. Reprinted by permission of the Behavioral Research Council.

The publishers wish to express their thanks for use of the following material:

Page 48. Portraits of Plato and Sigmund Freud, The Bettmann Archive. Portrait of the author, courtesy of the author.

Page 105. Portrait of Guiseppe Zangara, United Press International.

Page 106. Portrait of Less Harvey Oswald, United Press International.

Page 154. Photograph of Mount Rushmore, Sam Falk from Monkmeyer Press.

Page 155. Photograph of Abu Simbel, Monkmeyer Press.

Page 258. Photographs of old and new housing, courtesy of the author.

Page 358. "The Plagiarist," a caricature by Pigal, Historical Pictures Service.

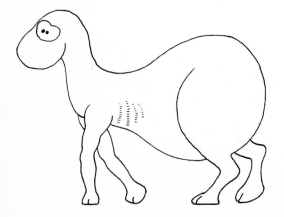

Dedication

To Uncle Charlie,
as kind a man as ever
graced the earth,
who travelled from
town to town
(wherever trains stopped)
with his satchel and gloves,
a professional fighter
with a calling card:
"Charles 'Kid' Lucca,
Not the Champ,
but will fight
anybody who thinks he is."
Why, America?

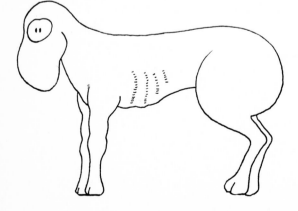

Preface

Once upon a time, when I started up a journal called *PROD**, some friends called it the *Mad Magazine* of Political Science. No doubt a similar kindness will be visited upon the present book. I call it *Politics for Better or Worse* because it reflects a career of hope-despair, knowledge-ignorance, activity-withdrawal—one of those love-hate relationships that compose so many love (hate) affairs. Philosophically, you might elevate its image by calling it an existential, phenomenological, pragmatic trip through a duststorm of facts and theories.

The scope of the book is broad; I can't help it. It was intended to be a text that would introduce political science to everyone, but I can see the book infiltrating into general introductory courses in social science, elementary courses in social problems, courses in American Government, American Society, and American Civilization, elementary courses in political philosophy, and so on; I dream of "adult" education courses using it, of schools of education, of underground readers in Athens and Paris, and of serializing it for *Psychology Today, The Rolling Stone*, and the *Village Voice*.

Alfred de Grazia

New York City

* *Political Research: Organization and Design*, later the *American Behavioral Scientist*, whose editorship I surrendered in 1965.

Table of Contents

POLITICS
FOR BETTER
OR WORSE

Introduction

As a boy I somehow got the idea that prayer was a fine thing, but you should not pray for too much lest God be angry. I think that the idea is ancient; the Greek gods, for instance, were supposed to be jealous of a man who asked too much of life or who was too able. So I shall begin my book with only a small wish, namely that you understand this introduction, or, if not that, that you skip it without further ado and come back to it when all else is done.

*   *   *   *   *

Political science, like sociology, deals with *human relations.* Inanimate things and nonhuman animals are left, for the most part, to the *natural sciences.* Political science can take any encounter between people and fit it into its scheme of things, just as a physicist can take any atom, or a biologist any cell, and teach some basic rules of science from it.

When *Al shakes hands with Bill,* a political scientist can begin talking about the principles of *conflict* and *cooperation* or the *equality* of the two men (equals shake hands; where it is believed that men are *unequal,* as in a *caste* system, they do not; the giving of the right hand originated as a sign of *good faith* since a man was giving up his stronger arm to the other, rather than swinging a battle-axe at him; etc.). Hence, we say, any human encounter can be the *data* of political science.

Data in political science can be *indirect* as well as direct. From judging what is occurring in actual encounters, we move to judging or inferring what may be occurring *in men's minds* during, prior to, or subsequent to encounters. When the death of Talleyrand, the famous French diplomat, was reported to his lifelong diplomatic antagonist, the equally famous

19

Austro-Hungarian diplomat, Metternich, his first words were, "I wonder what he's up to now."[1]

Political science deals also with *words,* or, in a broader sense, *symbols,* in two ways. The first is as *data,* because so many human encounters are through communications. When a newspaper describes "a friendly meeting between the Soviet and West German Ambassadors," the political scientist wonders about the word "friendly," what it means, and what the two men are talking about.

The second way in which words interest, and bother, political scientists is as *semantics.* Like other scientists, political scientists have to communicate with each other and must use symbols (usually words but sometimes mathematical symbols) for the purpose. So they constantly warn one another about the dangers of using words loosely. "Define your terms!" implies that it is necessary to explain any important word so that you and the people you communicate with are using the same word to refer to the same things. If two boys are referring to some girls as "cows," and grandmother happens by, she will get some strange notions about the sex interests of the new generation.

So much for *data* and *language.* Now, as to *techniques,* there are a great many varieties of these, and I think that their description had better be left to other books, except where a few techniques have to be explained in order to make a point.

* * * * *

Twenty years ago I wrote a book on the *Elements of Political Science* (New York: Alfred A. Knopf, Inc., 1952). It is still in print in its original form. It was designed for elementary students, but has been used mainly by students studying for degrees in political science. There is very little that I

---

1. The story may not be true. But, as the Italian expression goes, "Se non è vero, è ben trovato," meaning, "Even if it's not true, it's believable." In the pages of this book, there are many "hypotheticals," that is, examples that clarify but are not *data* because they do not refer to actual happenings. We just used one, as "when Al shakes hands with Bill."

would change in that work, were it to be revised. It is about twice the length of this book, but its scope is only one-third as broad. The difference between the two works shows what I believe must be different about political science today.

I am convinced that political science can no longer be introduced solely as the objective analysis of political events. The world is being ravaged by sicknesses of authority, institutions, and technology. This dreadful condition is ever more apparently the result of a lack of goals; a political consensus, founded upon an ethic of man, is lacking.

I feel that the time has come to pull together our views of the good society and to set standards for present and future generations. Students have been aware of this need well ahead of their professors, I fear, even when the former were simply emoting, lamenting, and striking.

Accordingly, I have decided to give equal time to the statement and discussions of the *principles* on which political life *should* be based. I mean to confront fully and frankly the moral problems of the age and to take a stand on them. The field of political philosophy has long been the concern of numerous members of the teaching profession, and some of them no doubt will exclaim now, "Aha, the prodigal son returns!" If so, I hope that they will treat me as well as the prodigal son was treated.[2]

The method of presenting principles here is to put them sharply before you, to show what facts I would face, and what principles are relevant to dealing with such facts. The first two key elements of this book, then, are description and principle. The third key element is application. Simply to state a factual condition is *pure* science. To put the fact to use, however, requires a goal, and this useful goal-directed activity is called *applied* science. (The distinction between the two holds true for any science.)

Permit me to offer an example, the first of many in this book. Indeed, the whole book is based on the same system.

---

2. In any event, there is a difference, I think, between the way ethical and moral principles are handled here and in the "good old days" before political philosophers suffered their crushing defeats at the hands of the administrative scientists and political behaviorists.

PROPOSITION:

People learn many ways of interpreting
politics and behaving politically
as young children even though they are
not aware of it, and they carry these
ways into adult behavior.

PRINCIPLE:

People should solve their political
problems through rational and
peaceful collaboration.

POLICY:

Youngsters should be taught rational
and peaceful collaboration in solving
the kinds of influencing and governing
problems that occur early in life
—in the family, church,
playgrounds, and schools.

Thus, we have a fact in the form of a general descriptive proposition, then
we declare a preference that can be related to the fact (that is, a principle),
and finally recommend how to control the factual conditions by the
application of the preference to social institutions. It is all simplified, of
course, but you can grasp the idea. As a second example (with comments)
we have:

PROPOSITION:

Almost always, when Communist parties
have become partners with other parties
in running a government,
they have seized control of the government
and suppressed the other parties.

Comment: This is a *pure* proposition in political science. It is neutral and can be accepted by men of differing political views as a fact that cannot be disregarded.

   But—it is not completely reliable. The number of instances on which it is based is small, perhaps fifteen. Also, the generalization fails in the cases of Finland, France, and Italy where at times the Communists were participants as a party in the governing coalition. At the very least these cases require explanation. Also, a number of cases consist of countries that were near the Soviet Union, "under its guns" literally. Further, the statement is historical, and historical conditions change.[3] And, finally, it is a little suspicious that someone like the author should select this proposition out of thousands to use as an example; if a person talks incessantly about a certain subject, you have to begin considering whether his obsession masks a prejudice.[4] But hold off making a judgment for now, because you will see that I am not obsessed with this idea at all.

---

   3. For instance, I am now not sure that the Italian Communist party would hold together in a power struggle, nor that its leadership would supress any central, liberal, or socialist opposition, nor that its membership would support such an attempt.

   4. By the same token, when a person (or press or group) studiously avoids a relevant subject, you need to be on the alert for a prejudice, also.

PRINCIPLE:

A person should live a life in which
free opportunity, personal safety,
and access to knowledge are assured,
and these goals should have priority
over other goals.

Comment: This is an ethical statement. Although it does not explain what kind of basic philosophy of man is being advocated, it is obviously related to how a government is run and how a government should behave. It suggests, if you are thinking about the early proposition concerning Communist parties:

POLICY:

Communist parties should be kept out
of coalition governments, unless the cost
of doing so is disastrously high.

Comment: This can be said in many ways. In substance, it is an *applied science* proposition that says to assist humanity in its ideals of freedom, it is important to block the power drives of groups that are known to suppress opposition. There may also be other reasons for the same policy, both good and bad, and scientific or unscientific.

Each of these three statements—the *proposition,* the *principle,* and the *policy*—should be discussed at greater length, and in this book ample discussion will follow all such statements. In fact, Part Two of the book is built around discussion of such triads. Part One gives a rapid scheme for political science as a whole.

It may sound complicated, but we are still in low gear in communicating with each other. Perhaps this verse will explain it all:

3-P's

**In politics or show-biz,
a Proposition's what is;
a Principle's what you wish won;
a Policy, what's to be done.**

*   *   *   *   *

We explained at the start that practically an infinity of human encounters can be used as the data of political science. Therefore, we must limit ourselves to a few of them.

There are also a great many propositions, moral principles, and applications that might be used for presenting political science to you. But just as we must avoid trying to discuss all events, we should avoid trying to cram in all generalizations about them; otherwise, we shall cause bewilderment. Treatment of the great many propositions, principles, and policies (the "3-P's") would have to be shallow; comprehension would be difficult; and the instructor would have to be a veritable encyclopedia.

The 3-P's in the chapters that follow are chosen on grounds of their importance to a science of politics, political ethics, and public policy. I would not argue with anybody who says that *more important* sets could be made up; let him or her do so; we would all benefit. But I would argue that the present lists are far better than taking potluck.

As to the *overall* scheme of political science presented in the first section, this is only one of several such schemes, but I believe that it is one well adapted to assisting intellectual development and cutting through masses of detail. If you were to take down a stack of texts on political science from the library shelves, you might enjoy fitting the general scheme of our first section into the frameworks of its predecessors such as Plato,

Aristotle, Aquinas, Machiavelli, Hobbes, Locke, Mill, Marx, Pareto, Merriam, Mosca, Michels, Dewey, and Lasswell. You should conclude this book knowing a system of political science analysis, and knowing twelve of the broadest propositions, twelve of the moral standpoints on which current controversy centers, and twelve proposals, which, if adopted, would change the political world. That, I believe, may be enough for one course.[5]

5. I might as well disclose the discouraging news that all of political science is not between these covers. The harsh ideals of the Author are exposed in a page of the Appendix, where he lists the courses he would recommend to those who go beyond the present course. Turn back while there is still time!

Part One

Political Science
in
Three Lessons

Lesson Number 1

Classic Comic Strips

In this age of television and billboards, it is only fitting that we should teach political science "quick and dirty."[1] Therefore we present the core of political science in a comic strip, not so lewd as some we've seen in *Evergreen Magazine,* but not so square as "Little Orphan Annie" either.

1. AUTHORITY AND WANTS

"A power over a man's subsistence amounts to a power over his will."

The Federalist No. 79 (1788).

---

1. The phrase comes from "quick and dirty" research projects, in which a scientist has to study some events fast, through a hastily improvised, not quite according-to-Hoyle rule—like finding out what the people of Chicago think of Mayor Daley before releasing a report attacking his conduct during the Democratic National Convention of 1968. Of course, Mayor Daley could act quick and dirty, too, and not in this same scientific sense.

2. SUBJECTION

"If the need be so manifest and urgent, that it is evident that the present need must be remedied by whatever means be at hand . . . , then it is lawful for a man to succour his own need by means of another's property, by taking it openly or secretly; nor is this properly speaking theft or robbery."

St. Thomas Aquinas, *Summa Theologica* (1266–73).

3. ELITE

"Hierarchy always exists, save perhaps among very primitive peoples who live in dispersed units like animals. It follows from this that a community is always governed by a small number of men, by an *elite,* even when it seems to have an absolutely democratic character."

Vilfredo Pareto, *Manuale di Economia Politica* (1919).

4. MYTH AND ALIENATION

"If on the one hand . . . the separation of social functions permits a felicitous development of the spirit of detail otherwise impossible, it spontaneously tends, on the other hand, to snuff out the spirit of togetherness or, at least, to undermine it profoundly. . . . Thus it is that the same principle which has alone permitted the development and extension of general society threatens, in a different aspect, to decompose it into a multitude of incoherent corporations which almost seem not to be of the same species."

Auguste Comte, *Cours de philosophie positive* 4 (1830–42).

5. REVOLUTIONARY IDEOLOGY

"There is the authority of the extraordinary and personal 'gift of grace' (charisma), the absolutely personal devotion and personal confidence in revelation, heroism, or other qualities of individual leadership. This is 'charismatic' domination, as exercised by the prophet or—in the field of politics—by the elected war lord, the plebiscitarian ruler, the great demagogue, or the political party leader."

Max Weber, "Politics as a Vocation" (1918).

6. PERSONAL MOTIVES FIND PUBLIC RATIONALIZATION

The political man displaces private motives onto a public object and rationalizes the displacement in terms of public interest.

Harold D. Lasswell (paraphrased), *Psychopathology and Politics* (1930).

7. RECRUITMENT AND APATHY

"A citizen is in general one who has a share both in ruling and in being ruled; this will not be identical in every kind of constitution, but in the best constitution it means one who is able and who chooses to rule and to be ruled with a view to a life that is in accordance with goodness."

Aristotle, *Politics* (about 350 B.C.).

8. NONCOMMUNICATION

"Man must, except in the nonexample of 'wolf-men,' maintain contact with other men throughout life. He must engage in communicative activity in the light and in the dark, upwind and downwind, in situations of dyadic intimacy and at audibility-absorbing distance, in situations that require absolute quiet, and in situations where competitive wave lengths drown out or distort his own oral contributions or reception. . . . And, above all, he must not destroy the conditions whereby the young can incorporate a language that he, as an adult, neither understands nor is able to teach. . . . Man . . . is a regulated multi-sensory station in a transmission system, a multi-channel interactor."

Ray L. Birdwhistell, "Communication," *International Encyclopedia of the Social Sciences* (1968).

9. CONFRONTATION

"The history of a revolution is for us first of all a history of the forcible entrance of the masses into the realm of rulership over their own destiny."

Leon Trotsky, *The History of the Russian Revolution* I, xvii (1936).

10. ORGANIZED PARTISANSHIP

"Disaffection or disloyalty can be got rid of by putting down the leaders; for in the absence of a leader or leaders, the people are easily governed and they will not take part in the intrigues of enemies."

Kautilya, *Arthasāstra* (between 300 B.C. and 400 A.D.).

11. A CONSTITUTIONAL FORMULA

"Every constitution . . . is a result of changes in the balance of class forces; it expresses the will and interest of the classes in power, guarantees the principles of such social and state order as is advantageous for and agreeable with the interests of these classes. . . . The Soviet constitution embodies the principles of socialist democracy, it is a genuinely democratic institution."

A. I. Lepyoshkin (1962) quoted by Carl J. Friedrich,
"Constitutions and Constitutionalism" (1968).

12. REVOLT OF THE MASSES

"During the eighteenth and nineteenth centuries, 'the people' had learned that it was sovereign, but did not believe it. Today the idea has been changed into a reality, not only in legislation, which is the mere framework of public life, but in the heart of every individual, whatever his ideas may be, and even if he be a reactionary in his ideas, that is to say, *even when he attacks and castigates institutions by which those rights are sanctioned.*"

José Ortega y Gasset, *The Revolt of the Masses* (1932).

13. FORMAL *vs.* REAL CHANGE

"People always have been and they always will be stupid victims of deceit and self-deception in politics, until they learn behind every kind of moral, religious, political, social phrase, declaration and promise to seek out the interests of this or that class or classes."

V. I. Lenin, *The Three Sources and Three Constituent Parts of Marxism* (1913).

14. IRON LAW OF OLIGARCHY

"The democratic currents of history resemble successive waves. They break ever on the same shoal. They are ever renewed. This enduring spectacle is simultaneously encouraging and depressing. When democracies have gained a certain stage of development, they undergo a gradual transformation, adopting the aristocratic spirit, and in many cases the aristocratic forms, against which at the outset they struggled so fiercely. Now new accusers arise to denounce the traitors; after an era of glorious combats and inglorious power, they end by fusing with the old dominant class; whereupon once more they are in turn attacked by fresh opponents who appeal to the name of democracy. It is probable that this cruel game will continue without end."

    Roberto Michels, *La Sociologia del Partito Politico nella Democrazia Moderna* (1912).

15. PASSIVE RESISTANCE

"If the injustice is part of the necessary friction of the machine of government, let it go, let it go. . . . [If an unjust law] is of such a nature that it requires you to be an agent of injustice to another, then, I say, break the law. Let your life be a counter friction to stop the machine. . . . As for adopting the ways which the state has provided for remedying the evil, I know not of such ways. They take too much time, and a man's life will be gone."

    Henry David Thoreau, "Civil Disobedience" (1849).

16. STALE FORMULAS

"Power is not strongest when it uses violence, but weakest. It is strongest when it employs the instruments of substitution and counter attraction, of allurement, of participation rather than of exclusion, of education rather than of annihilation."

Charles E. Merriam, *Political Power* (1934).

17. REPRESENTATIVE GOVERNMENT

"*Political Power* . . . I take to be *a Right* of making Laws with Penalties of Death, and consequently all less Penalties, for the Regulating and Preserving of Property, and of employing the Force of the Community, in the Execution of such Laws, and in the defence of the Common-wealth from Foreign Injury, and all this only for the Publick Good."

John Locke, *Second Treatise on Government* (1690).

18. ECO-POLITICAL DEVELOPMENT

"Certainly, the politic and artificial nourishing of hopes, is one of the best antidotes against the poison of discontents; and it is a certain sign of a wise government and proceeding, when it can hold men's hearts by hopes, when it cannot by satisfaction."

Francis Bacon, "Of Seditions and Troubles," *Essays* (1597).

19. BUREAUCRATIC OPPRESSION

"I have in mind those 'Communists' who try to replace the creative initiative and independent activity of the millions of the working class and farmers by office instructions and 'decrees,' in the virtue of which they believe as a fetish. The task is to smash bureaucracy in our institutions and organizations, to liquidate bureaucratic 'habits' and 'customs.'"

Joseph Stalin,* *Leninism,* vol. 2 (1930).

*Even a stopped clock is right twice a day.

20. PLANNING

[G]enuine planning is an attempt, not arbitrarily to displace reality, but to clarify it and to grasp firmly all the elements necessary to bring the geographic and economic facts in harmony with human purposes."

Lewis Mumford, *The Culture of Cities* (1938).

21. SHIFT IN RULING FORMULA

"A considerable part of the remediable evils of present life are due to the state of imbalance of scientific method with respect to its application to physical facts on the one side and to specifically human facts on the other side; . . . the most direct and effective way out of these evils is steady and systematic effort to develop that effective intelligence named scientific method in the case of human transactions."

John Dewey, *The Public and Its Problems* (1927).

22. PROSPERITY AND EDUCATION

"If the death of peoples, the complete ruin of political organisms, those lasting and violent social crises that interrupt the course of civilization and throw men back toward the brutes, were in any real sense avoidable, the development and recognition of a real political science might certainly contribute considerably toward avoiding them."

Gaetano Mosca, *The Ruling Class* (1939).

23. THE NEW REBELS

"Man shall not live by bread alone."

The Gospel After Luke, 4:4 (1st century A.D.).

But:

"The state is no academy of arts; when it abandons power in favor of ideal strivings of mankind, it denies its own essential being and goes down."

Heinrich von Treitschke, *Der Staat.*

Dear Reader:
    Here you are! A space for *your* great political thought. Write it down. Now we shall have twenty-five of them.

_____
_____
_____
_____
_____

A Model of Power

POWER AS A TYPE OF INFLUENCE

Two boys named Al and Bill are hanging around downtown. We quote:

Al: How about going over to that Republican campaign office and loading up on those matches they give away?

Bill: You mean the kind with Garfinkle on them?

Al: Yeah.

Bill: Who needs them?

Al: We're not doing anything here.

Bill: Hey, wasn't that chick Alice coming to see your sister this afternoon?

Al: Yeah.

Bill: You know, she turns me on. Let's go find her.

Al: OK. We can stop on the way for the matches. Last time I got a whole year's supply.

Bill: OK.[1]

This, friends, is an illustration of influence.

Al has influence over Bill in any transaction in which Al determines Bill's policy regarding something.

---

1. Al has a rather common motive; he's in politics for what it does for him, but he is like a bee that alights on a flower and while sticking its proboscis into the nectar gets its feet sticky with pollen, so that when it flits to the next flower, the bee's feet do the job for the flower that autolocomotion and other sexual organs do for other species. Similarly, Al is doing Garfinkle's job willy-nilly.

Note the following:

Transaction means that an exchange of some kind is occurring, ranging from mute subjection to an equal exchange of influences. In the hypothetical example given, Al tries at first unsuccessfully to influence Bill to go along to pick up the matches (Transaction no. 1). Bill (apparently nearly an equal) responds with his own initiative of a different kind (Transaction no. 2). Al cleverly combines Bill's motive with his own, and, in Transaction no. 3, influences Bill to go after the matches after all, but in the exchange has to spend time with his sister.

The word *determines* here means only that the initiative, formulation, and pressure to perform the Transactions (nos. 1 and 3) rest with Al, not Bill. Moreover, Bill, a free agent, influences Al in Transaction no. 2. Let's face it: Al and Bill are *manipulators.*

And let's have no nonsense against **manipulation.** All people manipulate their world unless they're dead, and some rare characters kill themselves to manipulate the world (e.g., the several people who burned themselves to death to express opposition to the Vietnamese government, U.S. policy in Vietnam, etc.). The important questions are always "What kind of manipulation? Of whom and by whom? And with what right or reason?"

When we say *policy* we mean "a course of action pursued." It can be an action, a response, etc. "Policy" usually means a group's action or plan or response, but we can use it loosely here in order to retain the word later on in talking about both individuals and groups. Policy demonstrates some *value,* some direction, some object (the matches in Transactions nos. 1 and 3; Alice in Transaction no. 2).

If this is influence, what then is *power?*

Power is a special kind of influence.

Power is compulsory influence.

Suppose Al has muscle, has used it in times past on Bill, and, in the dialogue that we have overheard is simply taking it easy; he does not use his *power* unless he has to and in certain showdowns. Al and Bill do not speak of it, but behind the seeming near-equality is the knowledge that somehow or other Al will get those matches and Bill will go along. THIS IS A POWER TRANSACTION, then, despite the gentlemanly nature of the exchange. Power becomes part of each of the transactions as a hidden force.[2]

In other words, *power* stands for *influence that can be enforced,* if necessary. Suppose Bill is influenced by Alice's beauty; he becomes excited. But if she says, "Love me, baby," he may turn off, and there is nothing she can do about it. However, if Alice were the Roman empress Theodosia, she might say, "Love me, Wilhelminus," and he had better love her, *or else . . . !* That is power.[3]

General Instructions

The ideas are simple, but the facts are infinite and the combinations of the facts are infinite. If, in a few words, Al and Bill have given us three or more transactions, you can imagine how many millions of transactions will occur in Al's and Bill's lives. And this is only a two-person transaction; Al and Bill often operate within groups of three, four, five, or a million persons. Now multiply them by three billion people and combine them in groups having **their own** systems of transactions, and you can imagine the volume of activity that can be related to the interest of a political scientist. But, of course, every science is like this: how many atoms are there in the ink on this page, in the cosmos? Therefore people search desperately for scientific generalizations about classes of things. Don't ever condemn generalization; condemn only **bad** or **incorrect generalization.** Remember that moral **principles** are generalizations, too. ("It is better to choose freedom over slavery," for example).

2. Interesting, isn't it, that human beings are so subtle as to conceal all kinds of motives and realities when necessary? Animals are much more direct (and stupid?), but you can understand why some people prefer dogs; their motives are usually clearly expressed. This all makes *the sciences of man* (psychology, anthropology, sociology, economics, history, aesthetics, philosophy, and political science) much more difficult than sciences about rocks, machines, and "lower animals."

3. One could go on about this. Suppose Wilhelminus thinks "when rape is inevitable, relax and enjoy it," but fear makes him impotent (preview: some power-driven people are sexually impotent because the same early fears that made them seek power as a compensation and reassurance made them sexually impotent). So he is axed, anyway. His situation is comparable to that of thousands of Vietnamese civilians who have heard a loudspeaker from an American helicopter telling them, "Abandon your village. It is coming under fire!" They would have liked to have done so, but the local Viet Cong was telling them, "Stay put and pass the ammunition!" Which brings up another proposition: *Power on the spot is more effective than distant power*, even if the distance can be covered in only minutes.

The Borderline Between Power and Influence=Ostracism

Once upon a time, striking workers beat up and even killed strikebreakers. That's power.

Nowadays, few people cross picket lines. Not that they're afraid of being beaten or killed—that's out of style now—but they do want the approval of their fellows. Solidarity. That's influence. But what happens when a worker insists on crossing that picket line?

Arthur Steele, as reported in the British press, tried it. A minor official in the union until he resigned in 1962 over a disagreement, he will be ready to retire from the Birmingham post office in 1974. But one day during the 1971 national postmen's strike he went to work for four and a half hours. And ever since then he has been completely ignored by his co-workers, except when they let the air out of his tires. They're mad at him, but he won't give up. He won't change his mind; he won't apologize; and he has no intention of quitting. He'll keep working until retirement day so he can get his pension.

Is that power? Or is that influence?

THE SPAN OF INFLUENCE

In Al's and Bill's transactions there exists a situation where two persons and their interests are directly involved. Each one feels that he should "make up the other fellow's mind for him," or "keep his freedom of choice" against the other party. But what is happening to Al and Bill affects third parties—the Republican party, the public, the matches manufacturer, Alice, and Al's sister, to mention a few. All are *directly related* to the power or influence transactions and many others are indirectly related. That is, power and influence here are *relevant* to many parties other than those directly involved. The competence of a pure and applied political scientist depends heavily upon his ability to see all who are connected with an event or an action.

THE PAYOFF[4] OF POWER

What are the motives behind peoples' actions? Why do people seek power? Or anything else?

We begin with a trip into "philosophical psychology." Here is a formula to remember:

A person (Al or Bill, for example) seeks to $\begin{Bmatrix} \text{assimilate} \\ \text{experience} \\ \text{adjust} \end{Bmatrix}$ some combination

of $\begin{Bmatrix} \text{1. power} & \text{4. affection} \\ \text{2. wealth} & \text{5. health} \\ \text{3. respect} & \text{6. knowledge} \end{Bmatrix}$ in relation to $\begin{Bmatrix} \text{himself} \\ \text{herself} \\ \text{others} \end{Bmatrix}$.

To Assimilate

First, one seeks to assimilate—to take into oneself, make a part of oneself, hold securely. It is the developing of the *mine,* the *ours.* All the senses are used for the process of injecting stimuli, transubstantiating the stimuli into a part of oneself. Just as the food I eat becomes a part of my body, so those things which I see, hear, smell, feel, and taste affect and become part of my spiritual being. But *spiritual* here does not imply ghosts or gods—rather it refers to that aspect of me that is not physical but is nonetheless vital. Its absence means death.

Despite the fact that I am constantly assimilating, and hence constantly changing, I do not assimilate everything in the world; there is a distinction between the *me* and the *non-me.* For some people the *me* is narrowly restricted, encompassing little more than the individual physiological being. For others the *me* is much broader; there are a few who proclaim "I am at one with the world," a Buddhist kind of idea meaning that whatever happens to any living (and in some cases nonliving) thing happens to oneself. This type of person has assimilated the entire world; everything is a part of his or her identity; for such a person there is no *non-me,* only *me.*

The boundary between oneself and others is often somewhat cloudy. Note the interminable casualty reports in war: **AMERICANS—16 DEAD, 37 MISSING OR WOUNDED;** THE OTHERS—SOUTH VIETNAMESE, 394 DEAD, 1964 MISSING OR WOUNDED; *Enemy, 3772 Dead, 6010 Wounded;* Civilians (Try to Find Out); elephants and trees(??). The self of many people to a degree

---

4. If you wish, you can use another term, perhaps one of the following: value, goal, end, end-in-mind, intention, plan, design, purpose, proposal, object, objective, subject, aim, target, quintain, or point. *Payoff* is rather fashionable among psychologists, economists, and political scientists.

assimilates their "own boys" and assimilates others to lesser and lesser degrees. If that is scandalous, there is the equally scandalous condition of a great many people who don't even assimilate "our boys."

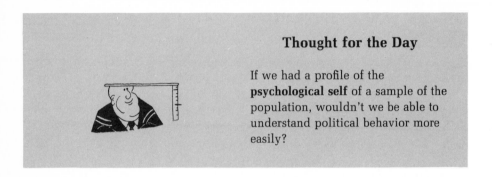

Thought for the Day

If we had a profile of the **psychological self** of a sample of the population, wouldn't we be able to understand political behavior more easily?

To Experience

Now, second, a person *seeks to experience.* People quest, create, invent, "expand their horizons." They attempt to know more about their environment. The stimuli that are assimilated into the *me* are not the only ones that have any effect on the individual. The majority of the people are not "at one with the world," and yet the world is still significant to them. The way that the world (i.e., the *non-me*) is experienced is closely related to the things that are assimilated into the *me.* For example, Casanova was a loving man; he assimilated the trait of loving into his being; the *me* of Casanova involved the process of loving women. What he *experienced* was many women; if you skip several chapters of his *Memoirs,* you can be fairly certain when you return to the book that he will still be chasing women. You'll find him, like Bill, making trade-offs of power, wealth, and prestige in return for affection (as he defines it).

The drive to experience and expand leads one into many areas, often at some expense to one's material and/or spiritual possessions. For some it leads to religious encounters and consciousness-expanding drugs. One cannot statically remain "just oneself." Assimilating leads to a consciousness of the *me,* a sense of integrity, but "genuine vital integrity does not consist in satisfaction, in attainment, in arrival. As Cervantes said long since: 'The road is always better than the inn.'"[5]

5. José Ortega y Gasset, *The Revolt of the Masses* (New York: W. W. Norton & Company, Inc., 1932), 32.

To Adjust

Now, third, a person seeks to adjust. To adjust means broadly to bring the "selfish" and the "nonselfish" into balance in the "soul." The problem of adjustment is that what one *is* often does not coincide with what one *wants to do* and what one *does* in the way of new experience. We have said that experience is related to assimilation, but the relationship is often not pure and direct. There are conflicting characteristics within the *me* leading to conflicting desires. When one desire is acted upon, the contrary desire must be dealt with. Adjustment aims to make that which is assimilated (the *me*) and the experience compatible. Adjustment makes your Identity whom you own, body and soul, compatible with your Identity "Mark II"—that which you would like to possess as your Identity.

In politics adjustment means creating a proper correspondence between those groups that you belong to and the groups that you wish to influence. It means defending your own against the claims of others to influence you and defending what you wish to do. Political adjustment stops certain actions and permits others to occur, according to the laws and courts. Giving everyone his or her day in court; equality before the law; and the rights needed to defend what he or she is, owns, and has made—these are specific illustrations of institutions of law created to satisfy the requirements of adjustment.

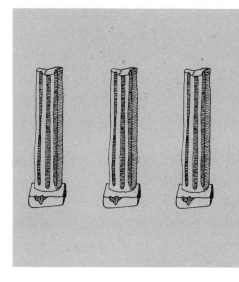

Three Trilogies of Self & Society

When Plato, whom many consider to be the most original of philosophers, sought to discover the meaning of the idea of justice, he constructed a theory of the soul and then a theory of government-as-justice-incarnate to go along with it. Let's compare it with our trilogy (assimilation, experience, adjustment), and while we're at it let's throw in Sigmund Freud's trilogy.[6] Freud did not project his three individual drives specifically into the social sphere, so we are rephrasing them.

---

6. Freud modified his trilogy late in life, as did Plato. So you can figure how much you can rely on *this* author sticking to *his* trilogy!

Plato's Idea of Self	Reflection in Society
Appetite	Ordinary People
Control	Officials
Intellect	Philosopher-Kings

Freud's Idea of Self	Reflection in Society
Id	Naked Power, Aggression
Superego	Social Restraints
Ego	Rational Policy

De Grazia's Idea of Self	Reflection in Society
Assimilation	Status Quo
Experience	Change
Adjustment	Justice

CATEGORIZING PAYOFFS

Now, the things that are possessed, expanded, and adjusted are the *payoffs.* These can be divided into six broad categories, as follows:

POWER: A person's drives are power-centered if he prefers his payoffs to be an increased ability to determine (and enforce) the policies of other people.

WEALTH: Here the preference is for payoffs in economic assets.

RESPECT: Fame and regard given by others are the preferred payoffs here.

AFFECTION: One seeking the many forms and tokens of affection has love-centered drives.

HEALTH: Here one seeks physical and mental well-being.

KNOWLEDGE: One seeks skills and information about human and natural conditions as payoffs for knowledge-centered drives.

It is alarming to see all people's desires so simplified. It raises serious questions: Why this Holy Six? Why not add two, take away four, split one, or throw the whole classification away?

ANSWER NO. 1.   Because you cannot talk about millions of human actions in the concrete as if they were all unique and different, *even though they are!* Confess it, the only way you can think and communicate is by generic words. When several preadolescents get together and one utters the word "parents!" the "ughs!" that arise spontaneously from the assembled primitives show that some important general meaning is being conveyed, although the specific image varies somewhat from one "ugh!" to another. (Meanwhile, the parents, no less primitive though outraged by their own inferior status and their being lumped together, are blowing the foam off their beer and saying "Politicians! Ugh!") So we settle on the "Holy Six," to reduce all actions to something manageable yet still meaningful.

ANSWER NO. 2.   You can add or subtract or amend as you please, but try to be useful. Don't add *money,* because we are cramming it into *wealth.* Don't add *influence,* because we are already using that term to describe a factor in the power transaction between two people—and, besides, influence can always be categorized under *power* or *respect,* depending on the situation. These terms have to be general and cover broad areas of human concern.

Here are many words that will signal the presence of respect in an influence transaction

honor, decorate, pin medals upon, crown, crown with laurel, award (fellowships, distinctions, magna cum laude, honoris causa, etc.), dignify, adorn, grace, distinguish, signalize, glorify, glamorize, exalt, raise, uplift, ennoble, aggrandize, magnify, exalt to the skies, immortalize, enshrine, deify, apotheosize, lionize, run after, esteem, note, regard, get consideration, appreciate, revere, venerate, cause awe, defer to, pay homage, adore, admire, idolize, worship, kowtow to, bow to, give obeisance to, salaam to, genuflect to, salute, value, prize, put on a pedestal; famous, well-known, far-famed, eminent, sublime, illustrious, brilliant, creditable, in good odor, in high favor, renowned, worthwhile, of high repute; somebody, big name, personage, social lion

Any type of payoff can be similarly rich in references or synonyms. And don't forget the opposites! Practically all of these words have antonyms expressing the absence of the value. For example, some words denoting *lack* of respect are in the box below.

dishonor, strip of one's medals, dethrone, disregard, drag through the mud, disgrace, condemn, etc., etc.

Combining Payoffs

No man is purely and absolutely centered on one value.

Hitler, for example, was strongly power-driven, obsessed with power, but he also had some other obsessions (fixed ideas) that he would not sacrifice even for the sake of power—for example, his belief in racism (a *respect* idea that caused him many losses of time, men, resources, *and respect* among outsiders in dealing with Russians, Ukrainians, Poles, Jews, and others) or his devotion to Mussolini (an *affection* idea through which he identified with his early model, and which cost losses later when he tried to support the Italian dictator beyond the point of a calculated return).

The same is true for "health fanatics," "snobs," "eggheads," "Don Juans," and others—there are exceptions to their obsessions, usually contradictory obsessions. If someone's personality is well known, that person can be described as having more or less fixed habits of pursuing his or her own peculiar combination of payoffs. (For example, "If I know Al, he's probably hanging around Republican Headquarters right now.")

Scoring Payoffs

Suppose you followed Al and Bill around for a while. Wouldn't you expect them to fairly consistently follow a pattern of payoff preferences? *Content analysis* and *case studies* in the social sciences in essence are systematic ways of following people around. For example, a political psychologist[7] may give a checklist like the one on respect above to a thousand students to determine the spread of their values and the intensity with which they hold on to them. He may also sit in his office and let a patient unload all kinds of associations, ideas, and dreams in the hope of discovering the pattern of values in the flow of words. This is not far from the research professor and staff (those doing all the dirty work) who are counting references in newspapers to the behavior of the Chinese elite in the hope of penetrating the leaders' "inscrutable," "mysterious," "Oriental" minds (which, actually, are no more inscrutable and mysterious than anyone else's mind[8]).

Incidentally, you will find that the social sciences are organized somewhat around these payoffs and their related institutions.

Payoff	Science	Institutions
Power	Political science	Governments, military groups, gangs
Wealth	Economics	Banks, markets, manufacturing
Respect	Sociology, anthropology	Social classes, castes, race relations, bureaucracy
Affection	Theology[9]	Churches, family, friendship clubs, brothels
Health	Psychology, biology	Medicine, clinics
Knowledge	Philosophy, education (pedagogy)	Schools

Note: History is in all of the categories (or should be) because what just happened a moment ago is now history, and what happened long ago happened in every field and may be useful to know.

7. What makes him *political* is simply that his studies center around power problems.

8. I am tempted here to remark that "people are all alike everywhere" since so much unnecessary trouble comes from thinking the opposite, but then I realize that "everybody is different" and much trouble

But note the many crossovers. The power aspects of churches are studied as political science, their social standing and bureaucracies as sociology, and their control of property as economics. There is no law against full and free crossing of lines in pursuit of a solution to a problem, though the establishment (or bureaucracy) in every field tends to regard "interdisciplinary work" as a kind of trespassing.

**The Haves and Have-Nots,
or the "Students-are-Niggers Test"**

Haves (10)	Have-Nots (0)	Score Yourself (on 0–10 scale)
Powerful	Powerless	_____
Wealthy	Poor	_____
Respected	Despised	_____
Loved	Unloved	_____
Healthy	Unhealthy	_____
Informed	Uninformed	_____
	Total:[10]	_____

POWER CONVERSIONS

Power Resources

We have noted that political science is basically organized around the payoff of *power.* We can call *power resources* whatever people possess that can be converted into power, whether it is a winning smile or a block of IBM stock certificates.

Of course, a person must be willing to convert his or her power resources to pure power. This motive varies greatly among people. Lacking an interest in power, a person will not wish to convert the assets of health or

comes from treating them as if they were alike. So I conclude with the self-contradictory generalization that "people are all alike everywhere, but everybody is different." It is not a natural law because a law should be more precise and cleaned of paradox. Still I recommend it as one of the most useful "rules of thumb" that you will ever acquire.

9. Some might contradict me and I would not deny it: that is, we also have psychologists, psychiatrists, "touch-encounter" therapy groups, etc., who are deeply involved in love-therapy, and some theologians seem often to be interested in everything exept love.

10. There must be something wrong with the test.

prestige into power. He or she may enjoy them too much as they are. Other persons will convert every ounce of resources they have into power; they catch a kind of "gambler's fever" that has led many into poverty, disgrace, and loss of love.

These power resources are already recognizable as the "Holy Six" values. A person's inventory of values shows to some extent how readily he can obtain power if he wishes to do so.

The type of resource (and subtype) has to be considered. For instance:

1. A Ph.D. in botany is a knowledge resource but probably not worth so much in a general power situation in the United States in the 1970s as a degree in law (we are not speaking of an election to the Council of the American Botanical Society). Nor does general power in Mississippi translate itself easily into power in Massachusetts; prejudices against both whites and blacks from Mississippi, not to mention legal obstacles and other local ties, would hamper the translation.

2. The crucial assets of a person who is being considered for a position on the Board of Trustees of the City University of New York may be South African gold mine stock, since many people want to boycott South Africa for its racist Apartheid policy.

Each person has his or her own *conversion pattern* or system of exchanging one or more values for one or more other values. (E.g., "Every penny he gets he puts into new clothes," or "He was completely dedicated to earning money until he was fifty and then set up a foundation to give it all away.")

Forms of Conversion

Note how the payoffs often take a usable intermediate form before a value is converted into power:

Power is often converted into power-in-use by means of penalties or sanctions, the auxiliary factor. "Pay your taxes or go to jail."

Wealth is often converted to power by means of cash or money as an auxiliary. "A senatorship costs $2 million."

Knowledge is often applied in a power transaction through skill. "Bryan's 'Cross of Gold' speech won him the Democratic nomination for President."

Respect is more readily convertible as prestige. "A famous name such as Rockefeller, Eisenhower, or Kennedy brings votes, appointments, nominations and special favors."

Love is often convertible as loyalty. "If Richard Nixon was good enough for Eisenhower, then he's good enough for me."

Health may become a power asset as sheer energy and persistence. "In negotiating with the North Koreans, you need infinite patience, a strong stomach, and a thick hide."

The convertibility of four of the resources—latent power, wealth, knowledge, and respect—for use in power transactions is great. Love and health are attached to individuals and are usually less easily generalized. But there are some famous cases where love between two persons is used to advance greatly the wealth, power, and prestige of one of them (Queen Elizabeth and Sir Walter Raleigh, for example). Nepotism, the placing of relatives in offices, is to some degree a conversion of family love into power and wealth.

* * * * *

It is helpful to compare what is said about converting political power resources with converting mechanical and electric power from one form to another.

1. The more potential or actual power available in a ready state, the easier and cheaper is the conversion. ("You can't beat city hall" means that an entrenched and ready power is tough to beat.)

2. The more resources available (expendable) for conversion to power, the greater the resulting power. ("He spent millions to get elected.")

3. The better planned (that is, the more intelligent, the more logical) the conversion, the larger the ratio of power output to resource input. ("Much of Curtis Le May's hard-earned prestige as an Air Force general vanished in a month of campaigning for Vice-President on George Wallace's ticket.")

4. The conversion results in some temporary loss of the original re-source, like heat or friction or dissipation or nonutilization of energy in a mechanical conversion. ("The giant corporations of America, despite the favorable impression they carry with the public and most politicians, spend many millions on public relations, institutional advertising, community relations, philanthropy, and lobbying." That is, to translate the favorable impression into active power requires an expenditure of much money and energy. Or "The qualities that made Mrs. Peabody a good companion and mother scarcely helped her with the job of being a politician's wife.")

5. The conversion of other resources into power can sometimes be reversed. In fact, most persons in politics and other power situations (family, church, club, college, etc.) are interested in converting their re-sources into power in order to reconvert power into other resources or more of the same resource. ("Croker retired as Boss of Tammany Hall to become a gentleman horse fancier in Ireland.")

Power Conversion Skills

Assuming you wish to convert one resource into another, what do you use as the *energy of conversion?* You convert the resource by some kind of skill into a usable formula.

For example:
If Caveman Arvag wishes to make love to Cavewoman Botsa (that is, "A" seeks to influence the love policies of "B"), he looks to his resources, which, when classified by the Grazian Inventory Scheme, amount to:

1. POWER: 1 club; 3 cousins with clubs; 1 overdeveloped bicep.

2. WEALTH: (above club worth 6 conches); 1 bear rug slightly used; 82 conches.

3. RESPECT: permitted by clan to utter 3 supersecret incantations.

4. LOVE: motherless; last woman disappeared in love feast with neighbors; has strong musk odor.

5. HEALTH: 2 excellent remaining incisors; can see well in dark; (also see "bicep" above).

6. KNOWLEDGE: finds water in unbelievable places; is logical; once tamed animal called by everyone "Aardvark" which disappeared with last woman; (also see "incantation" above).

Logically, he would run down the list:

Will his *Power* influence the love policies of Botsa?
   (?? Input: Botsa has 3 incestuous relatives with clubs.)

Will his *Wealth* influence the love policies of Botsa?
   (?? Input: The bear rug is quite odorless, and Botsa shares only a stinking sealskin with her small sister.)

Will his *Respect* influence the love policies of Botsa?
   (?? Input: None of her menfolk was awarded so much as access to confidential incantations.)

Will his *Love* influence the love policies of Botsa?
   (?? Input: The musky odor has its attractions.)

Will his *Health* influence the love policies of Botsa?
   (?? Input: Maybe he can steal her in darkness?)

Will his *Knowledge* influence the love policies of Botsa?
   (?? Input: Very heavy on this: see *Solution* below.)

Solution:
On a dark night, after numerous repetitions of the incantations until everybody gets sleepy, Arvag throws bear rug over Botsa, leaves 32 conches for her relatives, and carries her up a mountain widely believed to be waterless. There, by a little pond, he waits for daylight when his ravishing smile will excite her LOVE!

PROGRAM NOTE.   You can well perceive that each resource is also a means of converting another resource. The influencing of Botsa's love policies was finally achieved by a combination of resources of all six types. True, it is essentially a rape; that is, physical force (naked power) plays a key role. Still, other resources are used and particularly the role of knowledge, logic, and planning should be stressed.

To sharpen the point, think what would have happened if Arvag, instead of being an intelligent and trained person, were stupid and sought to rely simply upon brute force (that is, his power resources). He would have had his head bashed in by Botsa's relatives, lost his property, his reputation, his lovability, and his last incisors. . . . Sort of reminds one of the U.S.A. in Vietnam.

Special Conversion Skills

A skill comes out of knowledge. It is some learned way of using one's resources on people or things. You train your voice to reach the farthest gallery seats. You train yourself to be always courteous. You train yourself to hit the nail on the head every time (well, almost). You train yourself to look for a particular microbe under the microscope, watch for a star that should appear in your telescope, solve some equations, memorize, read rapidly, perfect a writing style, ignore hecklers while speaking in public, pay attention to the fine print of a tax report, speak a foreign language less barbarously.

We have already said that all kinds of action can be relevant to politics. (See, for example, page 19 of the Introduction.) Then all kinds of training can also be relevant, because you train in respect to a given prescribed set of actions. Think of all the verbs in the language. All these imply actions and most involve training. The box shows some of what a small dictionary gives as verbs beginning with the letters *P* and *T,* indeed only *Pa* and *Ta.*

P	T
pace, pacify, pack, package, pad, paddle, padlock, page, paginate, pain, paint, pair, pal, palaver, pale, pall, palliate, palm, palpitate, pamper, pan, pander, panic, pant, pantomime, etc. . . .	tab, table, taboo, tabulate, tack, tackle, tag, tailor, taint, take, talk, tally, tame, tamper with, tan, tangle, tank up, tap, tape, taper, tar, target, tarnish, tarry, taste, tattle, tattoo, taunt, tax

There are, of course, thousands of verbs in the dictionary, and nouns can also be converted into verbs. A dictionary writer who is hooked on politics could illustrate political usages in every case:

"The campaign was *paced* to begin slowly."

"The program to *pacify* South Vietnam is proceeding well (1968!)."

"The hall was *packed* with his supporters."

"The House and Senate agreed to *package* the provisions of the two bills."

"He was convicted of *padding* his *payroll*."

"He *paddled* against the currents of opinion most of his political life and died a statesman."

"The sheriff *padlocked* six bawdy houses, ten burlesque theatres, and one public bath yesterday."

"While he was being *paged,* the delegate was *paginating* his speech and was *pained* to hear his name *painted* in the most sombre colors by the previous speaker with whom he had agreed to *pair* in the final vote and with whom he used to *pal* around in college in the days before both had begun their careers of *palavering*."

Etc., etc.

There is a skill involved in doing anything. What skills are especially related to politics, that is, to converting resources into power? Certain words on the above list recur: *pacify, taboo, talk, target, tax.* These suggest power transactions.

Now, if power is present wherever sanctions are severe (in childhood, street gangs, schooling, in everything to do with armies and governments —about a quarter of one's life activities on the average) and, besides power, other forms of influence almost as forceful as power are present in every form of organization (churches, factories, businesses, labor unions, etc.) then

the resource-conversion skills
and the skills that make more power out of power itself
are many, <u>many,</u> <u>many.</u>

And, since we don't know how many, we must say simply: Don't be surprised at what combination of skills a person has, who has succeeded in his own area of influence and power.

Generally, the following hold true:

1. A leader shows some skill in the particular subject of his area. "An army officer usually knows one end of the rifle barrel from the other."

2. A leader has spent a long time in the surroundings from which his power develops.[11] "Genghis Khan was raised among horses." "Stalin patiently built a party bureaucracy that he could use against Trotsky." But "Wendell Willkie almost became President in 1940 from a career as a corporate attorney."

3. Two major groups of skills emerge among political leaders in the modern world.

A. Skills in communication

(Rhetoric, writing, oratory, persuasion, agitation, propaganda. In general, symbol creation.)

B. Skills in management

(Recruitment, organization, control. In general, combining and directing human and material resources.)

But then these same sets of skills are helpful in practically every type of career—selling girdles, making dog food, or organizing a gambling pool.

Perhaps it is time to look in on Al and Bill again, speaking of careers. We left them in early adolescence and catch them in early adulthood:

Bill: Where you going, Al?

Al: The usual place.

Bill: You gonna be a politician or something?

Al: No. I get a bang outa the people there. They're really something!

Bill: What do you mean?

Al: There's always somethin doing. Whyn't you come along? We get the *Facts*, man, the Facts, you know, on all the crooks in town.

Bill: No. Sally'll be mad.

Al: That's the way marriage is, huh?

11. This includes kings, nobles, and dynasties, whether hereditary or elective. King George III of England (that beloved figure of schoolboy history in America) was profligate, unreliable, uneducated, often crazy, and spoke the King's English poorly; but he was in the line of succession, and the English of the time had more important things to concern themselves with than the king. They were making money! And inventing things!

Bill: Heh,heh.

Al: Come on. Tell her you're looking for a better job, you know, through political connections.

Bill: OK.

Al has been hooked on politics. The next thing you know, he'll be explaining to anybody who'll listen that the Democrats are going to get rid of all the crooks in town. And it won't be long before he will be marked as a "comer" in politics with "his early acquired skills in persuasion, organization, and leadership on the crime problem" and a "naturally sympathetic manner that makes people trust him."

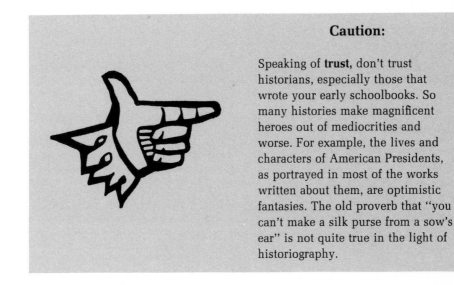

Caution:

Speaking of **trust,** don't trust historians, especially those that wrote your early schoolbooks. So many histories make magnificent heroes out of mediocrities and worse. For example, the lives and characters of American Presidents, as portrayed in most of the works written about them, are optimistic fantasies. The old proverb that "you can't make a silk purse from a sow's ear" is not quite true in the light of historiography.

The Propositions of Payoff Preference (or, why some prefer power)

In the case of Arvag's love, we said that a stupid man would prefer a pure power approach. But let's develop this point. What makes *A, Al, Arvag,* and Arvagians decide when to choose power as a means to an end?

1. People will use influence wherever they are trained or conditioned to believe other people can help provide, or should provide, or stand in the way of providing their preferred payoff. (This, of course, is extremely common behavior, though some people are more manipulative than others.)

2. People devote themselves to the types of *payoffs* that they are trained or conditioned to prefer or to believe will fulfill their wants. ("If you give a girl a gun instead of a doll, she may surprise you later on.")

3. People will use *power* as their *means* of influence when they want any kind of payoff very badly, when they are trained or conditioned to use power as their means (instead of other means of influence), and when they prefer power for its own sake (that is, as an end as well as a means).

We should add that payoffs need not be conscious. An affectionate remark can cure a person's headache sometimes.

4. People will seek power for its own sake when they are trained or conditioned to seek it, or enjoy it, or prefer it as a means of influence—even if they have no ends in view.

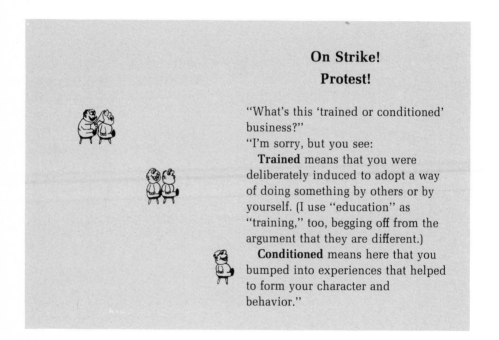

On Strike!
Protest!

"What's this 'trained or conditioned' business?"
"I'm sorry, but you see:
  Trained means that you were deliberately induced to adopt a way of doing something by others or by yourself. (I use "education" as "training," too, begging off from the argument that they are different.)
  Conditioned means here that you bumped into experiences that helped to form your character and behavior."

Where We Are and Where We're Going

It is time to conclude this Second Lesson in Political Science. You now know what constitutes power, how it is used, why it is used, how other assets are converted to power, and who is likely to exercise it. The Third Lesson disposes of all the heavy stuff of politics—groups, organization, authority, constitutions, and the like. When it's over, you will be dealing with millions of people!

Lesson Number 3

Organized and Disorganized Power

EXTENSION OF THE POWER MODEL

The next exercise is to train the mind to embrace all the actors of political life. The effect of the exercise upon you should be splendid; you will be able to conceive of individuals, of all kinds of groups, and of abstractions. "It is better than Yoga," writes Swami Bodekinanda, my student assistant.[1] You will be able to transfer propositions of political science from individuals to peoples and nations, and back again.

Here is the bare MODEL of Al's half of a power process which is familiar to you.

Al, in transaction with Bill, has WANTS plus RESOURCES, which, through SKILLS, he CONVERTS into POWER-READY RESOURCES and COMPELS[2] Bill to FULFILL THOSE WANTS, thus setting himself up for a second transactional cycle in which his WANTS and RESOURCES are somewhat altered—and so on in a great many cycles.

For women, use Alice and Belinda, and for women and men interacting, use Al and Alice, Al and Belinda, etc.

Now, for several people treated in separate transactions, change only the first line and read *Al, in transactions with Bill, Carl, Dave, Ed, and Frank*. Then you can describe Al over a period of time and make statements about his general behavior, such as, "Al is always hogging power."

---

1. You can imagine the power situation in which he finds himself!

2. Simply insert "influences" for "compels" to make this a definition of Al's half of an influence transaction.

Note: No groups exist in which all of the transactions are between one member and every other member separately,

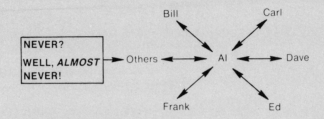

But, Proposition:

Members of a group may be more easily dominated and controlled if their only contacts are with the leader. And, marvelous to say, when you look about in politics, you find tendencies in dictatorships to break up all subgroups and associations so that everything has to pass through the dictator's hands. E. M. Forster wrote a short story almost half a century ago in which people were confined to cells, from which they dealt directly only with the unseen government.

A usual group has all its members transacting with one another in some fashion. Sociometrically, the transactions in Al's group could be drawn as below[3]:

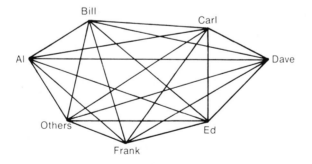

At the same time that group members have individual transactions, they have two-person, three-person, four-person, etc., simultaneous transactions.

---

3. Theoretically Al can transact with himself: "the struggle of good and evil within me," "the conflict of desires," etc. Everyone else can also transact with himself. Therefore, perhaps the formula below should read $2^n - 1$.

That is, Al converses with Bill, Ed, and Frank, as follows:

Al: Did you guys see the papers?

Ed: Yeah, what a laugh, 35 to 1 on the daily double.

Frank: You jerk, he means the newspapers.

Bill: Shuddup for a change. (Gives Ed a push.)

Al: My name was mentioned.

Frank: What for?

Al: Volunteers, Republican Volunteers.

Bill: Cool.

In this set of transactions, we find all members interacting with all members.[4] This gives:

Al—Bill	Al—Bill—Ed
Al—Ed	Al—Bill—Frank
Al—Frank	Al—Ed—Frank
Ed—Bill	Ed—Bill—Frank
Ed—Frank	Al—Bill—Ed—Frank
Bill—Frank	

Mathematicians put the possibilities elegantly and simply. They say: $2^N - N - 1 =$ the number of combinations of transactions that are possible in any group. Here, we have $N = 4$ members, and therefore, $2^4 - 4 - 1 = 11$ possible transactions. If Carl and Dave were added to the group, possible transactions of all combinations would have numbered $(2^6 - 6) - 1 = 57$. The number mounts rapidly, geometrically. If the group had twelve members and every member were transacting with every possible combination of other members the number would be 4083. "Ain't nature wonderful?"

What actually happens in any group is that very quickly patterns of transactions form and intra-group structure develops from these habitual patterns of communications within the group. These patterns mean that certain people limit the transactions of certain other people, that the meetings (collective transactions) are regularized, that certain behaviors are taken for granted or required. In other words the complications of group transactions are dealt with by reaggregating, specializing, and simplifying processes—the result being a structured or organized group.

---

4. "Author, where does Bill interact with Frank?" Aha! Notice how Bill picks up Frank's cue of treating Ed roughly. In other words, transactions can be nonverbal. They can also be indirect.

Because of the enormous number of possible and actual transactions almost everything said about the group's behavior is a generalization. When Al's network numbers a dozen, no one in the group, not even Al, who is becoming a professional "pol" of a low sort, participates in or knows of all the transactions of the group. What he hears about the group, if he has good intelligence reports, covers the more important internal and external transactions. Thus, the group has to be described with a set of generalizations.

"The group met often."   "Half the members had no political interests."

"The group was young."   "The group was largely unemployed."

"It was a political group."   "The group was informal."

"Al was the group leader."   "The group had a high morale."

etc., etc.

In each one of these statements, use of the term *group* means that some slice of the thousands of transactions going on has been observed, counted, sampled or reported about, and is now declared to be a characteristic of the group. *"The group behaves . . . "* means only that under certain conditions the group's members will arrange themselves in a certain way and act in a certain way. Thus "group Abel behaves peacefully toward other similar groups" means that somebody has observed that most of the symbols and actions or the most important symbols and actions of that group relating to peace or violence in respect to groups Baker, Charley, etc., are peace symbols and peace actions.

The more specific you can be about the group behavior, the more helpful your observations. For example, the following questions arise from the statements listed above:

A. How often is often? Did the same people always attend? How many on the average attended?

B. Do you mean the group was formed recently, or the average age of its members is low? Do old men belong at all? Are they the leaders?

C. Were its orientation, mission, recognized goals, members' interests, and leaders' interests all political? How broad a scope did its political interests have? etc.

Remember that every statement about a group has to be reducible to real behaviors or ideas of its individual members. Since it is impossible to move except at a snail's pace by describing every individual's action every time you wish to denote the most relevant and important actions coming out of the group or going on in the group, you use the shorthand term *group* and speak as if all members in it behaved uniformly. But never let yourself think this is the case, or else you will commit a grave scientific sin:

You will hypostatize the group.

(Not hyPOTHesize, hyPOSTatize. In other words, "you will ANIMATE the group." That is, give it a life of its own.)

The best way to avoid this ghastly crime is to:

Be as specific as possible.

What aspect of the group are you talking about? Not "the group" but "the group morale"—"the group's top leaders"—"the average age of the group members"—"the rank and file"—"the group's constitution"—"the majority of the group."

Now we are ready to place any aggregate in the model on p. 61. Instead of Al and Bill:

Altoona, Pennsylvania, beat out Billings, Montana, in vying for a Model City grant from the Department of Housing and Urban Development by virtue of a six-month, $30,000 lobbying campaign sparked by a professional staff in Washington. Altoona city officials declared following the decision that the lobby system worked well enough to keep it permanently in operation for follow-up and for other new projects. (The example is fictional.)

For nations, read Argentina and Brazil; for full abstraction, read *A* and *B.*

Whether political scientists concern themselves with huge aggregates ("The world's people . . . "), small groups, or individuals, the *model of power process* remains the same, and the same fundamental questions are asked. In other words, when you are asked what is going on between *A* and *B,* no matter what or who are named, apply the MODEL.

PARAMETERS OF POWER

In every case where you are called upon to describe the power process involving *A* and *B* show your virtuosity (virtue comes later) by adding to the description a summary of the *parameters of power.* Parameters are dimensions, boundaries, facets. The most useful parameters are four:

1. DOMAIN = the NUMBER of people affected by the exercise of power. (This is the sum of *B* where *B* is more than Just Plain Bill.) Thus: "The vote today by Congress to increase social security taxes affected 5,327,246 Americans." They are the *domain.*

2. SCOPE = the VARIETY OF ACTIVITIES of a given domain that are affected. Thus: "Congress authorized the Secretary of Commerce to require reports of capital spending planned by all corporations doing business abroad; until now reports were required only on assets held abroad."

3. INTENSITY = the PRESSURE APPLIED to direct the policy. Thus: "I,

Silligurd II, King of Slobbovia, by the Grace of God and the demise of Silligurd I, declare that, henceforth, any person guilty of conspiring against the person of the Crown be not only hanged, but also splayed, drawn and quartered, and fed to the carp of the castle moat."

4. DURATION = the length of TIME during which A's influence or power is felt upon the policies of B. Thus: "Stalin's despotic power lasted so long that he almost caught up with Hitler as the world's greatest mass murderer."

Put these four PARAMETERS OF POWER together and you have a measure of A's power over B, whether A and B are persons, groups, or nations—person over group or nation; group over person or nation; and nation over group or person.

Now we can construct a definition of totalitarian rule that makes sense. *Totalitarian rule is a rule under which a government or person in any group tries to determine all the activities (scope) of all people (domain) all the time (duration) with maximum pressure to obey (intensity).* This is without reference to good or bad effects, or what happens as a result.

What, then, is the opposite of totalitarianism?

Anarchism. *If no person nor any group nor any nation rules* B *in any way at any time, then* B *lives in a condition of anarchism.*

Query: Anarchism would appear to be a blessed state. Why are anarchists, then, shadowed anxiously by the police and sometimes put to death? We can think of reasons:

A. Some anarchists wish to convert their wants and resources into power(lessness) quickly, by bombing the authorities.

B. Some anarchists try to live peacefully as anarchists. This is a pain to those who support the existing system by military service, taxes, obedience.

*   *   *   *   *

Many of the transactions in which an individual is involved are power transactions, and the amount is increasing. I suppose, further, that he or she (this "he or she" business will be taken up later) is *influenced* in practically all the rest of his or her choices. The important matter is, perhaps, not freedom from all influence or even from power, but freedom from *influence that one dislikes and power that one dislikes.*

LIMITS OF POWER

Why am I moving on to the next subject without explaining more of this trap of influence and power we're in? Several reasons:

*Just because the subject is one of the most important of all doesn't mean that there's much detail to report from research on humanity's enmeshment in power and influence.

**This is a good time to write up your own profile or do a friend's.

***You probably don't really comprehend what you're ruled and influenced by.

****We'll treat it again later.

Limits of Power (We Repeat!)

1. What limits power?
2. Why doesn't it go up and up?
3. Is the natural tendency of society really totalitarian rule over everybody?

Bad News!

1. There is no foolproof limit to power except counterpower, often of the nastiest sort.

2. Power does tend to rise, because the easiest conversion is power-to-power; therefore power in any situation tends to accumulate and concentrate more intensely than any other value being converted to power.

3. Yes. See above.

Good News!

★   When people are brought up in a kindly atmosphere (kindly old *A*), they do not seek much power over others.

★   As power is applied, people may resist. If they cannot actively resist, they passively resist; finally they become rather useless vegetables, not good for much even when they don't cause trouble. (Reread the Declaration of Independence, 1776.)

★   Power is limited by its resources. "Would that the Roman people had only one head," said the mad Emperor Caracalla, and he did not have in mind to pat it.

★   Power is limited by the tactical skills of both sides. "If you get an injunction against me, I'll get an injunction against you." It is practically

Profiles of Intervention of the State in the Lives of Three Hypothetical Citizens

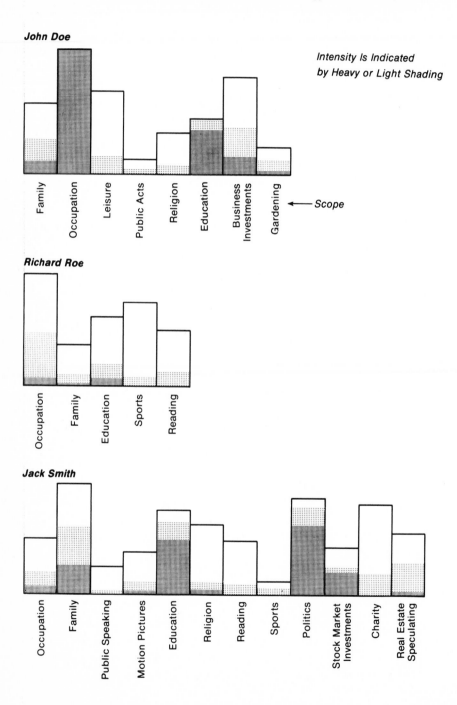

impossible to make all the calculations required to run people's lives for them.

★   Power can be limited by the "Rules of the Game." Where these rules limit what governors as well as governed may do, you have a "constitutional" government. In this game, the rulers, even if they are a majority, agree that they are prohibited from certain arbitrary exercises of power. "It is expected that each democratic party decry any violence in politics, even if it helps them."

★   The "Ideology of the Times" sometimes limits the growth of power. "The prevailing atmosphere in the Austro-Hungarian empire before World War I permitted great freedom of expression, despite many laws hampering liberty."

★   Human nature is not as rigid as vegetable or animal nature. It is not responsive to power alone. "People are flexible in evading laws they dislike."

★   There are hundreds of legal and extralegal ways of limiting power. Examples *(Legal):* There are elections; referenda; limited tenure of office; prohibition against certain kinds of behavior, such as arrest without warrant, and against certain kinds of legislation, such as Congress shall make no law abridging the freedom of speech or of the press. *(Extralegal):* Although opposition parties are not demanded by the U.S. Constitution, they rise up and "keep the ruling party honest" by providing an alternative choice. In Italy, the custom exists of marking each new Presidential inauguration with an amnesty to many convicts.

*   *   *   *   *

"Great, then. Nothing to worry about (I hope?)"

"Well, yes. Power still tends to accumulate and concentrate. There is no foolproof, limiting machine . . . But see here, you look worried. Why don't you go to the ballgame?"

"I can't. I have to keep my eye on that power every minute of the time."

"Are you sure . . . ?"

"Yes, yes, you are absolutely right. I know it, I feel it, right here . . . There's only one thing to do—root it out, chop it out. Down with power. We'll murder it! Leave no stone unturned! Search everyone! It's lurking everywhere! No one does anything without permission until we clean up this matter. Even if it takes a hundred years!"

"You know, Axelrod, Francis Bacon once wrote, 'A little learning is a dangerous thing.'"

"Arrest him, too!"

* * * * *

THE ORGANIZATION OF POWER

Al: "Al," she said, "you should have a political club. It will do you good. It will give you some stature." I said whaddayamean, and she said, "Well, it will give you a reputation for responsibility, and people will know you have some backing." "I got no money," I said. "That's just it," she says. "This will be better than money. Supporters—that's what counts."

Bill: Smart chick, huh?

Al: Damn right, she's smart. Her old man's a lawyer, but she runs him too.

Bill: What'll your club stand for?

Al: Who says it has to stand for something? It's a club; that's all. You know, when somethin has to be done, the club does it.

Al seems to be frightfully irrational, but that's because he never has had our Basic Course in Political Science and cannot fully analyze his own behavior. Actually, here he comes rather close. He says, in effect, that the proper kind of resource available to him is a social-political club. He has no money; therefore, he must develop a talent for organizing. He also perceives that this club should not have an overt specific goal. It has to be able to give its energies to anything that will help achieve the covert goal of helping Al's personal political fortunes.

A Curious Problem

Why do you need a (political) science about an activity when most of the highest achievers of the activity (politics) don't study the science?

A. Some famous intellectuals may be poor at converting power resources, but high achievers (good converters of power resources) often learn from them nevertheless.

B. Many high achievers did study politics thoroughly—Pericles, Cicero, Machiavelli, Jefferson, Woodrow Wilson, Trotsky, Mussolini, Hitler, and Churchill, to name a few.

C. There is a division of labor; those who study often have little time for politics and vice versa.

D. Many traits and skills that go with an activity (such as inherited power, athletic prowess, charm, a liking for legal mumbo jumbo, etc.)

may not be possessed by the pure scientists.

E. The science is not advanced enough in certain areas to be useful. Sometimes the science is bogged down or in the hands of an establishment that deliberately or unconsciously blocks applications.

F. Any science is specialized, while any activity in life combines several fields.

But What Is Organization?

Suppose you walk across a field once. There is scarcely a trace of your passing. Suppose you walk across it several times. You acquire the habit. Now a path begins to shape up. Others will take the same path. We can define the path now as the effective pattern of human activity aimed at crossing the field.

The path is practically an institution.[5] Late arrivals just fall into it and use it; they don't know who began it. No one wants to start a new path. In fact, there is risk in doing so: how do you know a new path is better? Isn't one enough? A second path would appear to be trespassing; you meet your friends on the habitual path; the old path is easier.

So far, so good. But suppose conditions change; suppose the fishing and boating pond at the end of the path dries up, and a Pizza Palace opens up at a diagonal to the path. Now a period of confusion arises; people are hesitant; some go around the long way; someone tries to break a new direct path and is scolded for trespassing.

Ultimately, a new pattern will be set and people will feel better adjusted. Whether the pond should be allowed to dry up and the Pizza Palace to be established in its awkward location are debatable questions of policy; so also the question of change and the means of adjusting to it—how should it be observed, controlled, and accompanied by appropriate changes in organization?

5. Indeed, the Anglo-American common law recognizes the path now as a public road unless the owner of the field deliberately blocks the path once a year to prove his possession of it. Once a year in the borough of Princeton, N.J., Princeton University closes a number of paths and well-traveled streets to retain its private right over them.

An organization is an aimed patterned activity. It is a set of "collective habits." An institution is a complex, enduring organization. The Girl Scouts of America is an institution; the Saturday Afternoon Mycological Hiking and Hunt Club of Fricassie County is an organization.

Why Is Organization?

Why the NAACP?[6]
Why the Girl Scouts of America?
Why the United Mine Workers?
Why the Securities and Exchange Commission?
"If you want to get something done, you have to get organized." Well, OK, you can use this sentence. It has some meaning. It means:

1. Organization mobilizes power resources. (It adds up the disposable power resources of its members.)

2. Organization operates effectively. (If its goal is agreed to, it permits the patterning of collective habits toward the goal.)

But try this on: *"If you want to get anything done, you have to avoid the organization."* What this means is:

1. Most organizations are barely able to keep their functions ahead of their dysfunctions. The Iron Law of Oligarchy (see page 35) says that invariably the few rule the many, but this has many qualifications and exceptions (which we will leave for later on). The Law also implies that the leaders:

feather their nests
eat high off the hog
fiddle while Rome burns
let George do it
can't find the forest for the trees
festoon themselves in red tape
scratch each other's back
play the Pasha
muzzle protesters
make fetishes of details
become wed to tradition
worship the status quo

Obviously, since they are disporting themselves in such picturesque ways, organization leaders:

6. National Association for the Advancement of Colored People.

A. can give little time to what the rebels say the organization is really intended for, and

B. can rarely have resources left for their main job, even if they know what it is.

2. You get the organization to do what you want by:

A. bringing pressure to bear from the outside (not an easy task even if you quit it so as to oppose it more openly), or

B. finding the right people in the organization, whatever their job is supposed to be, who can get things done.

Loose Habit Groups versus Rigid Habit Groups

Loose Habit Groups: Type 1 Organizations	Rigid Habit Groups: Type 2 Organizations

Power conversion groups such as:
     free political parties
     revolutionary parties
     writers and communicators
     councils
     legislatures
     clubs
     conspiracies
     lobbies
     evangelical churches
     campus movements
     inventors
	Power control and output groups or groupings such as:
	     totalitarian political parties
	     administrative agencies
	     executives
	     military forces
	     ritual groups (most churches)
	     factories
	     university administrations
	     the Establishment
	     engineers

These are the pathmakers: they create new habits and break old habits; they are less patterned; they are more voluntary; power in the organization is more "up for grabs."	These are the path users; they perfect habits and insist upon them; they are less risky and more involuntary; power within is measured out carefully.

A little friendly advice: Don't knock yourself out trying to make a hard-and-fast distinction between all the examples of Type 1 and all those of Type 2. The classifications of political science are not usually pure.

Organizations of both Type 1 and Type 2 are partly planned and partly out of control (that is, they grow "naturally"). They sometimes grow like an informal club and then become planned like a political party growing out of an informal association (the old Federalist Party of the United States, for example). In either event, the plan does not last long; it becomes supplemented by practices that were unplanned and even unforeseen. (The U.S.

Army Corps of Engineers was not planned originally to be a large-scale peacetime works construction agency, but nevertheless it is.)

A plan for an authoritative organization is a constitution.[7] Constitutions, however, are not exceptions to the rule that organizations are "partly out of control." It is a rare political constitution that lasts over a generation; it is an even rarer constitution that not only endures but also reflects the realities of political behavior. (Need I remind you that the U.S. Constitution quite specifically gives to Congress the right to declare war, but that Presidential orders have directed major wars in Korea and Vietnam?)

A constitution says a lot of abstract things, like what should be done and who is to do it. But these are *words*. When we look at what has been *happening* we find that the way the Constitution is executed changes with the times. (An airplane is a plan for flying. The way it is executed will depend upon whether the date is 1915, 1925, 1940, or the present.) So the meaning-in-action of the Constitution's words was different under early federalism or late nineteenth-century laissez-faire or the present centralized welfarism, and at other times, too. Each time the centers of power, and the concerns of those who had most to say about running the country, shifted considerably, even though reverent lip service was given to the authority of the Constitution.

AUTHORITY

Authority is the foundation of society. Without authority, a society falls apart. No society, acting through its government, can physically force all its members to follow all its rules all the time. It has to rely as little as possible on physical coercion and punishments to influence behavior. But most of the time, a society relies on its authority to achieve popular obedience.

Authority is power believed to be rightfully exercised. Such power is thereby legitimate. Authority is thus obeyed simply because it is right.

Authority does not exist in the sky. It refers to real happenings, it refers to behavior that is authoritative. What makes the use of power "right"? What makes behavior authoritative?

1. The possession of power. There are a lot of power worshippers among us.

2. Fame, respect, prestige of power holders. We are dazzled by fame and cannot discriminate right from wrong.

---

7. Words! A constitution in this sense may or may not be "constitutional" in the sense of limiting the powers of government and protecting individual rights.

3. It's right if it has been done many times before. "Since time immemorial . . ." is a hard line to beat.

4. If everybody else believes it is right, who am I to disagree?

5. It's all very profound and mysterious, and it works wonders; no question it must be right. (Also, the charismatic version: he is very profound and mysterious and he works wonders. He must be right; no question about it.)

6. They earned their way; they got elected; they studied hard. They have a right to do what they're doing.

7. They do everything according to the rules.

8. "They are my kind of people." They act just as I would. I find nothing to complain about.

9. They use scientific ways of finding out and deciding things.

Destruction of Authority

Author: Your generation, more than most, is privileged (or condemned) to create its own authority. The present authority structure is disintegrating.

Reader: How do you know?

Author: I heard Al talking to Goldie Stein today. She was needling him about his political club. He looked bothered. It went like this:

Al: It's easy to say, but nobody's interested in party politics anymore. It's all revolution, now, or turn off. Maybe I ought to go back to college.

Goldie: Well, why don't you go to college, Al? You could still run your club.

Al: No, the college guys are all worked up over war and black power. Where's that going to get me? I'll get caught up in a revolution.

Goldie: Maybe that's the answer.

Al: I don't want anything to do with those bombing freaks. Not that I'm with the Establishment—they're just a bunch of hypocrites. What you've got to do is try to tell a colored guy about . . .

Goldie: Black.

Al: What?

Goldie: Black. You try to tell a black.

Al: Yeah, you've got to try to tell a black about the way things get done!

Goldie: Or a woman!
Al: That's right. But nobody listens anymore.
Goldie: At least college would be exciting.
Al: Well, after five years in politics doing nothing I could stand some excitement.

Al is upset because the traditional sources of authority are no longer respected. Power is being exercised by people who used to be unable to do so, using methods that Al finds unacceptable. What are some of the factors that led to the destruction of authority?

1. Tradition: most modern activists (e.g., blacks, women, youth, poor) have good reason to suspect tradition.

2. There is not enough consensus (agreement) about actions being taken (e.g., war, slums, race relations).

3. "The king has no clothes." The mass media and general public skepticism have stripped off many mysteries of authority; few believe that power has been earned and that it is deserved.

4. Corruption: officials are suspect; people now feel that they are being duped, cheated, and tricked by the authorities and that the law is a farce.

5. Uninspired policy: while problems mushroom, solutions are rare.

Some of these conditions seeped into the conversation between Al and Goldie.

When authority is disintegrating, two general possibilities exist:

1. A repressive regime—large doses of pure power to reduce turbulence and public argument (as in Cromwell's English Commonwealth, 1653–58; or the military coup in Greece, 1967; or the Russian intervention in Czechoslovakia, 1968).

2. A new form of authority—governmental reorganization that jibes with a dominating body of public opinion (as in revolutionary America in 1776–83 and the Jeffersonian-Jacksonian Revolution of 1800–40).

In this age, when all aspects of politics and social life are on direct display through the mass media and fast travel, it is unlikely that authority can remain in a suspended state of disorder for as much as a generation.

A new form of authority is possible.

People (by which I mean a large section of the public of technologically advanced societies) can identify strongly with a form of authority that:

1. Applies scientific method in achieving social goals.
2. Reduces the hocus-pocus of politics and history.
3. Gives therapy instead of punishment.
4. Has an active and adequate program for shaping the future.
5. Includes large groups of people as participants in making policies, wherever it can be arranged.

Postscript to Part One:

The Good of Politics

The lessons are not over. Here is one more, called Postscript. Excuse me for slipping it in, but it has to do with ideals. It connects all that has come before to all that follows after.

* * * * *

It is necessary to orient your politics to an idea of the good because unless you have a general direction in mind you will be wandering around aimlessly, doing no one any good.[1]

Let's play another variation to this tune. People orient themselves in the same directions (with the same general values) because all people are:

1. driven to form a complete, self-possessed world, but
2. also hungry for new experiences and an expanded spirit, and
3. continually adjusting themselves and their surroundings to various combinations of the need to assimilate and expand.

---

1. I have often wished that we might discourage "the wrong kind of people" from studying politics in schools. But this wish is banished by the realization that society in its present state cannot distinguish right from wrong, and furthermore, people change their organic chemical balances and attitudes, and anyway what has been political science so far has not been dangerous, but all too feeble a tool. We would also need to test biologists, business school students, military students, law students, and others. Power decisions are everywhere, and these people will make them too.

The society (culture) adds a great many specifications to this drive system. It molds the size of the oneness; it suggests what are new experiences; it provides the means of adjusting what one is and what one wants to be (adjudication); and also sets the penalties for exceeding the limits of possessions and experiences.

In addition, men agree on many specific proposals and projects because these seem not to affect their differences. For example, those voting for a Democratic President do so for many different reasons, some of which are connected with opposing goals ("politics makes strange bedfellows").

At this point we have historical man. Historical man has had a great many standards arising from his numerous societies. He also has had a great many problems because of his incompetence in applied natural and social science. *That is, he fights, starves, sickens, and generally suffers from cultural conflicts and also from ignorance and misunderstanding.*

It is clear (to me, at least) that man needs two REMEDIES WHICH ARE AT THE SAME TIME DIRECTIVES.

1. FUTURE HUMANITY NEEDS A NEW RULING CHARACTER (PERSONALITY)

2. FUTURE HUMANITY NEEDS A GREATLY IMPROVED APPLIED SCIENCE

Fortunately, both of these are related and interconnected. Both problems, that is, can be solved together. If we can concentrate upon the development of a new leading character-type and give this character-type the knowledge and skill to build the proper institutions for ruling, we shall be on our way.

THE NEW LEADING CHARACTER (whom I shall sometimes call *kalotic* from the Greek "kalon" meaning "the beautiful," "fine civic character," but whom you can call democratic if you don't mind a little confusion)—

1. has an open ego, that is, identifies with all of humanity and is sensitive to the feelings and behavior of others. (Benevolence)

2. is multivalued. He does not get stuck on one thing—like power, wealth, or love. (Polyvalence)

3. projects events, sees their consequences, and is ready to develop techniques to govern himself and others validly, reliably, and flexibly. (Science)

That's all?

That's enough! As Archimedes said, "Give me a place to stand, and a lever long enough, and I can move the world." Give us enough characters of these three qualities, and we can change historical man and fashion a better world.

* * * * *

Questions and Answers:

Is this person manipulative? *Of course.*
Does he do a lot of influencing of others? *Yes.*
Must he be a big leader? *Not at all, at least not directly.*
Can he be power-driven? *No.*
By "kalotic" do you mean "democratic?" *No. By "democratic" I mean "kalotic."*
Can a ditch-digger be kalotic? *Yes.*
Can a famous politician be kalotic? *Yes, despite his fame.*
Can a powerful politician be kalotic? *Yes, provided that his power enlarges and recedes in response to his necessary responsibilities and that neither change occurs because he is losing self-control one way or the other.*
Has this kalotic person ever existed? *Oh, yes, very often, but he's had rough sledding.*
Give an example of such a person. *Look in your mirror.*

* * * * *

We conclude, for the moment, with three scenarios of how a kalotic and a kakotic[2] (the opposite, of course) will make certain choices.

Scenario 1: Time 1789.

Motley crew formed of the wretched of the earth sails ship into interminable waters. Cruel captain provokes mutiny. Captain is set adrift but manages to survive. Men form colony on island.[3]

KALOTIC RESPONSE

Causes of mutiny investigated. Captains generally warned of ultimate right to resistance to tyranny. Rules of naval discipline and recruitment revised.

KAKOTIC RESPONSE

Captain given royal honors. Navy searches the seas for mutineers. Several are hanged.

Scenario 2: Time 1970.

Several hundred massacre victims washed down river in consequence of new war policy. Meanwhile, far away, three technicians are endangered when ship loses partial control but land safely.[4]

2. I guess that if I can use *kalotic* as my word for good, I can use *kakotic* as my word for bad. Both, incidentally, are related to the Greek words *kalo* and *kako*.

3. For full details, see C. Nordhoff and J. N. Hall, *Mutiny on the Bounty* (Boston: Little, Brown & C0., 1932).

4. For full detail on the Apollo 13 mishap, see "Emergency in Space," in *Facts on File* V. XXX, no. 1538 April 16–22, 1970, pp. 253–55 and p. 256 on massacres in Cambodia.

KALOTIC RESPONSE

Causes of massacre ascertained.
Direct preventive action
taken. War policy reviewed.
Personnel involved replaced.
Causes of technical failure in
other case technically studied
for correction.

KAKOTIC RESPONSE

Technicians given majestic honors.
Massacre ignored except
for statement of regret by clerk.

Scenario 3: Time "anytime."

One power-elite furnishes great armaments to weak power against its enemy
in order to expand its own domain. Other power-elite supports the other party.
General disorder ensues.[5]

KALOTIC RESPONSE

Hold grand conference of nations.
Offer large opportunities
(multivalued and constructive) to
involved parties. Condemn
armament transfers and employ
political-economic sanctions and
embargoes.

KAKOTIC RESPONSE

Convert all resources possible to
naked power in contested region.
Ignore quality and future
promise of the party interests
involved. Risk showdown of
regional or nuclear war.

5. This could be the Middle East crisis or the Cuban missile crisis or the India-Pakistan War, or a
dozen other affairs of the past few years. (*Facts on File* or *The New York Times* are regular sources of
news on such happenings.)

Part Two

Twelve Principles,
Propositions,
and Policies

Introduction to Part Two

We now move into a discussion of twelve sets of Principles, Propositions, and Policies. They all pertain to a general philosophy which you can call democratic, but I shall call *kalotic* because I do not pretend to represent everybody's ideas of what democracy should be.

The twelve sets of 3-P's had better be connected logically and importantly to the general philosophical idea, or else I shall have failed (and how many times can you fail in life before you become a general failure?). The general idea can be expressed in one long sentence:

The society of the future should be moved: (1) to develop polyvalent (multivalued) and benevolent (open-hearted) persons, (2) to organize all authorities by representative systems, (3) to produce goods by creative and scientific methods, and (4) to distribute them without vicious discrimination.

But since we are talking about a moving cyclical process in which each factor derives from and also supplies the other factors, the sentence should be visually conceived as follows:

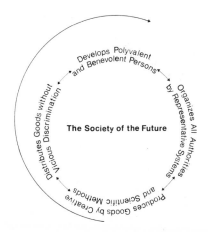

Each factor yields an output to all other factors and the society as a whole, and each factor receives an input from all other factors and the society as a whole. The entire system increases its self-realization as time goes on; the factors become clearer, more governable, and more effective, until a revolution is accomplished!

You are about to read a chart of twelve 3-P's. Read it down or read it across. Or, better, read each column of twelve statements down, and then read each set of 3-P's across. Once you've done that there are two points to be made about these twelve 3-P's:

1. There are hundreds of other principles, propositions, and policies in the ethical and political world. I have chosen these twelve because, in my judgment, they are closely connected with the general philosophical position stated on page 87.

Discussion. Look at the third principle, "Every person should be a leader." I might have said, "Every person should be a *follower*," which I also believe, but I don't think that I would get as far pursuing that principle as I would the first. I might also say, "Very few persons should be leaders." (Classically this is "Oligarchy is the best form of government.") But I don't agree with that; I believe it has many bad effects on mankind, and so I don't use it.

2. There is no compulsory and unique connection between each principle and the proposition and policy associated with it. Other connections *could* be made from a principle to different propositions and policies, or from a proposition to other policies and principles, or from a policy to other propositions and principles.

Discussion. Must Policy 3 necessarily and only be connected with Proposition 3 that "Leaders are critical components in networks of transactions that include cliques, activists, followers, and the counterpart network of opposition"? Now this questions not only whether the proposition is true (I will argue later that it is), but it asks if the given statement has a compulsory and unique connection with Policy 3 and Principle 3. And here the answer is "no" because this proposition would be useful to know even if I had chosen either of the other two principles that I mentioned above. That is, if you are trying to make followers of everybody, it would help you to know what the other elements are like in the environment of a follower—namely leaders, cliques, activists, and their opposing counterparts. Similarly, with the same principle, you could connect up with a different policy; that is, instead of stimulating groups to provide leadership opportunities, you could declare, "Set up leader training courses in every school." Not bad, but I happen to think my policy may be more important.

Chapter title	Principle	Proposition	Policy
1. Political Personality	Polyvalent and benevolent characters should preponderate in society.	People whose characters are rigidly formed are prone to behave as they see it, and become hostile when frustrated, and tend to be exclusive.	Pledge family, school, public, and governmental institutions to the continuing goal of a polyvalent and benevolent society, and weight their procedures accordingly.
2. Civic Activity	The demand and need for civic participation should be fulfilled.	The politically active persons in large groups vary in proportion to the total from 1 percent to 4 percent.	Promote participation in civic affairs from all components of a group by removal of disqualifications and by providing rewards and reducing losses for civic activity, so that the process of selection of benevolent leadership can be opened up.
3. Leadership	Every person should be a leader.	Leaders are critical components in networks of transactions that include cliques, activists, followers, and the counterpart network of opposition.	Stimulate groups to provide leadership opportunities to their members and inventory continuously the personal freedoms available within organizations.
4. Public Opinion	Personal troubles, the troubles of others, and troubles of the future deserve personal attention generally in that order; they deserve social attention in reverse order.	People generally tend to concern themselves with immediate and personal problems, regardless of importance to the larger group or society, or to the next generation.	Plan to handle future troubles now; organize institutions accordingly; conduct continuous propaganda to elevate goals by a half-century.

5. Vicious Discrimination	Society should eliminate discrimination arising from and contributing to the disqualification of persons for full social participation.	Every inherited or acquired trait by which human beings are distinguishable has been the occasion for political disqualification.	Provide equal opportunities to all persons in a group to achieve the group's values and correct those groups whose intended or invariable effect is to monopolize or curtail opportunities.
6. Society and Government	Good government should extend to embrace the social order.	A government of a certain kind coincides with a social order of the same kind.	Apply the same guidelines used to keep political institutions under control to every situation that potentiates and converts power.
7. Government Activities	Government activity, as distinct from public activity, should be minimized in scope, domain, intensity, and duration.	Every kind of activity has at some time been done through government; every kind of activity has also at some time been done outside of government.	Favor diversity over sameness in the organization and determination of public activities; maximize cooperative and educational means of executing governmental policies; introduce radical systems of activity devolution from state to publics.
8. Government Structures	Authoritative structures should represent both their own purposes and the general purposive character of society.	Social structures shape the distribution of power and other values within and among groups.	Impose a kalotic constitution upon systems of power and influence.
9. Wealth and Life Style	The aim of political organization should be to realize every person's credit.	The crediting of values and the provision of means for their exchange are generally illogical and nonkalotic.	Set up a system to reduce social waste and valorize every person's credit.

10. Law and Justice	Law should be whatever it takes to make future human conduct what we would like it to be.	The present system of law and justice profusely breeds laws, law cases, failures of law, and disgust and disrespect in regards to law.	Impose upon all penalizing powers the views of a future society where conflicts and offenses are treated systematically, equitably, and benevolently.
11. Obedience and the State	Obedience to authorities is recommended when the authorities are benevolent and beneficent.	More crimes result from obedience than from rebellion.	When authorities have to resort to "murder as a public good," they should be justifiably desperate (as under direct murderous attack themselves), and their retaliation should have justifiable consequences.
12. History of the Future	History should be continuously rewritten.	All social systems and movements write their own versions of history.	Rewrite history in accord with the visualized and desired future.

Chapter 1

Political Personality

If this chapter were to succeed, we should not have to go much further in political science. Political science would become a deductive science like Euclid's geometry, with which one starts with clear truths and uses reasoning to arrive at new truths. But, confessing in advance, the chapter is doomed to fail.

Assume that we could divide all people into two groups: those whose characters are *good* in every respect, and those who are *no good.*

But already I am saying something shocking—"divide all people"? What kind of totalitarian powers am I asking for? But you see, you already know the task is impossible. There is no earthly division between totally good characters and totally bad.[1]

In the real world every individual is a mixture of good and bad. The environment influences him or her to become better or worse, and he/she acts, being unable to foretell all the effects of any action. Sometimes the effects are better than anticipated and sometimes worse. All this produces a constantly changing environment and, therefore, the cycle is constantly being repeated—the processes always the same, the person always changing.

When the process of creating and utilizing bad characters gets out of hand, we may get results as horrendous as Adolf Hitler and Company produced:

1. The desire for a division between good and bad is one of the reasons why some people create "heaven." Unfortunately, not content with heaven, they reproject it back to earth and then try to force people into one or the other of the two categories.

Box Score

Good	Bad
Made some millions of Germans out of fifty million (the number is in dispute) feel for a few years that they were going somewhere.	About ten million murders and twenty million official killings. Terror and injury to two hundred million. Made Communism look good by comparison. Etc.

Repeat by the thousands (small and large):
> The Hyksos following the Middle Kingdom of ancient Egypt
> The Vandals of the late Roman empire
> Genghis Khan & Co. of the thirteenth century
> Stalin & Co. of the twentieth century

And so on throughout history. In fact, the true extent of misrule, even forgetting the person who growls at you to fill out tax forms properly, is so great that *man's capacity to believe in the better possibilities of life is marvelous and inspiring.*

*   *   *   *   *

"Well, then," says Alice. "You need only discover what produces the good effects on people and what the bad; then arrange your society to promote the good and discourage the bad!"

"Bravo, Alice!" Now we are back where we started. Let us see whether the theologians, philosophers, psychologists, jurists, sociologists, anthropologists, historians, and political scientists past and present can tell us:

1. What kind of character is to be preferred.

2. What kind of society has to be created to help the preferred character make policies for all.

*   *   *   *   *

Let us look at the scenario called *Pilate's Dilemma.*

Poor but eloquent young man is wandering around opening up men's souls, bringing various therapeutic effects to a variety of illnesses, paying little heed to symbols of rank and established "Truth," talking of a future spiritual existence to reward kindness, faith in the goodness of God, etc.

Pilate's Dilemma

Parts of the Personality Affected	Responses to the Young Man	
	Kakotic	*Kalotic*
Assimilation	He is taking away from me and my group.	He is giving me some new ideas of myself; he makes me feel good; I'm going to try to make myself more beautiful of heart and face the world differently.
Experience	There is only the way of the past, my way (which is, of course, the way of the laws as I interpret them).	There is more to the world than meets the eye. All people deserve consideration and help, even the authorities.
Adjustment	He is a criminal, the worst sort because he downgrades the authorities (me and mine), not merely robs or kills a single person.	He is a good fellow. The officials should be more like him. The laws should have a broader, humane spirit. He should be booked to speak in Rome.

   The good young man is going to be received and treated differently depending upon the personality of those who hold power over him. And if the political system is weighted towards the *kakotic,* there will be one kind of typical justice and if *kalotic* another kind. So, that is the problem of *systems design* (constitutions, agency organizations, laws, rules). But *men and women* make laws and systems. Can Al, Bill, Alice, and Belinda make such a system? Can you? That depends upon your skills, but also upon your character. The chances of your mind working along kakotic lines in the Pilate Dilemma would be, I guess, about 20 percent; if you were a typical American, about 40 percent. You are less likely to be kakotic than the typical person because you are a book-reader with all the upgrading of sensitivity and enlarging of sympathy that goes with that.
   To the problem of your character and that of all others is added the problem of the system. The system adds to or subtracts from the chances

that, whatever people may be like, results will differ from what they intend. Therefore, regarding the problem only of people now, a kalotic system is, let us say, 50 percent or more kalotic in its efficiency at reinforcing kalotic personalities; add this 50 percent (goodness in the system) and 60 percent (my estimate of kalotic people in the system) and divide by two. There is a crude imaginary sum of 55 percent. Not good enough yet, Alice!

PRINCIPLE I

Polyvalent and benevolent characters should preponderate in society.

Meanings:

Polyvalent: many-valued and many-valuing; broad-minded and open-minded.

Benevolent: open-hearted and with good will to all; tolerant and well-wishing.

Characters: consistent and persistent dispositions to act toward other people and oneself in specified ways.

Should preponderate in society: when policies are being made throughout a society to govern its behavior, they should ordinarily be made by the polyvalent/benevolent element.

Discussion

Polyvalent/benevolent people have a large capacity for extending sympathy to others and have a healthy self-respect.

They are inclusive; they take in other people and other ideas.

They have a desire to know what is going on in the world around them, and they use this information constructively.

When faced with specializations and specialists, they enlarge the facts, generalize, and see the whole picture.

They seek to please more than to punish, both others and themselves.

They are forgiving and understanding.

They appreciate creativity, invention, and science rather than regarding them simply as narrow tools to help them get what they want.

They assimilate novelty and change.

They are cooperative. They give and accept help.

They are flexible in making choices.

They are interested in the whole range of human activities, "the Divine Comedy."

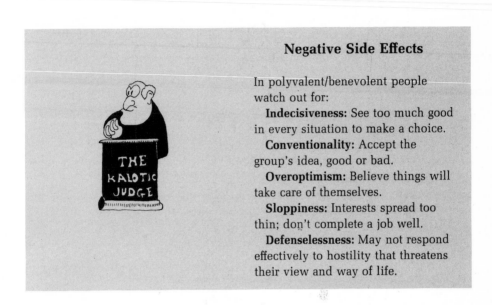

Negative Side Effects

In polyvalent/benevolent people watch out for:

Indecisiveness: See too much good in every situation to make a choice.

Conventionality: Accept the group's idea, good or bad.

Overoptimism: Believe things will take care of themselves.

Sloppiness: Interests spread too thin; don't complete a job well.

Defenselessness: May not respond effectively to hostility that threatens their view and way of life.

Social Effects

Polyvalent/benevolent characters, if preponderant, will:

1. seek to create balanced societies where every interest has a hearing, no interest rules the other, all interests transact rules with each other;

2. be concerned with the full range of human concerns in legislating—that is, with what all kinds of people need, with both local and world affairs;

3. be open to the full employment of scientific method in society and the state, thus reducing greatly the large loss and conflict that comes principally from ignorance, not viciousness;

4. try to conduct organizations that give full credit to all participants and clientele;

5. reduce the ritualism, ceremonialism, magic, mystery, and stratification that spread like dry rot throughout the ship of state;

6. be resistant to the allure of destructive and divisive leaders, no matter how they cloak their character and intentions.

Summation

We like open-minded and open-hearted people and the effects that they have on society and wish that we might breed enough of them to dominate groups and governments.

PROPOSITION I

People whose characters are rigidly formed are prone to force the world to behave as they see it, and become hostile when frustrated; and they tend to be exclusive.

Meanings:

Rigidly formed: holding the *me* closely and separating themselves from others, choosing new experiences along a few circumscribed paths, and holding fixed notions of power and justice.

Prone: tending to act this way unless others or adverse conditions prevent them.

"More than whom": should be understood here, meaning more than the normal person in the average of all societies but especially more than the *kalotic* type of character.

To force: to compel others to take the straight and narrow path with oneself, convinced of one's idea of right.

The world: all objects and persons that one has transactions with or forms opinions about through other sources.

To behave as they see it: having narrow perceptions and not seeing that others' perceptions might be true and good or truer and better.

To become hostile when frustrated: when others do not follow one's perceptions and rights, feeling abused and angry (instead of analytic, dispassionate, compromising, or accepting).

To be exclusive: making sharp distinctions between groups; putting people and events in boxes or categories unmindful that every person and event is in some sense unique.

"When they focus on public objects": should be understood here, meaning that many rigid people are not political, either in groups or in governments. They are interested only in things, machines, flowers, etc.

"And power is an important value": should be understood here, meaning that one has to acquire a taste for power. A rigid person is usually not polyvalent but concentrates upon a limited range of values.

Discussion

Where does the rigid type of character come from? We don't know for sure. Or, rather, we know some of the developmental psychology of

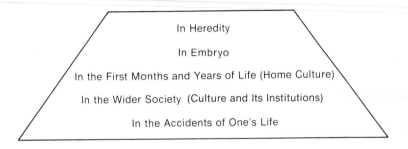

In Heredity

In Embryo

In the First Months and Years of Life (Home Culture)

In the Wider Society (Culture and Its Institutions)

In the Accidents of One's Life

rigidity, but the picture is still blurry and confused. While I'm consulting Brill's Dictionary of Psychology, take a look at the catalogue of synonyms for *broad-mindedness* and *narrow-mindedness* from Roget's Thesaurus.[2] It gives you an idea of the clusters of traits we are dealing with.

524. BROAD-MINDEDNESS

NOUNS 1. **broad-mindedness**, **wide-mindedness**, large-mindedness, noble-mindedness, "the result of flattening high-mindedness out" [George Saintsbury]; **unbigotedness**, unhideboundness, unprovincialism; broad mind.

2. **liberalness**, **liberality**, catholicity, liberal-mindedness; breadth, width, broadness, latitude; liberalism, latitudinarianism; **freethinking**, free thought.

3. **open-mindedness**, openness, accessibility, receptiveness, responsiveness, amenableness; persuadableness, persuasibility; open mind.

4. **tolerance**, toleration; **indulgence**, leniency *or* leniency, **condonation**, acceptance, **forbearance**, **patience**, long-suffering; **charitableness**, charity, generousness, **bigness**, bigheartedness, large-heartedness, greatheartedness, openheartedness; **sympathy**, **understanding**, sympathetic understanding.

5. **unprejudice**, **unbias**, unprejudicedness, unbiasedness; **impartiality**, **detachment**, **dispassionateness**, **disinterestedness**, disinterest; indifference, neutrality; unopinionatedness.

6. **liberal**, liberalist; freethinker, latitudinarian; broad man, big person.

VERBS 7. **keep an open mind**, be big, judge not, suspend judgment, **view with indulgence**, listen to reason, open one's mind to, see both sides, **live and let live**, lean over backwards, tolerate 859.5; accept, **condone**, shut one's eyes to, look the other way, wink at, blink at, **overlook**, **disregard**, **ignore**; "swear allegiance to the words of no master" [Horace].

ADJS. 8. **broad-minded**, wide-minded, large-minded, noble-minded; broad, broad-gauged [U.S.]; **unbigoted**, unhidebound, unprovincial.

9. **liberal**, liberal-minded, broad, wide, catholic, ecumenic(al), cosmopolitan, lib-

2. *Roget's International Thesaurus*, 3rd ed., (New York: Thomas Y. Crowell Company, 1962), pp. 342–343.

eralistic, libertine [derog.]; **free-thinking,** latitudinarian; free-speaking, free-tongued.

10. open-minded, open, accessible, receptive, admissive, responsive, amenable; **persuadable,** persuasible.

11. tolerant, tolerating; **indulgent, lenient, condoning,** forbearing, **forbearant, patient, long-suffering;** charitable, generous, **big,** bighearted, largehearted, greathearted, broadhearted, widehearted, openhearted; **sympathetic, understanding.**

12. unprejudiced, unbiased, unprepossessed, unjaundiced; impartial, dispassionate, detached, disinterested, impersonal, respectless; indifferent, neutral; **unswayed, uninfluenced,** undazzled.

13. unopinionated, unopinioned, unwedded to an opinion; **unpositive, undogmatic,** unpragmatic(al); unsettled, unrooted; uninfatuated, unbesotted, unfanatical.

14. broadening, enlightening.

525. NARROW-MINDEDNESS

NOUNS **1. narrow-mindedness,** littlemindedness, small-mindedness; **smallness, littleness, meanness, pettiness; bigotry,** bigotedness; **illiberality,** uncatholicity; **narrowness,** insularity, insularism, provincialism; **hideboundness,** strait-lacedness, stuffiness [coll.]; **shortsightedness,** nearsightedness, purblindness; **blind side, blind spot,** mote in the eye; closed mind.

2. intolerance, intoleration; **uncharitableness,** ungenerousness; unforbearance.

3. prejudice, prejudgment, **predilection, prepossession,** preconception, predetermination; **bias, bent,** leaning, inclination, warp, twist; complex [coll.]; **jaundice,** jaundiced eye; **partiality,** onesidedness, undispassionateness, undetachment.

4. class consciousness, class prejudice, **discrimination,** social discrimination, minority prejudice; **racism,** racialism, race prejudice, race snobbery, racial discrimination; anti-Semitism, redbaiting; **social barrier,** class distinction; **color line,** color bar; Jim Crow law; **segregation,** apartheid [Afrikaan]; desegregation.

5. bigot, intolerant, illiberal, little person; opinionist **512.7;** fanatic **472.17.**

VERBS **6. close one's mind**, shut the eyes of one's mind; **view with a jaundiced eye**, not see beyond one's nose *or* an inch beyond one's nose, see but one side of the question, look only at one side of the shield.

7. discriminate against, draw the line, draw the color line, redbait.

8. prejudice, prejudice against, prepossess, predetermine, **jaundice, influence, sway, bias**, warp, twist.

9. (present with bias) **angle, slant.**

ADJS. **10. narrow-minded**, little-minded, small-minded, narrowhearted, narrow-souled, narrow-spirited, mean-spirited; **small, little, mean, petty; bigoted,** bigotish; **illiberal**, unliberal, uncatholic; **narrow,** narrow-gauged [U.S.]; provincial, insular, parochial, confined; **hidebound**, creedbound, barkbound; **strait-laced**, stuffy [coll.]; **shortsighted**, nearsighted, purblind.

11. intolerant, untolerating; **unsympathetic**, nonunderstanding; **uncharitable, ungenerous; unindulgent**, uncondoning, unforbearing; deaf, deaf-minded, deaf to reason.

12. prejudiced, prepossessed, **biased, jaundiced**, colored, **partial**, one-sided, partisan, influenced, swayed, **interested, undetached**, undispassionate; class-conscious.

13. opinionated 512.22.

Now while some of my readers are circling to the right of the problem, others can begin circling to the left. In Ernest Jones' monumental book, *The Life and Work of Sigmund Freud,* we come across the following paragraph.

In 1908 [when he was 52 years old] Freud published five papers. The first of them, and the most original one, proved to be a bombshell and aroused more derision than anything he had hitherto written. It was a short paper, only a couple of pages, in which he pointed out that anal sensations in infancy, on the erotic nature of which he had long insisted, were capable of affecting character traits in a quite specific way. That any feature of one's character could proceed from such lowly origins seemed then to the outside world purely preposterous, although the truth of the conclusion is now widely recognized.[3]

3. Ernest Jones, *The Life and Work of Sigmund Freud* (Garden City, N.Y.: Doubleday & Company, Inc., Anchor Books, 1963), pp. 257–58.

Actually many people long before Freud had noticed the relation between the child's character and the same person's adult character. Why else bother with all the training of children to ensure that they behave like their parents? All societies everywhere have done so.

But the vast majority of people (including psychologists and political experts) could be made shocked and derisive because they were blinded. "Who? Me? Don't make me laugh!" Such is a common attitude toward a new, difficult, and embarrassing theory. People were:

1. Suppressing memories of many confusing or embarrassing infant activities although these memories persisted as active forces in adult behavior.

2. Acknowledging only some connections between infant and adult behavior.

3. Removing still other connections by using adult words that mean the same as words used to refer to infant behavior. (New fancy names appear such as "tenacity," "conscience," "respect for authority," "artistic ability," "religious devotion," "public opinion");

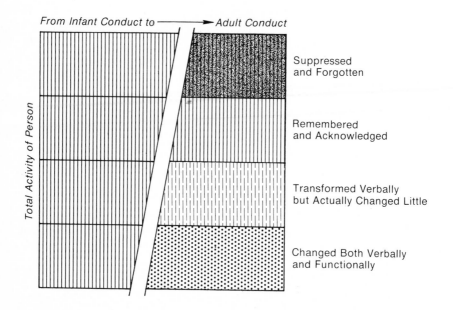

4. Really (but only in part) altering their traits by their life experience (actually, there *are* many changes through life, from infancy onwards, but *some* change does not mean *everything* is changed).

For example, some nasty things that happen to babies are forgotten both by them and their elders, even though the neurological system does *not* forget so readily. Thus, a child who is trained very early and intensively to control his excretions is prone in later years to respect habit, training, precision, neatness in his own behavior and that of others. If the same early discipline is carried on by threats, punishments, and shame, he is more likely, in later life, to expect to use threats and punishment for whatever behavior he deems good. Why select toilet training? Because it is one of the earliest prolonged exposures to pain and discipline of an infant's life. Try to think of others like it.

Indifference is another important factor in an infant's life. If a baby is not fondled often and at length and not treated to the company, sights, sounds, smells of friendly handlers, she or he may later be unable to suffer the closeness of others even while needing it. The "love-starved," after a point is reached, not only may not be able to ingest love, but may have a real inability to eat or "take in" other goods.

These two contrasting experiences (sometimes they may go together, poor baby!) will find their way into later political behavior.

To the contemporary scientific mind, this process seems logical, plausible, even deducible. The application of observation, prolonged over many years, however, is exceedingly difficult.

The first kind of training—harsh, punitive, imparting feelings of guilt that can easily find their place on objects of public concern (issues, leaders, groups)—is directly in line with our rigid type. The second type of training is apt to produce apathy, feelings of aloneness, coldness to the sufferings of others. In both cases "as the twig is bent, so grows the tree," and "the child is father to the man." Early training usually begets behavior and attitudes in line with the original thrust of the training.

A Would-Be Presidential Assassin

Giuseppe Zangara was wretchedly mistreated by his father, could not hold jobs, lived alone and unloved. He picked up antiauthoritarian ideas. Intense blinding headaches plagued him, and he heard voices and dreamed terrible dreams of his father. Voices told him to kill the President-elect, Franklin D. Roosevelt. He got a gun, fired it at FDR and missed, killing Mayor Cermak of Chicago instead. Though palpably insane he was executed.

A Presidential Assassin

Mom had a heavy hand in little Lee Oswald's life. Feelings of great inadequacy fought with megalomanic, world-conquering visions. The marines didn't help, nor did his various attempts to find ideological sustenance in Russia or Cuba, nor did his wife. She found him insufferable at times, ridiculed him, and one day he took his rifle and shot the President of the U.S.A. who was receiving the plaudits of a crowd from an open car. He was caught by the police and murdered by an irate vigilante who had serious psychological problems of his own.

The infant is a terrible dominator. He screams until his wants are met. If they are met reasonably well, he becomes gradually socialized to peaceful accommodation and later in life may not even think of using power over others except as a last resort. But power, remember, is the infant's first and last resort. He is absolutely helpless by himself but would like to be all-powerful. If he continues to feel helpless, owing to indifference and mistreatment from those around him, even when it is in the name of training, he may ultimately come to have an extraordinary respect for power and a craving for it.

Famous Characters Anonymous

When you begin to analyze single characters, you find them very special, and especially in politics (and history) people put out only the clues about themselves that they believe to be acceptable and popular. That is why intensive, confidential studies of people by personality psychologists are the best sources of our knowledge, and why the speculations I am offering here mainly serve to open up the problem of the relation between power and personality. We cast our mind over history and find highly varied characters. Here I share with you my speculations. (The names are omitted to protect the innocent.)

Senator "A" was a stern defender of the "old Roman Virtues" and ended all his senatorial speeches obsessively with the demand: "Carthage must be destroyed," until the Romans violated their treaty and destroyed the near-helpless city. (It was believed for a long time that the god Apollo had cursed the Romans for ruining "his favored city" unjustly.)

Dictator "B" was a great general and politician; Emperor of the French; crippler of France through devastating wars and centralized bureaucracy. Narcissistic overcompensator (that is, excessive self-love of an infantile type with a demand to be universally loved [he made it] and a fury of activity to compensate for small physique, some sexual impotency, provincialism [came from Italian-speaking Corsica]).

Mr. President "C" suffered from asthma; he compensated for his poor physique, poor vision, poor health by becoming a Wild West he-man. He was known as a law-and-order man and as a trust-buster, but his interest in these issues was to play a role, not to express indignation. In international affairs he was warlike and aggressive.

Mr. President "D" was a magnificently trained man, in time with the future, who had an enormous self-esteem ("God complex") that made him rigid and inflexible in crises over the power of fraternities at Princeton, the power of old-line politicians in New Jersey, and the power of the Senate in foreign affairs, specifically regarding joining the League of Nations. He forgot the United States was a republic with many demigods (e.g., Senator Lodge), misjudged public opinion, lost a big political battle, and went to pieces mentally and physically.

Mr. President "E" was a little-studied President, whose tight lips marked a tight character, a "tightwad," a law-and-order man in a circumscribed way, who rose to fame for breaking a police strike in Boston while governor of Massachusetts. As a national leader he exemplified beautifully how to ride in one direction (the inner-directed "old virtues") while the nation rode in another ("the roaring twenties").

Mr. President "F"—false type—why would such a rich big-spender, domineering, swashbuckling man (more a Renaissance type than an inner-directed, conscience [guilt]-driven type) make propaganda about turning off the White House lights to save electricity? (Because many millions of Americans save a few pennies by turning off lights—actually, they don't save any more, but the ritual gives a feeling of saving, a neat little gesture appeasing the gods of Thrift and Detail.)

Mr. President "G" was an orphan and a great engineer with a concern for individuals but an incapacity to excite love. Contrary to opinion, he was as much a "welfare state" man in action (not in speech) as his successor.

Mr. President "H"—I'd place him in the rigid category in his basic character structure but with a large surface layer of cool opportunism. His famous cleverness ("cuteness") is narrowly confined to conventional political norms, and exercised mechanically. Some indications are that he locks on an issue, "digs himself deeper," but he is aware of this trait and avoids its activation by determined opportunism.

Some of these characters are more clearly rigid than others. I cite only famous cases because they are conversation pieces; people have some recollection of them. Many other rigid types are carefully described in various psychological studies and novels. Millions of others exist.[4] You may not be able to imagine how many or to recognize the rigidity within yourself until you've asked ordinary people leading questions and seen the answers you get.

Imaginary Interview #924 of a Cross-Section of the American People

INTERVIEWER   RESPONDENT

"Do you think we'll ever have peace?"

"Not so long as the Russians aren't taken care of."

"What of the Chinese?"

"Them too."

"What about the Jews?"

"Well, you have to admire the way they get around things, but . . . say, where you from?"

"Around here."

"Did you see where some UFO's landed near Charlotte the other night?"

"Is that a fact?"

"Yep."

"Russians again?"

"No, not Russians. You don't think *they* tell us everything, do you?"

"I guess not."

"But you know, they're clean, these UFO people. Not a trace left behind."

"No litterbugs, huh?"

"No. Heh, heh. Lot of dirty pigs of our own. That's enough."

"How are you going to tackle this problem of pollution?"

"Simple. Make 'em clean up their own mess."

---

4. We do not see things as they are, we see them as we are. We all do this, but the rigid types do it to the point of real damage to others.

"You mean rivers and everything? The air. How will they do that?"

"That's their problem. Stiffer laws. That's all we need. Put a few of them in jail and you'll see what happens."

"Aren't the jails pretty crowded and stinking now?"

"Naw. Look, I'm no do-gooder. There's always room for one more, you know what I mean, heh, heh."

"What's your line of work?"

"I'm a riveter. But I'm really trained for a better job. Construction Supervisor."

"Doesn't the noise bother you?"

"What's that? The noise. No, it don't bother me none. The guys in the front office been holding out on me, though."

"For the Supervisor's job?"

"Yeah. I tell my kid to go in through the front office, not like his old man."

"Does he agree?"

"Sure. I guess so. He stays away from anything technical. He's going into business administration."

"But doesn't he want a real trade, a technical trade?"

"Naw, you know these kids nowadays don't know the meaning of work. They're ready to give everything up that's good and hard. I work twelve hours a day if I can."

"Why do you do that, the money?"

"Maybe. Sure I get tired, but it makes me feel better knowing I've worked hard."

"Who's the hardest-working person you know?"

"The President. He has a tough job. But politicians are a lazy bunch."

"I gather you wouldn't want your son to be a politician?"

"Him? Never! Anyway, he's not the type. Too bashful."

"Who has the more important part in raising a child, the father or the mother?"

"The mother. Absolutely. Course I remember in the old days, the father was the strict one. Whenever my father caught me fooling around, he gave me hell. But things are changed. You hardly see the kids any more."

"What did your father do?"

"He was a dairy plant manager. I've gone down in the world, huh?"

"Depends on how you look at it."

"Oh yes I have."

"Professor, is the opposite of a fascist a communist?"

"No, Belinda. They both have closed minds and belong to rigid doctrinal movements, though they oppose each other. They and their movements may begin as antiauthoritarian, but they end as authoritarian systems."

"Oh, can't you keep things simple?"

"One more point—the true F and C types have a low tolerance for ambiguity."

Political Personality Test

Force yourself to circle an answer one way or the other.

1. I look in the mirror a lot and am very conscious of my appearance. (Yes, No)

2. I make a lot of judgments about others being bad or good and right or wrong. (Yes, No)

3. I stick with my own kind. (Yes, No)

4. I become very annoyed when things keep changing or I don't know where I stand. (Yes, No)

5. There's a right way and a wrong way to do everything. (Yes, No)

6. I daydream at least once a day about having power and being a leader. (Yes, No)

7. You have to suffer a lot to achieve anything worthwhile. (Yes, No)

8. People have millions of secrets and I keep my share, too. (Yes, No)

Special Question:

9. Frankly, I haven't been myself for a couple of years. (Yes, No)

If the answer to 9 is *yes,* forget the test score and hope for the best. (The point of that question is that serious metabolic changes often occur in adolescence—and old age—producing marked symptoms of rigidity.) If the answer to 9 is *no* and you mark *yes* on seven or eight items, apply for a certificate disqualifying yourself from politics. If all answers are *no,* you may use the author's name as a reference in applying for campaign contributions. If you are somewhere in the middle, adjust yourself accordingly.

Now, if we were sure that tests such as this one identified *rigid types,* and if a large percentage scored high on *no,* and if we could prove many effects of importance were connected with these scores, then, *and only then,* might we begin to discriminate among people and say, "Look, please stay out of positions where you have to teach our children, or make decisions influencing other peoples' lives, until you can show that you have your rigid traits under control or until we have created such an efficient organizational system that you will be controlled no matter what you are prone to do."

We are not in this position yet, not in any general and systematic way. All we can say now is, "Take a look at yourself; here are some questions and scores that will help you understand yourself and others; here are some experiences that you will have later where you have to watch yourself and will be able to watch others."

How Rigidius and Rigidia Behave

What are such experiences and effects, looking at them now from the perspective of a rigid character. How will Rigidius and Rigidia act when faced with some typical political experiences and settings?

1. Rigidius and Rigidia will paint the world in sombre colors and act accordingly. (They will want to spend too many resources on defense, security, protection.)

2. They will see conspiracies of many types where conspiracies do not exist. (They will be stirring up ill will and diverting attention and energy to popular compulsions like "cleaning up the mess," "balancing the budget before anything else," and "red-baiting.")

3. They will keep secrets that need not be secret. (They will cause many public actions to be cloaked in privacy, depriving the group of the chance to change its mind, and so on.)

4. They will try to keep under control people and groups that should be left free. (Not being free themselves, they will suffer seeing other people free and will become experts on the *dis*advantages of all kinds of freedom.)

5. They will sacrifice their imagination and the search for alternative solutions, while pursuing one chosen solution to an excessive degree. (They will decide that a war has to be won; "There is no substitute for victory," they declare.)

6. They will keep government and power full of mysteries and magic. (Being prone to secretiveness and being respecters of power, they will not resent the dehumanizing effects of these practices.)

7. They will derive pleasure from the punishment of alleged offenders against society.

8. They will be antagonistic and aggressive toward groups to which they do not belong, while being overprotective of their own groups. (They will promote social schisms, often unconsciously.)

9. They will resent, and combat with righteous indignation, changes that do not conform to their narrow views or that are proposed by groups not their own. (They will have either warped ideas or no ideas at all of what goes on "on the other side of the tracks.")

10. They will be disturbed by small difficulties and get "hung up" on them, to the detriment of larger solutions, and will thus tend to be shortsighted in many areas. (They will "fiddle while Rome burns," engage in costly struggles over particular cases regardless of the general problem, block a group's progress toward a solution of problems by insisting on giving attention to legalistic technicalities or niceties.)

Three Extreme and Deadly Cases of Rigidity and Obsession

What would be some extreme cases where characters of the obsessive and rigid type acquired supreme power?

Dictator "A", for one. Raised comfortably from a physical point of view, but raised strictly and devoutly as a Puritan, he became a leader of the Parliamentary party when a corrupt divine-right monarchy was giving unbending resistance to social change. He organized an army efficiently—which was not done in those days—beat the royal forces, destroyed some of his own best troops who were too republican and anarchist, massacred large numbers of Irish Catholics and laid waste Ireland, dissolved the Parliament for not behaving according to his "God-given" ideas, and became Lord Protector until his natural death. His regime was harsh enough to make the English forget about republicanism for centuries.

Dictator "B", for another. Raised in poverty and uncertainty over his father's identity, he found a home in the German army; an Austrian, he became super-German and developed a sticky mass of racist and nationalistic obsessions that attracted a small following of fanatics in a country beset by many kinds of social problems. By violence and terror on the streets, his men elevated him to a position where he might rally a larger following and he ended up as legal chancellor. He destroyed the old governmental structure, set up a hero cult of Der Führer, and proceeded to annihilate internal opposition and to divide and conquer Europe. There was a pure line of precedent from the madness of his youth through all the years leading to his suicide.

Dictator "C", as a third extreme case. Earliest recollections of the dictator of the U.S.S.R. are of a narrow, suspicious, careful, unimaginative character. Stalin worked with Lenin as a back-up man rather than a front man; as Communist party secretary he moved his henchmen into strategic positions; he eliminated Trotsky, carried on successively worse purges of the leadership and party rank and file, invaded Finland, managed to survive the terrible destruction wrought by the Nazi invasion of Russia (which was all the worse owing to his paranoid ruthlessness), and died, to everyone's relief, after a dozen years of continued suspicious imposition of stifling regimentation upon Soviet society.

"It Can't Happen Here"

The psychology of "It can't happen here" comes out of the universal tendency of people to suppress bad memories, bad forebodings, and bad associations. It makes people dismiss "extreme cases" as irrelevant.

Will it help if I declare flatly that probably a fourth of all people who have ever lived have been affected directly by the type of case that we have presented here as "extreme," and that probably another quarter have suffered less severely during their lives from less virulent rule of the same type, and that virtually everyone who has ever lived has been affected in one or more of their groups by continual reinfection from the same processes? It is a rare American community whose history doesn't show some examples of "Little Hitlers" among its police, plutocrats, and politicians. The Calvin, Mussolini, Peron, de Gaulle, Franco, Castro, Mao, Ho Chi Minh, Chiang Kai-shek regimes, as well as others, "failed" to acquire the full set of qualities; all had at least some "extreme" elements and probably would have displayed more if it weren't for cultural differences, lack of resources, and/or outside resistance.

POLICY I

When you have identified a principle by which some aspect of life should be guided, and figured out a proposition describing human relations as they stand related to that aspect of life, you are ready to decide upon a policy. A policy is, in effect, an ordering of all the elements in a situation to bring about its desired transformation.

Assuming that we desire to promote a certain kind of character in politics, and that the situation abounds with unsympathetic characters, what do we do? In keeping with the fact that we have chosen to work on a general level of principle and proposition, we shall formulate policy on a general level, too. Also, in keeping with our intention to concentrate upon important rather than minor problems, we shall try to devise a policy that will measure up to the importance of the principle.

Let us then consider the following policy:

<blockquote>

Pledge family, school, public, and governmental institutions to the continuing goal of a polyvalent and benevolent society and weight their procedures accordingly.

</blockquote>

Meanings:

Notice that the first part of the policy calls for the domination of social elements by an attitude and goal, while the second part ("and weight their procedures accordingly") calls for attention to the structures of the same social elements. We shall not discuss this second part here, because much of the book will deal with it. Rather we shall discuss only the problem of *attitude.* And so we have only two brief notes here:

Pledge: assure that a goal and attitude are thoroughly agreed to. (We don't mean that everyone has to swear oaths every day.)

Continuing: social operations of all kinds over the life-span of the organization are imbued with the goal.

Discussion

We have determined that the problem of character in politics is important in every group and government, and that a major source of trouble in politics is rigid types who are politicized. What resources can be applied to reduce the number of these types and bring about the preponderance of the polyvalent/benevolent types?

1. *The polyvalent/benevolent types.* When informed of the nature of a situation and of the problem, they can turn their attention and energies to it.

2. *Specialized polyvalent/benevolent types who have skills appropriate to the situation.* These would include especially medical doctors, nurses, psychiatrists, psychologists, teachers of the young, family counsellors, social workers (in particular those dealing with dependent and delinquent children), and educators. Also included are people in the mass media—newspapers, magazines, radio, television, and a great many special journals, newsletters, bulletins, and so on.

3. *Many rigid and mixed types who are aware of their limitations and either can control their own actions, or are able to prescribe what is good for others.* "Do as I say, not as I do" is OK as long as it is offered humbly and honestly. A self-cured person very often is highly energized by his own therapeutic experience.

4. *All the constitutions and practices of groups that are congenial to the development of polyvalence and benevolence.* It is rare that a body of laws, rules, and practices is thoroughly one-sided. Nor are the laws ever complete. For example, an ordinary policeman obeying all existing laws still has a broad range of choices in dealing with people in many different situations. What he chooses to enforce and to advise depends upon his own character training.

5. *Practically all techniques of influence that can be employed in this type of campaign:*

A. The ordinary spreading of the idea, as with any idea that becomes current and fashionable via the press, movies, gossip, cocktail parties, picnics, classrooms, clubs, etc.

ETC.

It is about time to apologize for a word:

That wonderful word *"etc."* and its cousins, "and so forth," "and so on," ". . . ," "et al.," and "for example."

We must use these words a hundred times in this book. WHY? Any professor of linguistic style will tell you that it's not nice to let your elegant sentences dangle and dwindle into et ceteras. Scientists

will tell you that any proof that depends upon one or two cases and dissolves into et ceteras is no proof at all. They are right—an example is not a proof!

In apologizing for "etc." we may declare:

1. It is a way of reminding you that one example does not prove a rule.

2. It is a way of saying that additional evidence of the same kind could be brought forward.

3. It is a way of bringing in quickly at least one case to make an abstract point explicit.

And incidentally, what makes a brief example effective is not only its truth, that is, its correct representation of the rule, but also the audience's (your) receptivity. To speak of "the thrill of exercising power, as in voting in an election," will not have much meaning to people who don't know what it is to take part in an election.

B. A refocusing of research on human relations where a choice is possible, influencing the selection of research in directions that will clarify, validate, and help apply the theory of P/B preponderance.

C. Formation of special groups (such as countergroups, factions, or lobbying groups) wherever wrong-headed types dominate a situation.

D. Large-scale personal and group therapy. This is an age of widespread anxiety, of feelings of rootlessness and lawlessness, of lack of personal ties and affection. Ways must be found of bringing out the best in peoples' characters and we cannot rely upon the old institutions (schools, churches, neighborhoods, political parties, large companies, bureaucracies, Boy Scouts, etc.) to do it, at least not in the ways they have used in the past. Many forms of therapy have been invented to get people in affectional or just sane contact and communication with one another and with the larger society. Among them are:

(1) Better individual counselling. The priests, pastors, psychiatrists, guidance counsellors, advisers, social case workers, etc., need to be revived or reoriented to help *normalize* people, to make them feel better adjusted and less hostile.

(2) Sociometry, group counselling, encounter groups, sensitivity groups, therapy groups, rapport groups, etc. Numbers of these groups exist, often using bizarre techniques and usually with orientation. But usually they try to open up peoples' souls, to make them more affectionate and less hostile, to give people confidence and build their morale for attacking the frustrations of modern life.

(3) Role playing. Many means, including those listed in (1) and (2), can be used to get people to feel like other people, including those they consider enemies. The advantage of placing oneself in somebody else's shoes is that one's value system and one's good-will are extended to groups and people that are otherwise excluded and discriminated against.

E. The revival of good historical models. History, and especially semi-fictional or mythical history in schoolbooks, movies, and other media, can be a great teacher of character. The new character must be defined and then some of the old stories about Socrates, Jesus, Lincoln, and a thousand other characters must be rewritten to stress our preferred type of personality. So long as the television pours out happy visions of mass slaughter, the schoolbooks show pretty pictures of terrible battles as solutions of human problems, and the favorite sculptures of American town squares are old cannons or charging horsemen, the task of changing human character is obviously only beginning.

Groups of all types that operate according to polyvalent/benevolent principles should be praised and publicized. We can begin with the family—instead of elevating the patriarchal family ("the good old days when the man was boss"), or making a comic-strip fool of the men and women who are trying to run a family by polyvalent/benevolent principles, we should recognize, praise, and illuminate the good effects to all of society of the democratic (kalotic) family. Similarly with other of the institutions, praise and publicity should go to the side of every group that raises its members from one level of life experience to another. Each group to which a person belongs, beginning in infancy, is a developing and rehearsal of his personality for the next group that he joins.

F. Large-scale visiting and hostaging. The words *hostel* and *hostage* are related. When large numbers of people visit other people, inside and outside their own countries, they often take the part of and play the role of the other people. They are no longer useful pawns in the dirty games of chauvinistic and localistic politics. Also, it would take a relatively small investment of time and money to exchange a million Russian, Chinese, and American visitors for a year at a time; these hostages would make the ruling classes behave more responsibly toward one another and equip the visitors to explain the facts about the two countries to their own countrymen. Why this isn't done is part of the vicious circle of politics; the ruling classes of both countries are deeply prejudiced, negative, unimaginative, suspicious, and living in the ruts of history and routine; what they cannot perceive, ipso facto, cannot exist.

G. Recruitment policies of all organizations (who is let in the door). Again, the vicious circle has to be broken. If polyvalent/benevolent characters are excluded at the door of a church, school, profession, agency, company, or club, then the group will be reinforced in its own vices and become more and more up-tight in its policies and internal and external behavior.

Reasonable Expectations

We do not wish to give the impression that all social life will be turned into a breeding and propaganda machine for a particular ideal man. No, that would be a monstrous conception. What we are saying is essentially this: every society educates its people ideologically and civically. We as individuals learn, without noticing it, to support tons of social atmospheric pressure. Now we want to change the quality of the pressure in order to change some of the characters and the role of certain characters in society. Therefore we have to name the groups, persons, and techniques that set the pressure gauges, and suggest to them some new settings more in accord with our ideals of government. It's a great deal to achieve, but one shouldn't feel that it is some additional burden of pressure.

Nevertheless, all of this change of viewpoint and resulting change of influence cannot succeed entirely. The intelligent control of people's character is a most difficult task. You can imagine all the reasons that will be discovered for doing nothing or very little, or talking big and doing little.

The resources in terms of people and structures are huge but a great many people will be dropouts in their efforts. Think merely of all the propaganda that is put out on the subject of brotherly love, good race relations, etc., and how much good it does. Many times the effort to create new character will not bring great change. Fortunately, we are better equipped now than ever before to set in motion desired changes. And change in regard to character can also be supported by changes in structure and laws, which we shall discuss.

Chapter 2

Civic Activity

If most masters of political science have said that "the few rule the many" and most people who call themselves democrats say that "democracy is rule by the people," we are obviously in some trouble—real trouble or trouble with words or both. With the help of some statistics and our own way of looking at politics, and, to be sure, with some shuffling of words, I think that we can solve the problem. I should warn that in the process, some readers will lose their virginal idea of democracy. Let us begin.

PROPOSITION II

The politically active persons
in large groups vary
in proportion to the total
from 1 percent to 4 percent.[1]

1. See p. 136 ff. for the derivation of this figure.

Meanings:

Large groups: any group whose members number over 1000. This definition can be argued forever. I am talking here about large groups, because
of wide fluctuations in the activity in small groups. Note also, that I am
not talking about *leaders,* but only about *activists,* who may have a
lower rate of performance and achievement.

Examples of large groups: We should be clear as to what kinds of groups we
mean:

Schools, school districts
Businesses, business associations
Church sects, affiliated churches, large parishes
Cities, towns, counties, states, provinces, nations
Armies, bureaus, agencies
Political parties, major factions, movements
Large clubs, fraternities
Each group has its own political/governmental system. Each group includes
few active and many passive members, but groups differ in proportion of
activists.

Among small groups the *family* is particularly interesting. There are many
kinds of families, and in all of them government is a big problem. Compare
the patriarchal family of the biblical or Roman type with the American or
French nuclear family, where egalitarian or child-dominated or matriarchal
government occurs frequently. And it's of no use to argue that a family is not
politics and government. Some of the most marvelously organized decision
systems and most prolonged, vicious, and conflict-filled systems of government are to be found here.

But let's not stop at the family level either. We should also consider "the
government of the passions"—that is, the individual's own internal government and, yes, politics. Again let us not quibble. At one time, the atom was
supposed to be the final reduction of all matter; nowadays, a considerable
part of all physics devotes itself to subatomic structures and events. Similarly, a person can look into himself or herself and discover a universe of
hierarchies, factions, liberties and restraints, theories of self-control, self-
imposed sanctions, etc. Indeed, psychology can be regarded largely as the
study of government of the self.

Persons: all persons. Children, therefore, are included wherever they
belong to a group, even if the group cannot or does not give them a
chance to participate in decision making. Under these circumstances,
their presence will, of course, lower the *proportion* of *activists.* It is

necessary, therefore, to watch the statistical parameters of the group. Are *customers* part of an industrial group, say the automobile industry? (The "average American" has as big a stake in the conduct of the automobile industry as he has in Vietnam!) Are slaves to be counted as part of the population for purposes of calculating the proportion of activists? (Absurd? Recall the hot debate at the Constitutional Convention of 1787 over whether slaves should be counted in determining state population for representation in Congress.) So there remains a problem of definition of group membership that must always be settled before a discussion begins.

Politically: whatever has to do with power and the governing influence in a group. This should be clear enough by now. We are here speaking of people acting to influence and dominate group decisions (and restraints on decisions). Obviously, in every group, people are active; they eat, work, play, talk, and carry on in many ways that are not political, but these types of activity do not concern us here.

Active: engaging in actions beyond a certain norm or average point that is somewhat arbitrary, but also very real. Like the population of the group, this must be defined in each case or set of cases under consideration. Thus, how many masses per year must a person attend to be an active Catholic or Episcopalian? Need you merely give money to the Community Chest welfare drive in order to be considered as active in that organization, or must you collect money from others? Must you be at least a shop steward to count as active in your union? If some part of the student body of your college goes on strike and shuts the campus down, are you active by staying home, by studying, by hanging around the library building, or must you do more, either for or against the strike, or something unrelated to the strike, like writing to your friends elsewhere describing its evolution? Are you active in politics if you vote regularly?

We conclude that we must begin by inventorying all types of political actions, finding out which of them each person does, and giving everyone a score. We can then say: "If you score over X, you are an activist in this group."

How else can you cope with the problem? We must go this way as far as we can, and where we cannot find the facts, we still have to think about the problem in this way. Then, finally, we assemble everybody's scores and determine the politically active proportion in this group (like "2.23 percent" or something on that order).

Note that if we want to enlarge the proportion of "active," we simply move the X up or down. Thus, if we define "the politically active" in Great

Britain or the U.S. national government or elsewhere as anyone who usually votes in general elections, we shall get a high proportion of the population—perhaps 60 percent. Setting the gauge at X must therefore be a decision that we make according to what we want to do. And what we want is to divide populations up into different types of influentials to learn more about political behavior and public policy, and what's wrong, and what might be done about it. So we set the gauge according to our feeling of where is most useful. I confess it: it is a hunch (or hypothesis) about where the important breaking points and shifts in behavior occur. You are welcome to your own hunches.

The Types of Activity

AGITATING	Every specific political activity can be placed under
ORGANIZING	one of these headings. Thus both casting a vote and
DECIDING AND	reporting on the conduct of officials can be grouped
EVALUATING	under Deciding and Evaluating. Both a political argu-
EXECUTING	ment with a friend and a Presidential message can go
	under Agitating.

RECALL: Power (and influence) can be measured by *Domain, Scope, Intensity,* and *Duration* (pp. 65–66). Activities of all types can be classified according to this scheme and thereby activities of *low impact* can be distinguished from those of *high impact.*

AGAIN: This is an *empirical* process. You have to find the facts. This is also a *sensing* process. You have to sense where a dividing line between *powerful* or *influential* and *non*powerful or *non*influential would be.

Types of Activists

This chapter is not focused upon leadership, but upon activity. Hence, we are talking especially about what is usually called the "active citizen" or the "good group member." Leaders, it should be remembered, are included among the active citizens and good group members. Thus, if we were to do all the inventories and scoring that we referred to on page 123, we should probably be able to divide every large group, including the nation, into the following categories:

1. LEADERS

Leaders are in control of decisions. The larger the group, generally, the smaller their proportion of the total. Examples: U.S. senators; corporate presidents; bishops; generals; movement chiefs. There may be about 5000 such leaders in the United States.

2. INFLUENTIALS

Influentials directly affect the leaders and their decisions but can be put off for a time or are sporadic in their influence or cannot command the full sanctions that a group possesses. Examples: newspaper editors, lobbyists, the "outs," large stockholders, staff officers, consultants. The U.S.A. probably contains some 10,000 such influentials.

THE
ACTIVISTS

3. POLITISTS

Politists are moderately influential, do the everyday work of power and influence, watch, talk, criticize, know, are in and out of the process, supply the "henchmen." Perhaps 4 million Americans are politists.

In addition to the activists, we have two other categories.

4. ORDINARIES

Ordinaries are the aware, somewhat interested, routinely involved body of the public in a large group. There is heavy exchange with the politist personnel. About 75 million Americans might be called "ordinaries."

5. INDIFFERENTS

Indifferents are the politically apathetic, unaware, uninvolved. They are in the group because they must be, to make a living as in a company or a labor union, or for hereditary reasons (as in a nation or many religions), or because somebody influenced them to join. Some 65 million Americans would be called indifferent.

The PUBLIC, depending upon how you wish to use the word, can include all five groups, or all except no. 5, or can distinguish between no. 1 and nos. 2, 3, 4 or between no. 1 and all the rest.[2]

---

2. Add about 60 million Americans under 18 to the various numbers of the five groups and one arrives at the total population. The young would be almost entirely in groups 4 and 5. See my *Elements of Political Science* (New York: Alfred A. Knopf, Inc., 1952), Chapter 3.

The American Activists

To make the situation more vivid and to show how the estimate of 1 percent to 4 percent is derived, let us run an exercise from the American governmental arena.

THE AWARE: Awareness is the first step in political activity. Yet a great many people do not take that step, despite continuous media bombardment from childhood on "good citizenship."

A sample of American adults was interrogated about sixteen public issues of 1956, a Presidential election year. These issues included sending soldiers abroad, firing suspected Communists, school segregation, medical care, and aid to education—major problems of the generation in fact. Those who held a simple opinion on one or the other side of the issue and knew in general what the government was doing about it ranged from a low of 45 percent to a high of 78 percent.[3] It is not far off to say that one third of the adult population (one half if you include the whole population) are unaware and probably should be classified as indifferents with regard to their national citizenship. The proportion that holds an opinion about a President is higher than the proportion that holds an opinion about their congressman.

"In politics it is intensity of opinion that counts—never mind whether it is informed." Right? Counts for what? Very little, except to continue the masquerade of popular knowledge in the face of a tragedy of ignorance.

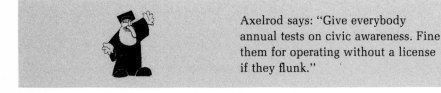

Axelrod says: "Give everybody annual tests on civic awareness. Fine them for operating without a license if they flunk."

THE VOTERS: Considering the long anguished history of the suffrage, you would think that most people would vote, and they do. That is, about seven out of ten in a Presidential election vote for the President—less for every other office. In some local elections you get down to one out of ten voters casting their ballots. This is some measure of the indifference and/or disgust of persons with the political process.

---

3. Angus Campbell et al., *The American Voter* (New York: John Wiley and Sons, 1960), 172–75.

Axelrod says; "Make them vote. You make them fight; you make them pay taxes; why not make them vote? Belgium, Australia and other places do."

SCORING A RANGE OF ACTIVITIES: Voting, like knowing about issues, is a single activity. Some part of the people do more than talk and vote. They work in different ways in politics. The table that follows lists the percentage of American adults in a given sample who were found during the 1964 Presidential campaign at each level of activity, from complete inactivity

Political Activity of Adult Americans

Score	Percent of Adults Making the Score	Number of Cases
0	0	0
1	2	34
2	3	53
3	7	106
4	10	159
5	13	211
6	28	437
7	16	258
8	6	95
9	3	43
10	1	23
11	1	17
12	—	4
13	1	6
14	—	4
15	—	0
16	—	0
Unusable	8	121*
Total	99**	1571

*My hunch is that if these cases were analyzed by other means, they would push the percentage of activists (scorers of over ten points) down to about 3 percent of the adult population. If the total population, rather than just adults, were counted, the percentage of activists would drop again to about 2 percent of all Americans.

**The total is less than 100 percent due to rounding off of fractions.

to high activity.[4] On pages 129–30 is the scoring system that was used to give each respondent his or her score. Perhaps the most remarkable feature of the table is the decline in political activity upon moving from the modest scores of 5 to 8 to the higher scores of 9 to 14. Also, the large number of inactive citizens in the range below 5 is worthy of note. The picture of American public life suggested by the chart shows the "average man" to be far from a "model citizen" as painted by a Fourth of July orator.

The examination was not meant to be difficult to pass, but only a small minority of citizens made high grades. About 13 percent of the 1450 respondents scored eight points or more. But if you will examine the scoring system on pages 129–30 to see what it takes to score 8, you may very well agree with me that to call a person scoring less than 10 an "activist" is like calling anyone who can carry a bag of groceries home an "athlete." The "active" score of 10 or more was achieved by 54 people—fewer than 4 percent. These are politists and include the leaders and influentials.

Many of the contacts of the government with the whole public are filtered through the politists. Much of the control and influence exerted upon the most active and powerful sector of the people—the political leaders of the government—emanate from the politists. All the United States citizens eligible to vote might conceivably be politists; but the fact is that the active public is today made up of perhaps 4 million Americans out of a total population of 210 million.

As might perhaps be expected, the body of politists as a whole has traits that place it midway between the ordinary and indifferent citizens and the highly influential citizens. The politists, in comparison with the less active citizens, contain a greater proportion of well-educated upper-income, white persons of skilled and professional occupations living in urban centers.

A study of a Michigan city by Professors Ralph H. Smuckler and George M. Belknap indicates also that the politists are more aware of technical and administrative problems of government than are the less active citizens, even when both groups are interested in the same type of problem.[5] In psychological terms politists have a greater *reality orientation* in that they see the way the governmental machinery actually meshes. The activists also are concerned more with local community problems as well as national problems, whereas the less active citizens tend to be interested solely in national affairs.

4. The analysis was designed by the author and executed by Mr. John Appel in Survey Research Center Study 473 (1964), University of Michigan at Ann Arbor.

5. *Leadership and Participation in Urban Political Affairs* (East Lansing, Mich.: Michigan State University Governmental Research Bureau, 1956).

How Americans Were Scored on Political Activity

Possible Points	Area of Activity	Description of Scoring Method (based on what respondent said he did)
3	Voting	A person scored one point if he voted in 1964, and one additional point if he said he sometimes voted in the past, or two additional points if he always or almost always voted in the past. Persons who were under twenty-one in 1960 were given one additional point if they voted in 1964, thus scoring two points.
2	Media use	A person scored one point if he read a lot about the campaign in newspapers or magazines or both. He is given half a point for reading both not very much. Another point was given for radio or television listening or viewing under the same rules.
1	Persuading	One point was scored for answering "yes" to the question: "Did you talk to any people and try to show them why they should vote for one of the parties or candidates?"
1	Financial contributions	Giving any money or buying tickets or anything to help the campaign for one of the parties or candidates earned one point.
3	Attending meetings	The respondent scored two points for going to one to three political gatherings, meetings, dinners, or affairs of that nature. An additional point was given for attending four or more of these events.
1	Party work	One point was scored for doing any other work for one of the parties or candidates.
1	Political	Belonging to any political club or organization earned one point.
1	Wore campaign button	Wearing a campaign button or putting a campaign sticker on his car earned one point.
2	Letters to public officials	The respondent scored two points for writing four or more times in the last four years; one point for writing one to three times.

How Americans Were Scored on Political Activity

Possible Points	Area of Activity	Description of Scoring Method (based on what respondent said he did)
1	Letters to the editor	One point was given to anyone who ever wrote a letter giving any political opinion to a newspaper or magazine.
16	Total possible score	(In totaling individual scores, wherever a person scored a fractional sum, the half points were rounded off alternately to the next higher or next lower whole number.)

Violent Politics

War is politics waged by means other than domination, adjudication, argument, bargaining, elections, or co-optation (the appointment of new rulers by old). It is violent politics between nations. Civil war is violent domestic politics. So are terrorism, political threats, kidnappings, beatings, assassinations.

Terror is nothing new in American politics. Every day's newspapers carry some account of political terror. Coverage in newspapers depends largely upon who is being terrorized. Over American history, probably an average of 25 percent of the population has been subject to political terror. You need only figure that blacks and Mexican-Americans, who number about 15 percent of the population, were systematically terrorized until very recently. Add to them 10 or 15 percent of the population who have lived in political machine-dominated, company-dominated, or gangster-dominated areas, where beatings, killings, ballot thefts, and intimidation were the order of the day against political opposition. No, terror is not new. But when the terror touches the well-to-do and the "Establishment," the press, which is a sensitive part of the Establishment, reacts in shock; terror becomes NEWS!

Politicizing the Universities

The same is true of politicizing the universities. Politicians and administrators line up to denounce the "politicizing" of the college campuses, and "politicizing" means using the campus as a forum for agitation of issues not otherwise *centered* in the campus. The impression is given by the Establishment (meaning those who control the institutions, public agencies, large companies, press, and universities, and those who represent them politically) that politics and universities don't mix well, and are not part of the American tradition that has produced such great centers of learning.

One may nor may not agree with the principles of either the new agitators or the Establishment, yet the universities have always been politicized. Here is a comparison of the old politicalization and that which is complained about from on high these days.

TRADITIONAL POLITICALIZATION	CONTEMPORARY POLITICALIZATION
We do not count internal university politics, which witnesses some of the bitterest and most sophisticated political warfare in the world.	
A. Operating institutes, courses, etc., to train present and future employers how to control their labor forces better.	A. Asking or assuming the liberty for student-faculty groups to imitate *but in opposition* a number of the traditional external political practices of universities listed in the left column.
B. Teaching and research for government agencies and administrators to control the population better.	B. Seeking some small slice of the university money pie to do the above, which, since the money pie comes from government so often, raises an external political issue.
C. Propaganda on all manner of Establishment beliefs and doctrines.	C. Trying to convert, by internal pressure, some of the traditional political policies of the university.
D. Training centers for the major parties.	D. In some cases forcing a university to reverse one or more elements of its political behavior, using both the limited means of pressure granted by the authorities and forbidden demonstrations, sit-ins, vandalism, and

TRADITIONAL POLITICALIZATION Cont'd	CONTEMPORARY POLITICALIZATION Cont'd

CONTEMPORARY POLITICALIZATION — continued:

disruption of classes. Also, unionization of employees and faculty is growing.

(In principle there is no change! If *your* ox is being gored, you cry out against politicalization. If the reverse, you demand representation. In fact, the support for and leadership of the Establishment are being threatened by new forces. Naturally, the tactics of the "outs" will differ from those of the "ins." And, insofar as the loss of scholarly tranquillity is alleged, when the boat begins to turn, it rocks; and its sleepy passengers cry out in alarm.)

TRADITIONAL POLITICALIZATION — continued:

E. Agitation and propaganda for various religious sects with strong political positions (e.g., prohibition of alcohol; opposition to divorce and birth control).

F. Defense and war consultation and research including G1 (Personnel), G2 (Intelligence), G3 (Operations), and G4 (Supply) types, sometimes closely affiliated.

G. Cooperation with local governments in biased and preferential social programs.

H. Preferential treatment to the children of privileged classes and ancestries.

I. Providing space and publicity for debates on all (reputable) public issues by all (respectable) parties.

TRADITIONAL
POLITICALIZATION
Cont'd

J. Exhorting members of the university to participate in civic and political activity.

K. Recruiting for the military forces.

L. Destruction of the humble abodes of the poor in adjoining neighborhoods.

M. Rewarding and bestowing honors upon political leaders and other Establishment leaders of many types.

N. Investing university funds thoughtlessly in ways that reinforce the social structure, but not necessarily the "goals of the university."

O. Operating pro–United Nations, pro-UNESCO organizations and numerous proethnic (e.g., Maison Française) and proreligious centers.

P. Furnishing representation and contingents of faculty and students to a great many outside and foreign movements, conferences with political biases, etc.

Q. Extending legal and social services to the poor (rare).

R. Fighting off unionization of college employees and faculty.

S. Applying entire campuses to war in time of war (but no campus has ever been applied totally to peace in time of peace).

T. Collecting taxes for the governments.

TRADITIONAL
POLITICALIZATION
Cont'd

U. Lobbying for subsidies, exceptions, and many other kinds of
legislation favored by the university governors.
V. Permitting (or restraining) faculty or employees to run for public
office and manage political campaigns and politically related enterprises.
W. Declaring various holidays.
(How many southern schools
observe confederacy days?)

A Few Novel Forms of Participation

The Vietnam War, the black civil-rights movement, and the general disgust
with authorities in the 1960s swelled the ranks of the political activists in
America, especially among the young who ordinarily are not so active as
their elders in conventional political affairs. Perhaps as many as 1 percent
more were added to those ordinarily active.

Along with the increased number of activists came some novel forms of
political participation. The old tactics may not prevail forever. Elections are
often slow, cumbersome, vague in their meaning, and mainly fought by only
two political parties, which, like the famous Chinese armies of long ago, are
not supposed to fight too hard, but rather to put on a show of fight and
settle the matter in the least costly way. Lobbying has usually become a
bargaining between elected legislators and leaders of heavily organized
interest groups such as unions.

Actually, many of the new tactics are bolder variations of techniques
employed in conventional political campaigning. If an encyclopedic history
of applied social science is ever written, it will show many variations but few
basic inventions. Thus, during World War I the poet Gabriele d'Annunzio
taught himself to fly a plane and flew over Vienna dropping leaflets on
behalf of the Italian cause. But even then this basic method of distributing
propaganda had already been used by balloonists. Half a century later

another variation was added: Mr. A. Benson flew over Jackson, Mississippi, and dropped copies of the U.S. Constitution to wake up local residents to the rights that he and other blacks demanded.

On October 22, 1966, a "Yellow Submarine" filled with bread, balloons, flowers, wine, and peace messages was launched from the 9th Street Hudson River Pier to protest continued Polaris missile launchings.

During the week of June 8, 1966, at Amherst College, a number of students walked out on the commencement address by Secretary of Defense Robert McNamara, to protest American participation in the War in Vietnam.

In the late 1960s a number of persons began to withhold a proportion of their taxes corresponding to the proportion of government funds going into military affairs.

On Sunday, May 4, 1969, Mr. James Forman of the National Black Economic Development Conference interrupted communion service at Riverside Church in New York City to demand, among other things, that churches pay "reparations" to Negroes for "exploitation."

In the summer of 1969, air traffic controllers handicapped air travel considerably by excessively exact observance of regulations in order to call attention to their demands for better working conditions and instrumentation.

On Earth Day, April 22, 1970, conservationists across the U.S. engaged in various activities including scattering Coke bottles on the lawns of the Coca-Cola Company and burying a car.

Since a sit-in by black students at a Woolworth Company store in Greensboro, South Carolina, in 1960 to obtain better treatment as employees and customers, there have been a great many sit-ins, kneel-ins, lie-ins, pray-ins, wade-ins, read-ins, and teach-ins on various issues.

There have been many thousands of riots, student strikes, marches, and confrontations in the new age of *stressed democracy.*

Stressed Democracy

Confrontations, riots, strikes, sit-ins, passive resistance, planned disobedience: the use of these techniques could be called *stressed democracy* when intended to force governmental and other establishments to act. Tactics are available against them.

Counterdemonstrations of the same sort can be arranged. For example, strikes have been used by parents and students who oppose the considerable inconvenience of attending poorer schools in far neighborhoods for the sake of integrating black and white students at school. Construction workers in a couple of cities have forcibly broken up the disruptive marches of Vietnam war resisters. Police have been in fact used as counterdemonstrators in many places under the pretext of controlling demonstrations.

The letter of the law can be enforced against legally questionable pressures such as sit-ins in universities, public buildings, and roadways. Police and national guard troops are usually employed, often supplementing private police and security forces.

Public opinion can be mobilized by the mass media.

Despite these possible means of opposition, the spontaneity and morale of those who have employed unconventional tactics have been far greater than those of their opponents, and these techniques are not so easily used in reaction, as many believe is or ought to be possible. Until modern politics accepts some of the reforms prescribed in this book, we shall continue to experience waves of such tactics.

1 Percent to 4 Percent?

Returning from what the activists are doing to how many there are, we have shown that 3 percent or something like that is true of the American national public. Can we not then assume that the percentage must be smaller in state and local governments, where the glamor of world events and mass media and flags and soldiers and $100 billion budgets is missing?[6] The question there is whether 1 percent is too high a minimum? Are the activists of Tuscaloosa, Alabama, or Battle Creek, Michigan, less than 1 percent of the voting population? It is doubtful, because, in the first place, there is a carry-over from national politics. That is, persons are carried over from the one level of civic activity to the other. People in Tuscaloosa who work in national politics also have local interests. Then, too, some hundreds of appointive nonpaying and paying positions exist in such cities. Local elections bring out friends and neighbors of candidates who aren't interested in national politics. Local referenda, special votes to approve borrowing money for more sewers, or more library books, etc., involve persons in local activity. I suspect that a similar percentage of activists can be found in business and other countries, as well.

SCHOOL DISTRICTS?   The activists are probably about 1 percent here. For the figure nearest your home, call your local school superintendent.

GENERAL ELECTRIC COMPANY?   Here the hierarchical principle is at work. Take one in one hundred employees as a policy-making executive of

6. Correction: The U.S. national government alone is now up to a $225 billion budget! But did you notice the "error"? If not, why not? That's $500 for every man, woman, and child in the country—quite an error!

some importance, add a labor leader for every two hundred employees, add a few important stock-holding groups (portfolio specialists from pension trusts, insurance companies, banks, and a few individuals), add a few government officials who are part of the GE family because they do nothing but regulate some important phases of GE activity, and you have something between 1 and 2 percent; that is, perhaps about 500,000 persons belong to GE's "jurisdiction," of which about 7500 might be counted as GE activists. We are not using customers as part of the population, though certainly important purchasers should be included (like the agents of the French government, which buys GE nuclear reactor plants and brings to bear certain needs through its franc-power).

OTHER COUNTRIES?   Of course, where you have compulsory voting, you can't give credit for that activity but have to use other measures of activity. Furthermore, there are great differences between societies, and the figures available to us are rarely comparable.

Why the Magic Figure?

The "Law" of Limited Activism is not so mysterious. It is explainable on several grounds, some of which we have understood already:

1. Few people are inclined by training and temperament toward political problems and political power—whether in a state, a union, a university, or a church. They seek other payoffs.

2. Politics has a high attrition rate. It is discouraging and uncertain; it involves human conflict, often of a discourteous kind; its rewards are often small; and therefore many people drop out after a little experience with it.

3. Many people are disqualified for politics within their groups. There is discrimination on many grounds in most groups, beginning with racial, ethnic, religious, and educational discrimination—both in law and in fact (de jure and de facto)—and going on to all kinds of special tests. Civil servants in most governmental jurisdictions are forbidden to engage in certain kinds of politics. Radical politics is exciting, and could bring in many participants, but radicals are discriminated against.

4. Leadership becomes entrenched in office and uses its privileges to maintain power and discourage unfriendly activity. (For example, about 90 percent of those congressmen who seek reelection are actually reelected. Most labor unions have no opposition factions of any consequence.) Hierarchical doctrines of administration and leadership, though they may be old and unproductive, dominate almost all groups and keep power concentrated in a few hands. There is little joy in politics without power.

5. The great difficulty of changing the policies of any large group discourages continuous activity.

Thus the figure of 1 percent to 4 percent should no longer surprise you. Bear in mind, however, that the character and skill of this small activist group determines the kind of government we shall have. Anything that can be done to shape this activist category to our needs will reflect itself in the shape of the whole society and culture.

PRINCIPLE II

The demand and need for civic participation should be fulfilled.

This vague principle can only be acceptable if we specify the demand and justify it, and if we specify the need and justify it, and then relate the demand and need to each other.
Meanings:

Demand . . . for civic participation: the unfulfilled desires of persons to take part in politically oriented activities on all levels of government.
Need for civic participation: the number of people required to perform adequately the functions of the public and government in society.

Where Demand Is Hiding

It may seem strange to talk about an unfulfilled demand for civic participation just after showing how few people want to participate and do participate in politics. But if you will reexamine the five reasons behind the "Law" of Limited Activism, you will see that two of them (3 and 4) imply that participation would be heavier if certain obstacles to it were removed.

Unquestionably there is a blocked demand for participation owing to prejudices of a racial and ethnic sort. You can be sure that, whenever any group agitates as a minority within a larger group, it does so because the principal group refuses to allow many of its members to succeed on their merits. You would have much less voting by citizens of ancestry *A* (Japanese in Hawaii, for example) for candidates of ancestry *A*, if there were not so many non-*A*'s (Hawaiian Caucasians, for example) who vote against *A* candidates because of the candidates' ethnic background.

You can be sure that there is a suppressed demand among civil servants to be more active publicly simply by observing that there are laws prohibiting much of that activity. Such laws are enacted to take care of another kind of problem, that of efficient bureaucracy and fair administration for all, regardless of political party. Still, in most jurisdictions, the reform was undertaken too enthusiastically and, as a result, several million Americans, and precisely those who know most about what is happening in many areas of government, are disqualified or discouraged from political activity.

The entrenchment of leadership, or the perpetuation of oligarchy, also discourages participation. Persons intending to seek public office for any reason whatsoever are discouraged and discriminated against by those already in power. The leaders are experts at all sorts of legal and illegal tricks for eliminating potential competition. To make matters worse, most people have been taught, in and outside school, that the most effective leadership is leadership by the few. "Avoid conflicting authority"; "There must be somebody on top to decide"; "Don't break the chain of command"; "No one can serve two masters at the same time"; and so forth. These ideas, like a slave-psychology play into the hands of those who have power and let them justify the exclusion of all but a few persons from a share in decisions.

We conclude that there is a pent-up demand, nor is it a trivial or incompetent demand. The size of this demand may reach 50 percent of the number of activists already engaged; that is, if satisfied, it might raise the proportion of activists to 4 or 5 percent of the population.

Why can't I be on the nominating committee, too? I have a college degree.
Flubber, here, has been hanging around headquarters for 12 years, Chester. Maybe next year.
Committee Nominating the Committee nominating the Candidate for Dog Catcher.

I've shook hands with every leader, but no one's ever asked my opinion.
Chester, are you being a trouble-maker again? Anyhow, they've got some big contributors to worry about.
VOTE

What's a big contributor?
Well, here's this years list: $1.00 or a month's work gets you a handshake. $50.00 gets you a letter complimenting your civic virtue. $100.00 gets a dinner and being seen with the candidate once. $500.00, meet his family. $1000.00, you can climb in bed with him. You've heard it said, "Politics makes strange bedfellows."

The Five Needs

Would this satisfy the need for *activists?* There are five needs that require activist manpower in a *kalotic* society (please recall that *kalotic* society is my kind of "democratic society" and maybe yours; if it isn't yours, play the game anyway).

1. The activists form the breathing, aerating, circulating element of the society. They must be numerous enough for this purpose. They must number not only enough to *fill all the political positions and offices* but to provide another couple of layers of replacements. There must be enough so

that hacks, bums, and nuts do not get public posts by default. It is awfully dangerous to have no *public reserves*. America today is in this position.

2. If sufficiently representative, the activists give a *broad foundation of consent and representation* to the activities of the influentials and leaders. If they come only from selected and special parts of the population (like the well-to-do, or lawyers, or bureaucrats), the consent that the government works on is only partial, and strains and stresses to the political order arise out of the passive and active resistance of other elements of the population, especially in this day when most people are unwilling to concede to any special group the authority to rule them.

Useful and necessary ideas and feelings (you could call them *publicly inspired political and social inventions*) must come from all parts of the population. Rarely is a ruling class so imaginative that its members can plan what is best for everybody. The rulers must be jostled and prodded by persons who are very different from them. This promotes polyvalent and benevolent leaders, and upsets and discourages rigid-compulsive types.

3. A large activist group is needed to *insure opposition.* That is, a group of persons should be actively engaged in criticizing the government in all of its particulars, proposing alternatives, and offering themselves for positions of power and leadership. The presence of a large opposition keeps the rulers of the moment thinking about what they will do when they have to leave office; it keeps them more honest in their dealings; it does not, contrary to what many people have thought, make them liable to destroy the opposition to avoid criticism. The weaker the opposition, the more an elite cherishes thoughts of wiping them out or at least ignoring them.

4. A large participation enables more *public control of the government.* This it does by giving the governors the impression of traveling and acting in an arena shared with other performers rather than in a vacuum. Wherever they turn, they find persons with awareness and opinions. In all sectors of decision making, even those remote from mass view, some elements of the public have seeped in to watch, criticize, applaud, and join in.

5. A fifth function of a large activist sector in the public is to *protect the society against external enemies.* (Internal enemies of the society are fended off by the four means listed above.) Niccolò Machiavelli was only one among many tough-minded observers who found that republics were harder to overthrow than principalities or tight oligarchies, because the removal of one or a few leaders was immediately countered by the rise of other leaders, and by the decentralized opposition of many small leaders. I am not sure that this reasoning is correct, though I sense that it is.

Nazi Germany wiped out several republics, and, although their underground opposition continued, it would not have sufficed to eject the foreign conqueror. The same is true of the Soviet intervention in Czechoslovakia in

1968 and Hungary in 1956; strong popular movements with heavy nationwide participation opposed the foreign power. However, we also note that there were pro-Soviet movements of considerable size in each country, and, besides, the Soviet Union had enormously more powerful armed forces.

The constitutional tendency of republics to ward off foreign conquerors is not guaranteed to be successful under all circumstances. And, of course, one should not think that either a small participation or a large one will ward off a bombardment by nuclear missiles; we can surmise that in a nuclear disaster that is not absolute, a republic (that is a country with many activists) can recover its strength faster than a despotically ruled country. But that is small consolation.

Any estimate now of the *need* for activists has to be crude. Let's say that, if the "true" demand is 4 or 5 percent, then the demand is still not sufficient to fill the *need* which we guess is about 6 percent of the population. A kalotic society—open, protected, stable, competent, dynamic—may require that 6 percent of its people engage in political and civic activity continuously. This is as close as we can come now to satisfying the principle.

It's Time to Attack the Author's Figures!

Author, what's this 4 percent, this 6 percent, and so on? You use some impressive figures in this book. Are they accurate?

As accurate as I can find or estimate given the fact that I cannot find the data that I want most of the time. And as accurate—where I do locate them or generate them—as is necessary to serve our purposes. As Aristotle wrote, about twenty-five hundred years ago (note the loose figure, which is accurate enough to stress the antiquity of the remark), the wise man is as precise as his material allows.

Unfortunately, the numerical data about politics are often of **poor quality,** and where they are of good quality they are often **not relevant.** You could find the exact number of state officials in Virginia, say, but you cannot cite that kind of figure if someone asks you, "Who rules Virginia?" The figure is not relevant enough.

But often you cannot even find any basic number to begin with; how many politicians are alcoholics, for example, or how many radical students of today are going to become the conservatives of the future?

Meanwhile the mathematical capabilities for handling and analyzing data have become exceedingly fine. Computer programmers stand by with their palms itching to handle tons of data. But if you do not have accurate and relevant data to give to them, it's as the trade saying goes: "Garbage in, garbage out." Only if counters count what they are supposed to count (validity) and all that they need to count (completeness), and what is worth counting (relevancy, saliency), do we get what we want as quantified scientific material.

It is also well to remember that figures are really adjectives, although often more exact and complex than other adjectives. If you are not overawed by numerical symbols, it helps sometimes to fix on a number rather than an adjective to describe a certain condition. The symbol "6 percent" may be preferable to the word "few" or "some." Given what we want to do, our kalotic philosophy, and what little is known about the "true" need for activity, we make an expert, though rough, guess at 6 percent rather than 5 percent, which seems too few, or 7 percent, which seems to be too many or too hard to achieve.

Why not 6.5 percent or 5.9122 percent? It would be foolish to state too specific a goal. Take "the four-minute mile" in running. For years, the record stood at four minutes, one and four tenths seconds, and everyone was panting for a new record. To "achieve the four-minute mile" was specific enough—reachable, understandable, simple; it wasn't just "faster" (the one-minute mile), or uselessly precise (the three-minute, fifty-nine-second mile).

One more word, though, before leaving the principle and taking up the policy. I trust that you understand that the demand for civic participation is *in itself a good, in itself a worthwhile goal* of people. It is right that men, women, and children should ask for a share of power and influence, just as they should ask for a share of wealth and a share of affection and a share of education and respect and medical care. If no one has ever looked at you with contempt, disbelief, and hostility when you have asked to take part in a decision, then ~~you have been exceedingly~~ privileged (no, the very words that come to one's lips are a slave's words) you have been given your due in life. Almost no one in the world has been so lucky.

Still *another* word! Don't concern yourself with the nightmare of over-participation of the normal population, but only with the overparticipation of misfits. Knowing what we do know about the urge to participate in decisions and power, we can say that to free the normal desire to participate will never cause a mass rush into politics and civic affairs, whether in the nation, the city, school affairs, corporation politics, university politics, church politics, or even family politics.

POLICY II

> Promote participation in civic
> affairs from all components
> of a group by removal of
> disqualifications and by providing
> rewards and reducing losses for
> civic activity, so that the process
> of selection for benevolent
> leadership can be opened up.

Meanings:

Disqualifications: not holding seniority rights, being too young, being female, being Catholic, being too poor to run for office, etc.

Providing rewards and reducing losses for civic participation: maintaining pay, getting free time off, keeping or gaining new benefits on another job for doing a civic job too, paying for civic jobs, preventing retaliation for participating in opposition politics, etc.

The process of selection: both active choosing of benevolent leadership and the provision of an environment that induces such selection (in the sense of biological evolution where a process of "natural selection" of the fittest goes on to a certain extent).

Total active participation is impossible and bad.[7] But "nature" (the "Law" of Limited Activism) cuts participation to a small proportion.

Civic Participation

A major step forward in the U.S.A. would be a Charter of Civic Participation which could take the form of a constitutional amendment, a law (since the Constitution may well imply all of the desired conditions), and resolutions without penalties by the authorities in the different executive, legislative, and functional institutions of the country. Of course, the initial force behind such official actions must come from independent persons who search out the undesirable conditions, prescribe the ideal, and bring pressure to bear upon the establishments for the enactment of the proper rules.

This Charter, in its many, many forms, should declare in essence that all large-scale organizations are public in nature, that they all have a duty to provide full and equal opportunity to their members to join in the decision-making processes of the group in a meaningful way, and that they are bound to find means of doing so with all reasonable speed.

To take a humble example, the choir should have something to say about the choice of the choirmaster and of the songs; at the same time, the parishioners ought to have some influence regarding the songs they must hear. Awakening some of the choir and some of the parish to the possibilities of representation in choosing the music of the service will raise the general level of participation of the congregation in the religious ceremony. In the case of a university, it has recently become possible for the first time in five hundred years to consider the student body as a participating element of the university community. The level of voluntary and meaningful participation by students has certainly risen.

In brief, one views participation as permeating the whole internal government of a group; thus conceived, participation is freed and spreads. As more people are involved, the character of participants normalizes (all types enter in); the tenor of the language of power improves (it is less secret, snobbish, and specialized); the character of elected or other representative persons is enlivened by wider contacts.

A government without numerous voluntary participants is like a bush that is strangled.

---

7. Why "bad"? Think what confusion would ensue if 10 percent of the people decided to run for office.

148

Rating Organizations

Does any government (or large-scale group) you know of
do the following?

Name of Organization _____ (you supply) _____
A. *Discouraging and Disqualifying Participation*
    1. Make it tough for some members to make their voices heard?
_____
    2. Get rid of dissenters? _____
    3. Discriminate racially, religiously, ethnically, socially, financially so that some members in fact cannot participate in the decision-making process? _____
    4. Keep the mass disorganized? _____
    5. Perpetuate the myth that leadership always knows best? _____
    6. Have easy techniques of squelching advice? _____
    7. Scorn people who criticize the organization? _____
    8. Promote the acquiescent ones? _____
    9. Promote rigid and compulsive characters? _____
    10. Provide false substitutes (games, recreation, "society news" instead of complete news) rather than real participation in the serious governance of the organization? _____
    11. Etc.?

B. *Giving Rewards for Participation*
    1. Give recognition to those who contribute ideas? _____
    2. Make allowances for time spent and energies devoted to the larger political functioning of the group? _____
    3. Provide facilities and conveniences (e.g., rooms, mimeograph machines) for people who wish to think about, discuss, study, and recommend improvements? _____
    4. Etc.? _____
Note: You can be fairer if you answer each question with a score of 1 to 5, rather than by "Yes" or "No." In any event, if you rate "A" heavily on "Yes" and "B" heavily on "No," you are judging an organization as unfit for our kind of society.

Chapter 3

Leadership

You are on your way to a wedding and a character stops you. "By thy long grey beard and glittering eye, Now wherefore stopp'st thou me?" you exclaim. And he answers your question with a question (which makes you think he is a Talmudic scholar), "What kind of person can solve the political problems of this scrofulous society?"

To gain time, and because it is also reasonable, you reply:

"Well, tell me the problems and I'll describe the person." (For, after all, if you were an employment agency, and somebody telephoned you saying "I need three workers," you'd be sure to ask whether he wanted waiters or bank tellers.)

"Hmmm . . . ."

But, in a flash, you are back at him.

"The worst problems of our society are the following:

1. Many people are alienated and loaded with hostilities.

2. Technology has gotten out of hand.

3. The governments of the world are stagnant and cannot agree with one another.

4. The poor are multiplying; where they aren't hungry, they are exhausted by the complexities of life."

"Right, right," he is saying. "You took the words right out of my mouth."

Grandma Knows Best

"Therefore," you say, after a solemn pause during which you gaze at the sky and then look directly into his mad blue eyes, "you need:

People of creative benevolence;
applied scientists of technology;
and applied scientists of management."

"Of course," he says.

"But that's a big order. When do you need them?"

"Yesterday. I mean, right now."

"Ten thousand years might do it."

"What!" he shrieks. His veins and eyes bulge.

"At the present rate of progress maybe eight thousand, maybe a hundred thousand. You see . . . ."

"Get out of my way." You aren't in his way, but that isn't what he means.

"Wait!" you exclaim. "The chicken and the egg . . . what comes first, the chicken or . . . "

But he is gone.

What you were trying to say is the "good leaders" and "good society" are connected like the chicken and the egg. You can't say which comes first. The two come along together. It's difficult to change people without changing society but you can't change society without changed people to change the society. So you say "ten thousand years," meaning that maybe some beneficial mutation will occur that will permanently alter both leaders and society simultaneously.

*   *   *   *   *

But now, let *me* explain. You are quite right in the problems you list to the graybeard and right in the kinds of men and women you need to bring about their solution. However, you may be unduly pessimistic. And, anyhow, there's nothing to do during the next ten thousand years except try to fox nature. In "the natural course of things" people might have sprouted wings during the past million years, but rather than just sitting around waiting for that to happen, they taught themselves to fly artificially. By the same token we might as well try to alter society now rather than wait for nature to *maybe* do it for us.

Two factors are in our favor. We think we know what we need, and the means for supplying the needs are practically available. So now I shall proceed, as I swore I would, by presenting another set of "3-P's"—this time it concerns leadership, which is closely related to activity. First of all, note that:

You can't evaluate a leader (or create a leader) without setting up the goals that he should pursue.

This idea has already influenced many pages of this book. It is the **fundamental** idea of **all applied science. To do something scientifically, you must not only be scientific but you must know what you want to do.***

Irrelevant Detour

*This is so true that in order to do **nothing** scientifically you have to know that you want to do nothing. Only then can we have the science of do-nothing (a very difficult applied science, by the way, with useful applications) in solving "problems" created by too much leisure time, in refraining from useless or harmful overdecisions in all kinds of human affairs, etc.

Enough said. The proposition of leadership is:

PROPOSITION III

Leaders are critical components
in networks of transactions
that include cliques, activists,
followers, and the counterpart
network of opposition.

Meanings:

Critical components: most essential parts of the process being studied. The
way things get done in human relations can scarcely be understood
without postulating leaders.

In networks of transactions: in the dense and ever less dense interactions
that the leader engages in with others. (See pages 62–63.) For example,
modern sociologists have developed various techniques for showing
that leaders are centers of spiderwebs of intragroup relations. Like this
drawing in which each dot represents a leader, subleader, or follower
ramifying from the principal central leader.

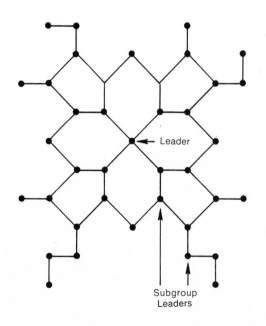

That include cliques, activists, followers, and the counterpart network of the opposition: roughly the order of density of interaction between the leaders and their groups. The *clique,* or henchmen, or colleagues, or associates, or staff, or whatever are the heaviest interactors; the *activists* we have already observed to be the larger group surrounding the power and influence centers; the *followers* are the equivalent of the larger public, the ordinaries; and the counterpart *network of opposition* is something *new.* This last seems a strange element to include; after all, are these not the ones who deny the leader and whom he is engaged in defeating or opposing? Yes, but . . . The leader leads the opposition despite their will, and sometimes they follow willingly. It is doubtful if the United States leaders (specifically Kennedy as President) would have been led into such costly diversionary decisions as the manned flight to the moon if the Russians had not momentarily gained a propaganda victory by putting a man into space first. John F. Kennedy is quoted as exclaiming at a meeting of his top advisers (clique):

If somebody can just tell me how to catch up. Let's find somebody—anybody. I don't care if it's the janitor over there, if he knows how.[1]

Leaders lead their opposition leaders.

If you examine the behavior of General Motors Corporation and the United Automobile Workers Union over a period of time, you will see that each responds to the other's every movement—price changes, wage demands, complaints, profits, costs of living, changes in leadership—until without question you must include them in the same leadership network, each leading the other. Such behavior, which is indeed typical of all groups that have any relations with external groupings, makes the opposition become more influential among the leadership than some of the leaders' own followers.

The phenomenon of leaders leading opposition leaders is also seen, often pathetically, in war, where the soldiers on both sides are exquisitely and painfully aware and studious of their enemy's behavior. One of the most difficult states of mind to inculcate in officer training is the continuous attention to the state of mind and behavior of the enemy in order to use the enemy's wants against him. Apology: "War is a great teacher of mankind," said the philosopher Heraclitus twenty-five hundred years ago, and, alas, we have been seeking better teachers ever since, to little avail.

1. Quoted from Hugh Sidey, *John F. Kennedy: Portrait of a President.* In "Why We Went to the Moon" by Hugo Young, Bryan Silcock, and Peter Dunn, *The Washington Monthly,* 2 (April 1970): 28, 34.

Situation Theory

If you retain these meanings of "leadership," then you can understand the Situation Theory of Leadership—that is, leadership cannot be understood by studying lone individual leaders; one has to study the leader's group networks and the groups with which the leader's group is contending. You cannot understand a black nationalist leader without understanding the men and women around him or her—what they want and insist upon, what they supply to and take from the leader (for each leader is different), nor can you understand a black nationalist leader without knowing the character of the judges, courts, police, and public (both black and white) with whom both leader and group interact.

To illustrate the point we first study the *individual leader*.[2] *Bacchus, Apollo,* and *Hercules* are three leaders. We are going to assume all hold identical positions as leaders of ancient cults whose function is to give advice to three different city governments. And we assume that they are

2. The following discussion is adapted from Alfred de Grazia, *Elements of Political Science* (New York: Alfred A. Knopf, Inc., 1952), 95–98.

having equal success although possessing markedly different qualities, as we see in the table below. It is very difficult to make any generalization about the qualities necessary for leadership, even though the situation is simplified to the point where only four traits are given for each man. You ask rightly: "How does Hercules lead the same kind of group as Bacchus when they are such different people?" And you answer, again rightly, "It must be because of a different distribution of qualities within the group." The hope of drawing general conclusions from studies based on comparisons of individual leaders is vain—except about positions requiring the most specialized kinds of abilities, such as the knowledge of Latin, which can be tested.

BACCHUS		APOLLO		HERCULES	
Genial	(a)	Wise	(b)	Strong	(c)
Some Wisdom	b	*Friendless*	– a	*Unwise*	– b
Weak	– c	*Some Strength*	c	*Fair Organizer*	e
Some Money	d	*Poor*	– d	*Wealthy*	(d)

If we now make a diagram to include each leader's group, we have, according to our theory, the following kind of picture, provided that the groups perform identical functions with equal external results. (Remember, we are still making assumptions, not talking about real groups. We are "theory building" or "model building," you might say.)

List of Qualities

ⓐ	Genial	a	Some Friends	−a	Friendless
ⓑ	Wise	b	Some Wisdom	−b	Unwise
ⓒ	Strong	c	Some Strength	−c	Weak
ⓓ	Wealthy	d	Some Money	−d	Poor
ⓔ	Organizer	e	Fair Organizer	−e	Poor Organizer
ⓕ	Trait X	f	Some X	−f	No X
ⓖ	Trait Y	g	Some Y	−g	No Y

Leader-Follower Groups

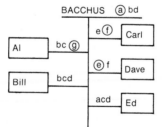

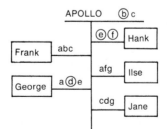

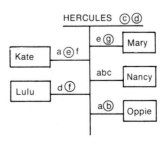

There are now three groups, composed of six members each. Bacchus, Apollo, and Hercules are viewed *with their followers.* Each follower has certain qualities, and it will be seen that in every case the followers provide what the leader lacks. Thus, Bacchus is genial, but weak; three of his followers (Al, Bill, and Ed) have some strength. Bacchus is possessed of some wisdom; that wisdom is supplemented by that of two followers (Al and Bill) who also have some wisdom. The same balance exists in the groups of which Apollo and Hercules are the leaders. We see that each group produces the qualities needed to equal the cumulative balance possessed by the other two groups, and even adds new qualities (*f* and *g*).

We assume that all traits, such as geniality and wisdom, help produce the right kind of "vibrations" and transactions in the group; the trait is a behavior-in-process; a trait is to behavior what structure is to function (two sides of the same coin).

Leadership, therefore, is a function of the group and cannot be understood by merely studying the leader. Leaders who occupy identical positions will seem to possess inexplicably diverse qualities when they are studied in isolation from their followers. This is true whether by "followers" we mean a large inert mass or a small group of followers who are, in their own right, leaders of still other groups. Thus, according to our theory, an attempt to find uniformities in the traits of American Presidents would be doomed to failure unless it also studied the people around the President. A satisfactory comparative study of World War II leadership in America, England, and Germany would have to include not only Roosevelt, but also Hull, Hopkins, Marshall, Morgenthau, and Byrnes; not only Churchill, but also Attlee, Eden, and Bevin; not only Hitler, but also Göring, Goebbels, Himmler, and Speer. Only then could we observe how the collective qualities in each group add up.

At the same time, this method detracts nothing from the importance of the leaders. It leaves the admirer of great leaders free to marvel at the unusual combination of qualities that great leaders commonly possess, enabling them to bring several critically necessary qualities to a situation to which their best lieutenants bring only one or two.

But our theory will not permit us to confine our study to the leader and his own particular group. The following diagram illustrates what happens if we do. Two groups belong to each party acting in a given situation with reference to goal *X*.

In this figure we have two coalitions that we assume are equally successful in achieving goal *X*. It will be noticed that neither the qualities possessed by the top leaders nor by the group of *leaders* of the comparable groups *A* and *C* are identical. That is to be expected from what has been said

Two Equal Coalition Leaderships

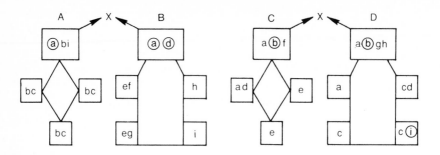

Trait	Total A	Total B	A + B	Total C	Total D	C + D
a	2*	2	4	2	2	4
b	4		4	2	2	4
c	3		3		3	3
d		2	2	1	1	2
e		2	2	2		2
f		1	1	1		1
g		1	1		1	1
h		1	1		1	1
i	1	1	2	—	2	2
	10	10	20	8	12	20

*ⓐ= 2, that is, a strong trait.

above. If one adds up the qualities possessed within each of the comparable *groups A* and *C, these* do not add up to the same sum. The process of adding leadership qualities has *passed over the single group boundary.* We must examine the sum of qualities possessed by group *A* together with its allied group *B,* and by *C* together with *D,* and only then do we see that the cumulative leadership qualities are the same in the two double groups. These qualities, however, are so distributed that neither the study of individuals nor the study of single groups can explain the diversity of the leaders.

What our theory asserts here is not startling. *The theory is that the supply of qualities of leadership appropriate to a given situation may be a function of more than one group.* A classic example of this theory is found in Polybius' discussion of the separation of powers in his history of the Roman republic. He wrote that Rome had become great largely because of its balanced constitution, which contained elements of monarchy (the consuls), aristocracy (the Senate), and democracy (assemblies of plebs). Governance in accordance with the best interests of the nation was guaranteed by a combination of the strengths of the three branches of government: weak consuls could be buttressed by strong Senates, harsh Senates modified by popular protest. A study of consular leadership alone, ignoring the Senate and plebs, would show a puzzling succession of men of very different traits and backgrounds.

Similarly, in regard to the United States, a study of the Presidents alone,[3] or of the Presidents with their cabinets and "kitchen-cabinets," will not reveal an intelligible pattern of Presidential leadership qualities. To the study of the President's group must be added the study of the other leadership groups of the United States that influence the decisions of the President. Within these groups we should study the top people, their immediate cliques, and their relation to their followers. We should have to add up their leadership qualities, add to them the qualities that come from the President's group, and determine from that sum the leadership equilibrium of such a structure. We should expect this final sum to be the same for equivalent situations. One may constantly expect, however, differences in the leadership qualities of, say, the President's group, or any other subgroup, at different times.

The empirical work required in studying any leadership situation by the method implied in this theory is, of course, very great. Some may say that we are shutting out an elephant in order to admit a whale. To this the reply may be that difficulties are never avoided in science. It is as difficult to make painstaking studies of foolish things as of important things. Another answer is that the best biographical studies do proceed in the manner we have outlined. Carl Sandburg's several-volume biography of Abraham Lincoln is an example. Seeming contradictions in the behavior of the leader can be resolved often only by unraveling a difficult knot of circumstances that contains ultimately all the contending influences in a given situation.

Leaders Without Groups?

THE ARTIST AS LEADER.   Any civilization worthy of the name has a number of creative artists and scientists. Most of them feel lonely, isolated, and misunderstood. Here is the plaint of one of them.

---

3. This was systematically tried once in the late '30s by Harold F. Gosnell, who with several rambunctious research assistants (including this author), put together a list of all the traits that any scholar or journalist had said were typical of American Presidents. Then we began intensive studies of all materials

The Rest

O helpless few in my country,
O remnant enslaved!

Artists broken against her,
A-stray, lost in the villages,
Untrusted, spoken-against,

Lovers of beauty, starved,
Thwarted with systems,
Helpless against the control;
You who cannot wear yourselves out
By persisting to successes,
You who can only speak,
Who cannot steel yourselves into reiteration;

You of the finer sense,
Broken against false knowledge,
You who can know at first hand,
Hated, shut in, mistrusted:

Take thought:
I have weathered the storm,
I have beaten out my exile.[4]

The voice is that of young Ezra Pound. In another poem in the same collection, "Commission," he inventories the classes of the oppressed in modern society: "the hideously wedded," "the bought wife," "those who have lost their interest," "the adolescents who are smothered in family," and others; he says, "Go my song . . . go in a friendly manner, go with an open speech."

Ezra Pound contests with T. S. Eliot the honor of premier polymath among the superbest poets originating in American culture. A "crazy traitor," Pound experienced political punishment by decree of madness.[5]

on each President to discover uniformities. The study expired when the researchers discovered it would fail and as its members ambled off to war, but the by-products, as often happens in research projects, proved of value: some statistical data for a book on political parties, an article on the personality of Franklin Roosevelt, and a lot of free-floating facts that caused some harmless fallout over the years.

4. Ezra Pound, *Personae* (New York: New Directions Pub. Corp., 1926), 92–93.

5. Especially popular in the Soviet Union as a tool against resistance by scientists, intellectuals, and artists. See Thomas S. Szasz, *The Manufacture of Madness* (New York: Harper & Row, Publishers, 1970). Dr. Szasz reviews the history of social persecution of the insane and mentally ill, those thought to be insane or mentally sick, and those dishonestly labeled as such. He urges doctors to protect their patients from social persecution and criminal prosecution.

Brought to America for trial after World War II from Italy, where he had lived many years and had praised fascism, denounced Jews, and attacked American culture, he was given the choice: be tried and almost surely condemned for treason or be examined and adjudged insane—in either case, prison of a kind. The old man's lawyers chose the latter and only years later were a few friends able to spring him from the hospital.

PRINCIPLE III

Every person should be a leader.

To what degree? When? How? Where? Why? All good questions.

1. *To what degree?* A leader is a critical component in a group system. A leader moves the group more than the average, sometimes a great deal more, having more than average influence. Various common statements get at the point:

"Without their leader, that bunch can't do anything."

"Things have slowed down since Orestes Papastratos went on vacation."

"It's a one-man team."

"They take turns leading."

"After he was chosen, he rested on his oars."

Etc., etc.

In other words, the degree to which a person is extraordinary and therefore a leader is something to be measured or at least thought of in measured terms.

2. *When?* Whenever he or she* is ready; whenever possible; whenever

*These personal pronouns like "herself" give me trouble, but what can I do? Practically every language is male chauvinist, lacking a set of usable, bisexual pronouns. This tends to discourage the reader from thinking that the author is talking to and about women as well as men.

Someday we may have a new set of words; instead of

one	he	she
one's	his	her & hers
one	him	her

perhaps we will say

se
shis
shem

Today "one" or "one's" can sometimes be used to avoid gender. But how do you say, "Every person knows (one's?) (shis?) place"?

chosen; whenever he or she must act in a crisis; whenever he or she is degenerating into a slave or automaton.

3. *How?* By all the techniques of leadership that the person can command; by helping set and clarify the group's goals (major or minor). By boosting the morale of the group through persuasion, propaganda, example, and positive evaluation and reevaluation of the group progress. By finding new resources for the group (recruits and material). By watching the outer social seas through which the group is sailing and keeping it alert. By choosing or helping to choose coleaders, top leaders, lesser leaders, specialist leaders.

4. *Where?* In any one or more groups in which a person finds herself or places herself. Recall the groups mentioned on pages 72–73 and 122. There are perhaps 20 million groups in the United States counting political groups, work groups, voluntary groups, church groups, etc. Leadership is involved in all striving toward a goal.

5. *Why?* or better yet, WHY BOTHER?[6] A person cannot be thoroughly human (that is, polyvalent and benevolent) unless se (Remember the box!) succeeds in expanding the "me" and "mine," seeking new experiences, and adjusting shis world to that of others—that is all part of *kalos,* the beautiful life; it brings shem happiness. And if you think this isn't political science, let's go back to Lesson One to Compte, Lasswell, Aristotle, Birdwhistell, Trotsky, Kautilya, Ortega, Michels, Thoreau, Merriam, Locke, Stalin, Mumford, Dewey, and Mosca. Or, more briefly:

6. The "five needs" for political activism, above, pages 142–43, should be reviewed here.

7. The "Founding Fathers" (a childlike term for the tough-minded gentlemen who in an astonishing

**One needs to be counted in lest one be uncounted,
counted for nothing, or counted out.**[7]

"OK. I'm a leader sometimes. I emerge from my hole, and I do what I can to influence others. But I'm not much of a leader. Most of the time I'm a follower, because mostly I like to string beads, knit sweaters, and fix cars. What I want to know is: How do I obey? I don't like most leaders. When do I disobey them?"

On Obedience—the Ethics of Followership

Obedience is now an old-fashioned word because of the spreading distrust of authority around the world. It has become plain that there are many kinds of obedience and disobedience; only at the extremes of human character do you find persons who obey without question and disobey unhesitatingly.[8]

If you agree with the objectives of a group, you should obey because cooperation is required in many tasks, large and small. The organization of cooperation cannot be achieved without leadership. Challenges without inherent corrective directions are mere abuse. The leadership has to be credited with the right goals; it has to give direction, both positive and negative; it must administer rewards and penalties.

If the actions of government are judged to be incorrect, then dissent is to be invited. But the leadership must be allowed to continue until it is apparent that better alternatives have been discovered. Providing evidence that they are using the best known methods of achieving a correct or corrected policy contributes to the leaders' authority; if they do not do so, they become disqualified to receive obedience.

If the value or priority (as contrasted with the correctness) of the leaders' actions is challenged, then they should run the rapids of change. They should submit to arguments, petitions, referenda, elections, and all other means of promptly affecting their views. The means of pressure should relate to the urgency of change, the significance of change, and the reluctance of the leaders to change.

It seems reasonable to assert that: (1) *if leaders know that they can be easily challenged, they will act so as to reduce the number of reasons for challenge;* and furthermore (2) *to the extent that each person can be a leader, everyone will have less need to be one.* That brings us to:

---

tour de force put together the U.S. federation under a Constitution) were accustomed to the phrase "to be jealous of one's liberties."

8. The organization rating scale on page 148 above will help.

POLICY III

Stimulate groups to provide leadership opportunities to their members and inventory continuously the personal freedoms available within organizations.

Comment: Policy III is closely related to Policy II regarding the increase in civic participation (see page 146). The means of increasing the number of activists will increase the number of potential and actual leaders in all sorts of groups. You will recall that there was no concern about activating too many people; it is also unlikely that we would create too many leaders. The serious problem that besets most nations and groups is that their system works to put forward too many of the *wrong kind* of activists and leaders.

The Dangers of Charisma

Humankind is still possessed in large part by great fears and by beliefs in individual incompetence and helplessness.

Humankind is therefore prone to elevate to the status of gods or great magicians any person who catches the popular imagination as a "hero."

This happens especially on the tribal and national levels—the most dangerous levels, because these are where the lethal weapons are stored. Hero worship also occurs in various institutions where the elevated individual may be a labor union leader (e.g., James Hoffa of the Teamsters' Union); a church leader (e.g., Mohammed); a police officer (e.g., J. Edgar Hoover of the FBI) and so forth.

These people and many others were charismatic, that is, they spun off into a heroic space in which they simply could not be challenged by ordinary people and means. Like Franklin D. Roosevelt, Nehru of India, and Joan of Arc, their tenure could not be successfully challenged; their actions would excite a large favorable crowd without benefit of cool criticism; and their opponents would find it hard to obtain a hearing and would be tainted by sacrilege. I am suggesting no judgment about heroes as persons, certainly not about those exemplified here. I am only stating that the leaders in a group should use whatever means are known and inventable to reduce the effects of charisma.

We say in this book, "There is a good kind of authority which is arrived at by various means such as using the scientific method in achieving agreed-upon human aspirations." We say, furthermore, "This kalotic authority, which is needed to bind the people of a group together and give them morale and confidence, is limited in its hold over our minds by its very nature and by various structures and frameworks that we approve of or propose in a number of chapters." We say, finally, "When this kind of authority is largely absent, a worse kind of authority makes itself felt. Maybe this worse kind will always be present to a certain extent. But one of the most important jobs of political science is to limit as much as possible the seeping in of antikalotic authority."

One kind of antikalotic authority is an overdose of charisma, too much personal hero worship, or the "cult of personality" as Soviet Premier Nikita Khrushchev once called it. Let us see how it works in a little scenario called "How god is played convincingly" (the propositions) and "How to play god convincingly" (the applications). If you watch the life (and death) of a great political hero, you are likely to see a number of the propositions and applications of the same or similar type working to create and develop charismatic authority.

Objective history colors good with bad, so it is significantly violated. *Heroes, therefore, often write their own biographies, or come out of obscurity, or have mysterious origins.* Persons identified in the popular mind with custom and tradition are highly regarded. *Heroes seek to envelop their past in favorite traditions, often inventing or letting stories be invented for the purpose. (After death, historians and storytellers take over.)* Social distance produces awe, and *a hero should not have common family squabbles or normal sexual preoccupations; one should be "pure."*

The language and symbolism of heroes are value-laden, unscientific, or impenetrable, and invite supporters who can preach them without embarassment and with great sincerity. *So speak or write an abstruse book, with many answers to life's questions, under extraordinary circumstances, receiving inspiration and even words from a mysterious source, whether it be a person or statistics.*

A terrible danger and a miraculous escape work well at the time and continue to develop historical embellishments. *This may be done by spending a time in jail; surviving a critical illness; being shot at and missed (or hit for that matter provided that the bed of martyrdom is readied); retreating into a wilderness or disappearing on a mission into another world; prolonged suffering as a soldier or captive; and undergoing some severe trial of muscle, will or virtue.*

By contrast, certain peculiar all-too-human touches add to the large dimensions of the hero. *Wearing common clothing after deserving glorious raiment; donning unusual but traditional garb, like a leopard skin or a cowboy hat; living on yogurt or a bowl of rice or practically nothing at all; winning the love of animals—such behavior sorely tempts the popular mind that sees in it a connection with itself.*

Personal charisma has sooner or later to be supplemented by the official and legal blessing of the organized group, but a hero's flame is extinguished if he becomes merely another official or politician playing the game. The political activists and the inside-dopesters, such as the press, are the last to believe in untamed heroes. *Therefore, avoid taking public office, getting stuck on a job, or playing by the rules of the game. Set up "higher rules" that officials and politicians may not or will not accept. Be above the sources of your support; especially be above money; adopt the attitude that these must come, just as offices will come, in due course. Do not screen the character of your followers, as examining boards or employment officers would; it is enough that they believe in you and your mission.*

The best known technique for controlling the mystique of leadership is to provide constant circulation in leadership positions (rotation in office). This works not only in the old democratic political sense, as in the ideas of Presidents Jefferson and Jackson, but also in the modern situation of role playing in industry, government agencies, universities, schools, churches, and any kind of associations—in short, wherever the game can be played. That is, in addition to providing ample opportunity for "circulation of individuals in and out of elites," as Michels said (and as Jefferson and Jackson might have said), you provide regular occasion for the substitution of leaders for followers, in the offices of all groups in society.

It is remarkable how humbling and enlightening it is for a group leader to step down and assume the role of a lesser leader or follower while one of his subordinates leads. In Mao's China it is commonly demanded of university students, party officials, and various others that they go out into the fields to work alongside the peasants on occasion. And on kibbutzim in Israel everyone who is physically capable takes a turn working in the kitchen. In line with the *situational theory of leadership,* however, a correctly played game of leader rotation should permit (actually or by simulation) the substitution of a leading *group* for the regular leading group.

If you imagine this kind of game,[9] or practice it on a couple of occasions, you will also understand the simple meaning of the clause "and inventory continuously the personal freedoms available within organizations." For, you will feel the power of leadership and therefore the need for intelligent steering and brakes on leaders, just as when you drive a car (as against *reading* or *hearing* about driving a car). The personal freedoms we talk about are the aids to steering and the brakes on power. The inventory of them, their listing, publicizing, and celebrating, will keep the attention of the group on them so that they will not be forgotten.

---

9. Much more on extreme obedience is said below, in Chapter 11.

Chapter 4

Public Opinion

PROPOSITION IV

"Nero fiddled while Rome burned." There is nothing wrong with playing the harp, and Nero was rather a good musician and actor. However, as emperor of the Romans, he should have been doing something else. Perhaps, like the famous mayor of New York, Fiorello La Guardia, he should have donned a helmet and chased after the fire engines. At any rate, he should have tried to do something more in tune with the crisis.

Most people are Neros in this sense. In the language of Proposition IV:

> People generally tend to concern
> themselves with immediate and
> personal problems, regardless
> of importance to the larger group
> or society, or to the next
> generation.

A well-executed study by Professors Samuel Stouffer, Paul Lazarsfeld, and others illustrates this condition, which has been documented and commented upon by many others since time immemorial. Stouffer and Lazarsfeld interrogated a sample of Americans at the height of "McCarthyism" in the early 1950s, when many publicly concerned Americans believed that the U.S. Senator from Wisconsin, Joe McCarthy, was undermining the temple of American liberty and about to cause it to topple over.

The scholars asked a representative group of Americans what were the objects of their concerns. In reply, only a very small fraction of the American citizenry appeared upset either over McCarthyism or over the Communism McCarthy was attacking. They were worried about their health, the health of their families, their jobs, and so forth. Only after considerable prodding could they be brought even to mention the "McCarthy crisis"—much less did they intend to do anything about it. And, if they had been spurred into opinion and action, granted their feeble armament of information and therefore their need to rely upon sloganized thinking, many of them would only have reinforced the cohorts of Senator McCarthy. Thus, only a tiny "elite" considered the issue highly important and were prepared to do battle over it.

Yet *what others are doing* and *the future* are absolutely essential considerations of politics. Again, it's not that people are immoral for considering themselves first and thinking of their immediate concerns; people *should* take care of themselves as far as they can. The point is that a large-scale effort like government—or any other large-scale effort—cannot help and protect its people, indeed cannot exist, without a future vision and abstract concerns for a large part of the people.

PRINCIPLE IV

The principle can be put as follows:

> Personal troubles, the troubles
> of others, and troubles of the
> future deserve personal attention
> generally in that order;
> they deserve social attention
> in reverse order.

What nature has failed to place in one's genes—a complex social and political guidance system—one must supply artificially. Now, if nature gave us an instinctive social system that would be modeled upon our *ideal* of humanity, then we should be somewhat enthusiastic—*until* we realized that the principle of uncertainty would be lost, and then we would be miserable and uncreative.

Therefore governments, if they are to be more than mirrors of immediate passions, have to instill popular attitudes and create structures that reverse the normal preoccupations of mankind.

Search for a Policy on Opinion

Leaders must either persuade people to think about what is appropriate policy or set up procedures that prevent people's ordinary concerns from blocking group and future concerns.

In history, the response of leadership has usually been to exclude the people from the concerns of government; then the people, being cut off from the larger concerns of their countries or groups, become corrupted and mix up their own immediate and personal problems with the public good.

In countries where a democratic sentiment prevails, and where most people expect something from the government, the leadership has to try to give people a sense of "others" and "the future." This is often a thankless task, since "What are you doing for me today?" is the theme song of mass society. And the masses sing out loud and clear unless, as in communist and authoritarian societies, they are suppressed.

THESIS	ANTITHESIS
Politicians concerned with the whole and the future offer: postponement of gratification; redistribution of goods; attention to complex and abstract problems.	*Most people demand:* delivery of goods to *me* now; constant signs of care and affection for *me.*

SO

SYNTHESIS

Politicians are pressured to offer:

A	or	B	or	C
less postponement of gratification; less redistribution of goods; less attention to complex and abstract problems.		pretenses of accepting the antithesis while working underground to provide the thesis.		suppression of popular demands in order to succeed with their thesis.

Thus risking corruption by:

A and B	C

bringing about ridicule of so-called democracies on grounds that they are hypocritical. For example, examine the Speeches for All Occasions.

permitting leaders to say that, though they are undemocratic, they are forthright and frank.

Speeches for All Occasions

1. *On Accepting Candidacy to* _____.
Words cannot convey the gratitude I feel for the trust that you, who represent so faithfully the people of _____, wish to repose in me. I have given much thought to the question, and have asked advice from my closest friends as to whether I may be worthy of the honor and responsibilities of the position. In consequence and in all humility, I have decided that I must accept your nomination and bend all my energies to service of the _____ and the people. Thank you, my friends.[1]

2. *Visit of official party to* _____.
I am happy to be with you in _____ today, and am deeply moved by your friendly reception. [Pause for possible applause.] For a long time, I have been aware of the progress that you are making here in every sphere of human endeavor—in work and in culture, and I am aware too of the difficulties and problems that urgently require attention. I expect to discuss these problems with your distinguished leaders while I am with you, and to carry back to my associates in _____ new plans and projects for the benefit of the people of _____. Thank you and [choose one: "God bless the Queen"; "Viva Mussolini"; "Right On"; "May God keep you well"; or "Now we shall go to work."]

1. One of my favorite leaders was Admiral George Dewey, Commander of the U.S. fleet at the victory over the Spanish fleet in Manila Bay, in the Spanish-American War of 1898. Since the American politicians love military heroes, who gain votes cheaply and don't usually interfere much with their shenanigans (think of Washington, Grant, or Eisenhower), they duly proposed to him nomination for the Presidency. In reply, Admiral Dewey wrote: "I've thought of the duties of the President and I think that it does not take too much ability to handle them. . . ." That fixed him! The same great man, at the delirious moment of the smashing of an enemy warship, said to his hurrahing sailors: "Don't cheer, boys, the poor beggars are dying."

3. *Note of resignation when things are bad and you've made them worse, and you are told you had better get out.*

Dear M _____:

It is with the deepest regret that I tender to you my resignation as _____ because of the pressure of personal responsibilities that can no longer be ignored. At the time that I assumed my duties, it was apparent that we had inherited a situation acutely in need of reform. I am pleased to report that we have made considerable progress during my tenure in office and I shall hand on to my successor an operation that is much improved. This success has owed much to your leadership and understanding, and for that the people of _____, as well as I, can be profoundly gratified.

Sincerely yours,

_____

4. *In preparing to tell a harsh truth to your audience, such as that the F-111 has been grounded again, or that the five-year plan is four years behind schedule:*

"We are aware that the people whom we are addressing are too superior to the weaknesses of human nature to lose command of their temper for an instant. We should not hold this language if we were not speaking to men whom their virtues and their intelligence render more worthy of freedom than all the rest of the world."

That fourth speech is what Alexis de Tocqueville said was the typical way of addressing constituents in the American democracy of the 1830s.[2] De Tocqueville added, "It is true that American courtiers do not say 'Sire,' or 'Your Majesty,' a distinction without a difference. They are forever talking of the natural intelligence of the people whom they serve; . . . they assure him [the voter] that he possesses all the virtues without having acquired them, or without caring to acquire them. . . . The sycophants of Louis XIV could not flatter more dexterously."

Write your own universal messages on

5. Why the treasury is running a deficit.
6. The vile tactics of the opposition.
7. The need for young people to go into politics (addressed to old people).
8. The traditions that made our _____ great.
9. Law and order.

_____

2. *Democracy in America* (1st English language edition, 1835. New York: Alfred A. Knopf, Inc., 1945), Vol. 2, 267–68.

Exchange the messages with your acquaintances. If there is much similarity, it may mean that there is much repetition and sameness in the political process; then you can believe either: (A) that originality had better be avoided, or (B) that a little originality may get you a long way.

Still, despite difficulties, we must teach:

POLICY IV

Plan to handle future troubles now;
organize institutions accordingly;
conduct continuous propaganda
to elevate goals by a half-century.

That is, we accept the burden of democratic hypocrisy and reject authoritarian and communist suppression. For the suppression of opinion invites *larger* and *deeper* corruption; it still flatters the mass; *it does not educate people to their potential as respectable human beings;* and it does not permit a wholesome development of knowledge or science.

Every day the newspapers carry evidence of these facts. The Soviet government eliminates Jews from public office and makes it difficult or impossible for them to leave the country; the South and North Vietnamese are, as a by-product of their war, achieving the genocide of the Montagnard tribes; the People's Republic of China whips up the populace to curse the United States and/or the Soviet Union as the incarnation of evil; attempts in Poland and other Soviet satellite nations to protest high prices or lack of autonomy are broken up violently by government troops; and writers and scientists send out pleas for support from places as far apart as South Vietnam and Moscow.

Actions of these kinds can surely be observed in so-called democracies, but, if the student will take the trouble to count such items in a group of newspapers and journals over a period of time, he or she will surely find more of them in authoritarian and communist countries. (I exclude that peculiar American and South African monster of racism, even remembering the poor record of the Chinese Communist regime's Tibetan genocide,[3] the Soviet genocide of Cossacks in World War II, and other similar cases that make the accusation of racism valid also against other countries.)

Also, regardless of the form of the regime, the combination of national-

---

3. An editorial from the *Indianapolis News*, January 8, 1972, gives an example of how the left hand sometimes doesn't know what the right is doing:

"The refusal of the White House to approve release of a film on the Chinese Communist rape of Tibet indicates, contrary to administration assurances, that obvious concessions are being made to Peking as part of the recent softening of U.S. policy toward Red China.

ism and militarism causes nations to act differently beyond their borders than within them. Publics and their mouthpieces tend to be more docile than usual when foreigners rather than they themselves are abused and uniforms are paraded.

"The U.S. Information Agency spent $73,000 of the taxpayers' money producing "Man from a Missing Land." The film deals with the 1959 Chinese Communist invasion of Tibet—despite promises to respect that country's autonomy—the flight of its spiritual leader, the Dalai Lama, and his asylum in India. The episode was one which clearly illuminated the brutal and aggressive nature of the Red Chinese regime. . . .

"Bruce Herschensohn, USIA director for screen service, explained the film's shelving. 'The picture was finished about a month before President Nixon's announcement of his trip to Peking,' he said. 'It caught everybody by surprise. It is just one of those things that no one could have foreseen.' It thus becomes quite clear that suppression of the film is part and parcel of the recent effort of our government to treat Red China with kid gloves and to downplay American awareness of Peking's crimes."

Censorship

How do we manage to direct public opinion toward long-range goals and yet fight censorship? Censorship is, of course, forbidden by the U.S. Constitution. But before we wave the flag, we should add that in times of war censorship of opinion and news is allowed. Also, both press and other public and private agencies and companies frequently distort and suppress news, and they censor what their officers and employees say about their work. In addition, one cannot give away professional confidences without being subject to a possible lawsuit. Nor is libel permitted.

Among the drudges of newspapering, reporters and copy editors, the concept [of freedom of the press] is rarely mentioned. Anyone who has worked in the city rooms of an American newspaper knows that freedom of the press is usually freedom not to print—to spike, tone down or rewrite—or to plant stories as favors. For the working newspaperman, the working definition of freedom of the press is "The right to print or not print what a newspaper considers to be in its best interests, as these are defined by its directors and business office and their camp followers." This is more than a shout and a holler from the First Amendment to the Constitution, but is it entirely cynical?[4]

On Censorship as Obscene (or obscenity as censorable)

Censorship of obscenity, like restraints of all kinds, is what men who control laws do to make themselves feel better, richer, etc. Censorship gets a great deal of public support in the area of obscenity, most particularly by people who set themselves up as guardians of public morality. Perhaps in no other area has so-called due process of law been so little observed. Generally, until very recently, anybody speaking in the mask of a parent, teacher, policeman, or clergyman might grab and destroy what he called a "dirty" thing and would be above public or legal criticism.

Rarely has such a motley and poorly equipped crew been given such large discretion. Police seize and arrest. Prosecutors prosecute. Judges condemn and enjoin. Customs officers and post-office employees confiscate. Motion-picture corporations, grown rich on portraying violence and sexual excitement, set up their own censorship boards to skate along the edges of public indignation. Churches blacklist films. Books, magazines, and pictures are condemned by citizens' groups. Dozens of different types of agencies are set up in localities to censor films, books, and magazines.

The scene has been confusing, and the courts have been confused, too.

---

4. Samuel Abt, "The Papers and the Papers," *International Herald Tribune*, May 9, 1972, p. 12.

They don't want to take the attitude that the government of Denmark has finally taken, causing the ruination of "smut pedlars," namely abolishing all laws against pornography and obscenity. They are still trying to figure out how to preserve freedom of expression and keep American morals pure. Here is the sort of thing that happens. Geoffrey Wolff, a journalist and critic, is writing:

Officially, Irving Fishman, with a Bachelor's Degree in Business Administration, tries to keep you and me from reading dirty books and seeing dirty movies brought into New York from abroad. A movie he doesn't want us to see is called I Am Curious—Yellow. *The film arrived from Sweden December 30 [1967]. Fishman saw it January 4 and seized it to prevent its distribution by Grove Press, Inc. In legal terminology the movie was "arrested" but unlike people who are arrested it can't go free on bail until after the moral policeman's judgment is tested in court. . . . Irving Fishman swings a big stick. He seized the movie in accordance with Section 1305, Title 19, of the United States Code, which deals with the importation of pornographic or seditious material. Fishman looks at movies and if he thinks they are obscene we don't see them unless the court decides he is wrong.*

He was asked how he determines whether a work is prurient: "As to how I go about making that judgment this is just—it seems to me it would be based on the reaction I had to seeing the film. . . . I think my answer would have to depend on my own judgment, my own experience; I couldn't define it."[5]

At considerable cost, the publisher or film distributor in these cases carries an appeal from one court to another and may finally free his property. Here, as in other areas of human activity, the laws, officials, and the pressure groups surrounding the lawmakers and enforcers, bring about the destruction of legitimate business and create rackets and bad products. The drink, drug, gambling, and literature scenes all share this common misfortune. Men and women are made worse by the perversity of the laws; police increase in numbers and powers; the quality of whatever product is involved gets worse and more costly; energies are diverted from basic social problems to these highly flammable areas and fuel is poured upon the flames.

"True" obscenity and sexual crimes are perversions of the value of affection. They arise out of the denial by the authorities—parents, teachers, lawmakers, and law enforcers—backed by frightened and indignant people, that an impulse to enjoy sex should exist. Sex crimes are like stealing, terrorism, alcoholism, mugging, and vandalism, in that they all come out of a background of societal fraud and injustice against the person's need to identify with, experience, and adjust to power, wealth, respect, affection, health, and knowledge—the six major values of life.

---

5. In Edward de Grazia, *Censorship Landmarks* (New York: H. H. Bowker, 1969), xviii.

The Indignant Ignoramous: Menace to Science and Progress

We cannot expect to satisfy everyone with this answer to the population's lust to legislate against sin. Again and again people will want to declare, "Author, aren't you excusing obscene people by explaining that the society is basically at fault? Aren't you giving them a justification?"

The question is important because it applies to the nature of all science and to every kind of liberty. So my answer is general and abstract.

1. Science progresses by analyzing the *causes* of events. This implies *liberty* to search for causes.

2. Until the causes of an event are known, you cannot be confident of your means of controlling it and your means of control may be destructive and even encourage (or discourage) events against your wishes.

3. Until the causes of an event are known, you may be making a poor moral judgment about it.

4. The preponderance of scientific evidence at this time is that our system of education in the family, school, and culture often suppresses freedom and excites abuses in so doing. The legal system then worsens the abuses and spreads out to stifle other liberties.

When the telescope was invented, the authorities agreed that looking at the naked heavens closely was unnecessary and indecent. "Tradition," "Centuries of Civilized Behavior," the "Divine Word," even "Science" itself, were cited against the practice. But Copernicus, Bruno, Kepler, Galileo, Newton, and others created modern astronomy despite such obstacles. Air travel, improved ship navigation, space exploration, and many other inventions and ideas were born out of the set of operations to which the telescope was essential. The scientific frame of mind conquered this area to a large extent.

In 1970, a National Commission on Obscenity and Pornography issued a report and recommendations on its subject. Essentially it said that, except for some restrictions for the very young, the multitude of governmental interventions in the area of obscenity and pornography should be abandoned. Now we quote several news reports:

President Nixon rejected "totally" today the month-old report of the National Commission on Obscenity and Pornography. He called its conclusions "morally bankrupt"....

"So long as I am in the White House, there will be no relaxation of the national effort to control and eliminate smut from our national life," the President said.

It was believed to be the first time in many years that a President had flatly rejected the report of a Presidential commission.... [6]

6. Warren Weaver, Jr., *The New York Times*, October 25, 1970.

Now another report:

"The warped and brutal portrayal of sex in books, plays, magazines and movies, if not halted and reversed, could poison the wellspring of American and Western culture and civilization," [Nixon] said. . . .

"The commission contends that the proliferation of filthy books and plays has no lasting, harmful threat on a man's character. If that were true, it must also be true that great books, great paintings and great plays have no ennobling effect on a man's conduct. . . ."

"Centuries of civilization and ten minutes of common sense tell us otherwise," he said. . . .

"Smut shall not be simply contained at its present level; it should be outlawed in every state in the Union. And the legislatures and courts at every level of American government shall act in unison to achieve that goal."

Nixon concluded by saying: "American morality is not to be trifled with. The Commission on Pornography and Obscenity has performed a disservice, and I totally reject its report."[7]

And then a reply:

The head of the Commission on Obscenity and Pornography has challenged President Nixon's rejection of the panel's recommendations.

William B. Lockhart, . . . dean of the University of Minnesota School of Law, said in Minneapolis . . . that "the President is unhappy because the scientific studies do not support the assumptions congenial to his viewpoint."

Lockhart said he thought the President had not had time to study the 800-page report but had been influenced by advisers who "led him to repeat some of the same tired arguments that have been advanced for a century about sexual materials."

These arguments are unscientific, "based on assumptions, guesses, and fears," Lockhart said.[8]

On the same day that Dean Lockhart replied to President Nixon, the New York City police raided twelve places dealing in what they called "hard core pornography."

Mr. Nixon's statements came when an election was only a week or so away, and in politics and war anything goes; that is a possible view. But probably he is sincere. Does he know, however, the causes of "true" obscenity and whether he or anybody else can spot it? Many of the "great books, great paintings, and great plays" he talks about, deal with "the warped and brutal portrayal of sex." In any event, he obviously believes that he or somebody whom he likes can eradicate the obscene.

Like Mr. William O'Brien, a certain higher clerk in the Post Office who confiscated an illustrated edition of the Greek classic *Lysistrata,* and when

7. Wesley G. Pippert, *Washington* (D.C.) *Star*, October 25, 1970.

8. *Chicago Daily News*, October 26, 1970.

asked the grounds for his opinion said, "Breasts, yes, but nipples, no. Buttocks, yes, but cracks, no!"[9] And we are back to Mr. Fishman, higher clerk of customs, and his impoverished criteria of morality.

The Future Be Damned!

Authoritarian and communist states seek to reduce the number of groups in the population. Franco's Spain has been notoriously hostile to the Basques, a nationality group that under free conditions could live there comfortably. Nasser expelled from Egypt several nationalities that were responsible for maintaining much of the Egyptian culture and economy, and he even persecuted the Coptic Christians, who are an ancient pre-Arab, Egyptian group. The reasons nationalists give are many; the *real* reason is that organized or "different" groups cause trouble to despots. "Different" people cannot be welded into a homogeneous pliable mass by the despots and their centralized bureaucracies.

Indeed, a principal problem of kalotic democracy is to assure interest groupings the possibility of organizing and pressuring the government. As we have already indicated, blacks, youth, and women will only be treated with respect and given a part in policy making if and when they become organized and lobby. Perhaps, for children and the future, we need a Lobby of the Unborn, as anthropologist Margaret Mead once suggested. (See p. 264.)

Short of that, one has to advocate the measures implied in our Policy. One way of "conducting continuous propaganda to elevate goals by a half-century" is to stress civic education in the schools. The elementary schools, unfortunately, have been snobbishly ignored by the intelligentsia and, as a result, such as there are of identity-enlarging and time-enlarging lessons are mainly chauvinistic and militaristic. In the universities—the pacesetters for the future—specialization of knowledge has brought about a civically unequipped, narrow type of moral and intellectual leadership.

If there will be difficulty mobilizing educators for this task in the schools, it may be imagined that the problem of generating futuristic forces outside of the educational world is worse. Practically no considerable interest group in America or anywhere else depends upon a future generation. Labor unions bring benefits here and now. So do corporations. So do the medical profession, the legal profession, and just about any other group now known.

True, there are voluntary associations for infant welfare, conservation of natural resources, and world organizations, but all of these are weak.

9. In Edward de Grazia, *Censorship Landmarks.*

Their members are few, they lack large staffs, their resources are meager. Considering that a great many future-experts believe that the world will face numerous disasters within the next fifty years, the disposable public opinion resources are pitiful.

The alternative or supplement to private resources is governmental energy and money. We have already said that politics, regardless of type of regime, forces leaders to think in terms of today's problems. So, unless new methods of choosing leaders were to be invented, little hope for the future could come from the politicians.

A second kind of governmental alternative would be to place resources for the future in the hands of permanent civil servants. Since they would not be elected, bureaucrats might be expected to take a longer view of social problems and their solution.

Against this appetizing idea, certain objections arise:

1. Politicians and politics, in the end, control the size and form of the resources of the bureaucracy. If they were, in a fit of futurist responsibility, to give over such resources, then presumably the effort could be carried forward without continual commitments on their part. (It is well known that bureaucrats do tend to hold onto powers and activities, once possessed.)

2. Bureaucracy, even when told to do right, cannot be expected to continue to do so without control, and yet we have said that this control would normally cause bureaucrats to limit their vision, not to expand it.

3. Particular bureaucracies are isolated from other bureaucracies. But problems of the future are not isolated. What value is to be obtained from an American plan to restrict petroleum consumption, if Japan does not do so? If fish life in the Mediterranean is being destroyed, who gets the countries that are implicated to join together to halt and reverse the process? The bureaucracies of the affected countries individually can do almost nothing.

IN SHORT, WHEN IT COMES TO THE NEXT GENERATION:

1. THE PEOPLE DON'T CARE.

2. THE PROFUTURE INTERESTS AND LOBBIES ARE WEAK.

3. THE POLITICIANS DON'T CARE.

4. THE BUREAUCRATS AREN'T TOLD TO CARE.

NOBODY GIVES A DAMN!

except a few persons here and there spending a total of a few dollars and a total of a few hours.

Why should I have to end a chapter on an optimistic note? I believe that there is no way of representing the future powerfully in national and world policy.

In consequence, I predict that future man will have a poorer material life than he has had, if he is prosperous, and, if he is poor today, he will have by no means a better life.

Coda

No, I cannot leave it at that. If pessimism were to prevail, we would not be happier for it; an optimist is generally happier than a pessimist. We should take every chance that we can to better human affairs.

We have said it before and will say it again.

Stress education for the future. Orient all disciplines to the future. De-emphasize history as such in favor of history written in a way to assist policies for the future. AND BE RADICAL! WEAK MEASURES WILL NOT WORK!

Chapter 5

Vicious Discrimination

To *discriminate* is almost to *distinguish:* that is, to tell the difference between two things. Thus, "Joey can't discriminate between red and green," or "Joey cannot discriminate between right and wrong."

But there is always a purpose in discrimination or distinctions. Obviously, there is some use in discriminating between the colors red and green. If Joey drives a car, he may hurt somebody while running through a red light under the impression it was green. Beyond this, there are aesthetic purposes; different color combinations afford a variety of pleasures.

But suppose we are in Mexico and we note that olive-skinned people are discriminated from red-brown-skinned people; the former are called "whites" and the latter "Indians." Now people who are "color-blind" contribute to breaking down a certain class structure where the whites are on top and the reds below. People who do discriminate and insist that the discrimination is important operate to preserve the privileges of the whites and the disqualifications of the reds.

There are various facets of discrimination to keep in mind:

1. The ability to perceive and verify discriminations among things and people is one step on the way to a highly useful and valuable kind of intelligence. (For example, the discovery that X rays can be distinguished from visible light; the discovery in painting that objects in the foreground can be distinguished from objects in the background; the discovery that personnel who are *people*-oriented make better managers than people who are *things*-oriented.)

183

2. Most people attach values to their discriminations. They prefer one part to another. (For example, some people prefer blue eyes, others brown; some like noise, some silence; etc.)

3. All rules of conduct (and therefore *all laws*) involve discriminations. (For example, note the basic discrimination between the lawful and the unlawful; the distinction between those eligible for pensions and those not; those who have *X* quantity of alcohol in their blood after a driving accident and those who do not; those who operate clean restaurants and those who don't; those who commit premeditated murder and those who commit manslaughter.)

4. A great many discriminations are: (A) incorrect, (B) exaggerated, (C) falsely understood, or (D) applied to persons categorically despite individual differences. For example:

(A) *Incorrect:* women have finer aesthetic feelings than men; or people without political party affiliations are more intelligent about politics than those who belong to a party;

(B) *Exaggerated:* the young have less interest in politics than the old (some but not much, and they are interested in different issues);

(C) *Falsely understood:* well-fed people are less likely to cause trouble than underfed people (they are more willing and able to assert themselves on various issues);

(D) *Applied categorically:* that Germans are readier to follow orders than Americans or Russians.

5. Many distinctions are often not made when they can be made and sometimes should be made—for example, the distinction between the use of cannabis (marijuana) and "hard" drugs; or the distinction between Nazis and Germans; or the distinction between a power-hungry politician and a politician who seeks actively to get things done.

Several consequences of these conditions are:

* 1. You cannot get rid of all discriminations without getting rid of all law and all science.

* 2. The task of correcting scientifically incorrect discriminations is immense. It is nothing less than making every person in the world into a first-class logician, scientist, and encyclopedist.

* 3. The task of changing the attitudes attached to both *correct* and *incorrect* discriminations is one of the largest and most important jobs facing applied political and social science.

It is difficult to change the hundreds of specific cases of discrimination whose total effect is to create or prolong dislike between people, such as the following:

The fact that many Americans eat corn should not cause so many Frenchmen to believe that Americans are only a step above horses. Nor should many Americans regard Frenchmen as exotic and remote because they may eat snails and frogs.

The popular Caucasian American belief that all Chinese look alike is an incorrect, subjective idea, since the Chinese obviously don't believe so (the Vietnamese—a branch of the Mongolian race—call Americans "long-noses"); but, in any case, it's an absurd ground for making vicious distinctions between Chinese and Caucasians.

If, to begin with, you don't deal with a character that is basically open, you can change many specific vicious discriminations, but the rigid and hostile character will find new ones to believe in.

Given these facts about discrimination, you can understand why this chapter is entitled "*Vicious* Discrimination." We cannot and should not try to eliminate discriminations. We should try to select correct discriminations and use them to create the government and society that we believe to be good.

PRINCIPLE V

Society should eliminate discrimination
arising from and contributing to
the disqualification of persons
for full social participation.

This principle should not surprise anybody. We are already committed to a belief in an open society with full opportunity for people of all types to participate in all kinds of groups. But the principle is violated in most countries to a fearful extent.

*   *   *   *   *

Bleary-eyed astronomers are heard to say, "No matter how often I look at the stars, I am amazed." Here is a proposition of political science which, no matter how often I contemplate it, amazes me.

PROPOSITION V

Every inherited or acquired trait
by which human beings are
distinguishable has been the occasion
for political disqualification.

Meanings:

Inherited: any quality, such as eye color or a propensity to heavy muscula- ture, which is transmitted through the genes.

Acquired: qualities, physical or mental, whose origins within a person occur after fusion of one's parental sperm and egg.

Distinguishable: discovered and named by some large number of people. (Or, and we must add this, they think they have discovered it.) That is, for example, people are tall or short (both an inherited and acquired trait, incidentally). Or, as another example, people stink or don't stink (a subjective-objective judgment that is often associated with the wrong trait[1]), etc.

Occasion: the excuse or reason for, or associated with, the disqualification.

Disqualification: a distinct formal or informal reduction in the influence- potential of a certain category of persons when compared with others who are equals in every other respect.

Every: "every category of difference has at some time somewhere . . ."

Now to the proof, which may be very difficult indeed.

Proof by Noncontradiction of Extreme Notions

* 1. *Try height as a disqualification!*
A. The Vatican's Swiss Guard had to be over six feet tall. This was a prestigious occupation for centuries that helped many a poor Swiss boy and his family get ahead in the world.
B. The New York Police Department required men of over 5'10" in height. This requirement seemed proper for "efficiency." (How could a small guy arrest a big guy?) It became obvious that the rule was discriminating substantially against Puerto Ricans who are on the aver- age shorter than most other Americans. The "cops on the beat," not to mention those behind the desk, make the great majority of judicial decisions in America, especially in conflicts among the poor. It became of considerable importance to the Puerto Ricans and their families to reduce this minimum height, and so it was finally reduced. Needless to say, offenders could still be arrested, since police wear uniforms and

---

1. Take an old New Orleans example: dock loading is sweaty work. Stevedores stink. Stevedores are black ("tote that barge, lift that bale . . ."). This is a trait of the work being done, yet it is associated in some people's minds with a racial stink and used as one more reason for backing up physical segregation. Incidentally, the kind of occupations that cause people to stink is more important, politically, than the smell itself. Kings and queens used to stink badly, by Ivory Soap standards, but that was a good smell, the stink of pomp and power. One is reminded of the time a lady reproached the famous lexicographer, Samuel Johnson, saying "Dr. Johnson, you smell," and of his retort: "No, my dear lady, *you* smell; I stink."

badges, and carry guns, handcuffs, and clubs, all of which assist arrests ("Too much so," say other critics).

C. Napoleon or General Giap could not have gotten into West Point.

* 2. *Intelligence*

A. If you can devise a test which you can persuade people to accept as a measure of "intelligence," you can discriminate against the low scorers. If it turns out that the test actually measures "culture" and "previous education" then you have a nice weapon to use, in the name of science, to discriminate against people of different backgrounds. Actually, U.S. intelligence tests have done just this, blocking blacks, immigrants, and poor whites quite nicely over many years from officerships in the army, admissions to academic programs in lower schools and to colleges, etc. Since these are avenues to political, economic, and social power, the "lower classes" are kept in place.

B. Well, now, how about high intelligence? Who discriminates *against* high intelligence? I am tempted to say that business, government, the armed forces, and practically all institutions discriminate against the highest intelligence, and with a large research grant I could prove this. However, it may be sufficient here to point out that candidates for public office in America rarely lay stress upon a high IQ or college degrees or refer to the opposing candidate as stupid, because a great many voters will clobber him/her for the presumption that high intelligence could influence one's conduct in office; Congresswoman Shirley Chisholm, candidate for the Democratic Presidential nomination in 1972, spoke of her near-genius IQ and her various academic accomplishments, but she quickly added that her reason for doing so was not to boast but to demonstrate that she had adequate qualifications so that, if she were a man and were white, the press would take her campaign seriously.

Sometimes you may wonder whether the fact that a politician likes animals can be more crucial than whether he is intelligent. When Richard Nixon was Vice-President and was accused of financial wrongdoing, he gained sympathy from the public by exhibiting his spaniel on television—the famous "Checkers speech." Two Presidents later, Lyndon B. Johnson lifted his beagles by their ears and triggered nationwide arguments over cruelty to animals.

Tom Paine, whom George Washington once said was worth a regiment (in gratitude for Paine's rousing revolutionary pamphlets) and at another time called "a dirty little atheist," wrote against property owning as a requirement for the right to vote, saying: "When a broodmare shall fortunately produce a foal or a mule, that, by being worth the sum in question shall convey to the owner the right of voting . . . in whom does the origin of such a right exist? Is it in the man, or in the mule?"

*　3. *Other types of examples*

People are politically discriminated against on grounds of foreign birth; residence in one neighborhood instead of another; dealing with the government (conflict of interest) or not dealing with the government (patronage system); etc., etc. It would take a lengthy discussion to determine whether such cases are extreme or ordinary. For example, wasn't it rather extreme of the "Founding Fathers" to write that only native-born citizens could become President? But I have never heard the question argued in principle.

Proof by a Multitude of Common Disqualifications

1. Family

Aristocracy in many countries disqualifies "commoners" and in democracies a famous name by itself often carries people to high places.

2. Economic class

A multitude of discriminations—both formal and informal—can be named, though in the twentieth century these are largely hidden and informal. Once wealth was *required by law* for high office; then (and now) it became *required in fact* because of the need to pay for costly campaigns.

3. Sex, race, youth, religion, etc.

For example, it was estimated that some 2.5 million votes were turned away from John F. Kennedy when he ran for President because he was Catholic. Barry Goldwater, too, lost votes because his paternal ancestors had been Jewish (indeed, he probably lost some Jewish votes because he was no longer Jewish; he caught prejudice both ways). Jews have been discriminated against in all conceivable ways.

It is necessary to note here a fact often forgotten: depending on how discrimination is practiced, a group can in some ways convert it into an asset, usually by using it for increasing drive, motivation, performance, and intelligence; Jews, Quakers, Mormons, Christian Scientists, French Huguenots, Armenians, "overseas Chinese," and other groups can be cited in this regard. "This is a hell of a way to run a railroad," for it depends upon uncontrollable and vicious practices to pull up the cultural and political level of a society.

Esther's Seduction of Artaxerxes

How old is anti-Semitism? The wise one will say, "Very old!"[2] and the sage will add that all forms of discrimination have much in common, and therefore many peoples have suffered from the same kind of persecution before and since the history of Jewish persecutions began. But because of the Hebrew respect for **the word** and **the book,** which passed into the heritage of the West (even while the Westerner was persecuting those from whom this respect was gained), the record of anti-Semitism is more complete.

Bible buffs will recall the following passages from "Additions to the Book of Esther" in the Apocrypha:

The Great King, Artaxerxes, to the rulers of the hundred and twenty-seven provinces from India to Ethiopia and to the governors under them writes thus: "Having become ruler of many nations and master of the whole world, not elated with presumption of authority but always acting reasonably and with kindness, I have determined to

2. I am impressed by the theory of Immanuel Velikovsky, who, in *Ages in Chaos* (Garden City, N.Y.: Doubleday & Company, Inc., 1952) and in personal conversation, has given reasons to fix the beginnings of anti-Semitism to a confusion arising after 1500 B.C. that mistakenly certified the Jews as related to the Hyksos, destroyers of Egyptian civilization and savage oppressors for centuries.

settle the lives of my subjects in lasting tranquillity and, in order to make my kingdom peaceable and open to travel throughout all its extent, to re-establish the peace which all men desire.

"When I asked my counselors how this might be accomplished, Haman, who excells among us in good will and steadfast fidelity, and has attained the second place in the kingdom, pointed out to us that among all the nations in the world there is scattered a certain hostile people, who have laws contrary to those of every nation and continuously disregard the ordinances of the kings, so that the unifying of the kingdom which we honorably intend cannot be brought about. We understand that this people, and it alone, stands constantly in opposition to all men, perversely following a strange manner of life and laws, and is ill-disposed to our government, doing all the harm they can so that our kingdom may not attain stability.

"Therefore we have decreed that those indicated to you in the letters of Haman, who is in charge of affairs and is our second father, shall all, with their wives and children, be utterly destroyed by the sword of their enemies, without pity or mercy, on the fourteenth day of the twelfth month, Adar, of this present year, so that those who have long been and are now hostile may in one

day go down in violence to Hades, and leave our government completely secure and untroubled hereafter."[3]

Then Mordecai swung into action. He shamed and persuaded beautiful Esther, herself a Jew belonging to the harem of the king, to plead the cause of the Jews. Esther adorned herself and boldly approached Artaxerxes. A complete switch in attitude occurred. Haman and his kind were all butchered, and the Jews were left in peace. Left in peace, that is, until the next persecution and the next. And, remarkably, very similar allegations accompanied later attacks, both against Jews and other minorities, down to the 1970s in the Soviet Union.

Proof by Crazy Cases

There is an old saying: "Every virtue contains its vice." Here is another saying that is rarely heard: "Every vice has sometime been a virtue in politics." By this I mean that any trait or behavior that you dislike has at some point in history helped persons or groups achieve preferred or high positions in politics. (Note: I don't mean that a leader *happens* also to have a vice; I mean that the vice positively *assists* in the achievement of power.)

Let's start with a list of common vices or handicaps that have helped people gain or hold power. There are innumerable examples of these in history and today:

Treachery (Hitler made a nonaggression pact with Stalin which preceded his all-out attack on Russia.)

Trickery (During World War I German intelligence shipped Lenin in a sealed car into Russia knowing he would foment revolution.)

---

3. *The New English Bible* (New York: Oxford University Press, 1962), 97.

Mayhem (The proslavery representative, Preston Brooks, who crippled Charles Sumner of Massachusetts with a cane in the House of Representatives was widely admired south of the Mason-Dixon Line.)

Kidnaping (Some people made heroes of the French-Canadian rebels who in 1970 kidnaped several officials and murdered one.)

Suicide (Japanese *hara-kiri,* an elaborate suicide, was practiced to leave an honorable political and military name to live afterwards.)[4]

Crippledness (Not only the misfortune pitied by voters nor even the display of war wounds for political preferment, but the actual self-infliction of wounds—e.g., tattoos—or the seeking out of certain types of cripples for political advancement—e.g., dwarf royal attendants—have been known at various times and places.)

Stuttering (Again, not the misfortune, but the deliberate cultivation of stuttering has been used to show one was "in"; various Englishmen practiced it because their king, George VI, was a stutterer.)

and

Envy	*Bribery*	*Evasion*
Malice	*Theft*	*Irresponsibility*
Disparagement	*Suppression of*	*Arrogance*
Flattery	*Liberty*	*Ostentation*
Cowardice	*Profligacy*	*Fraud*
Laziness	*Betrayal of Principles*	*Enslavement*

But, now, let's take up some "rarer" vices:

Human Sacrifice: This practice was extremely common in history; the gods were allegedly especially pleased by such offerings.

Cannibalism: Expertness at dissecting and extracting human organs and, sometimes, cooking them properly, has been in some demand in scattered parts of the human family in times past. It is rare, but not unknown, even now. The eater is believed to derive the political power of the eatee.

Emasculation: Famous examples of this not uncommon practice were the eunuchs of the Ottoman Empire who were supposed to become more reliable and trustworthy (especially with the harem) in executing their responsibilities.

Prostitution: Both male and female sacred harlots inhabited temples and enjoyed the perquisites of political power incidental to their influence over priests and laymen.

---

4. The *Chicago Tribune* of November 27, 1970, carried a report by Samuel Jameson about a Japanese author, Yukio Mishima, who sought to spark a coup d'etat by kidnaping a general in order to force the army to assemble a thousand troops, then urging the troops in a speech to revolt against the constitution, and finally committing hara-kiri in hopes of exciting them to immediate action. He failed, not without earning some praise for his actions.

Enforced Virginity: The opposite. The Roman vestal virgins would be killed if they violated their pledge.

Mass Murder: The Nazis operated their slaughterhouses in some secrecy, but ability in this endeavor was well rewarded, and graft from the sale of clothing, personal possessions, gold tooth-fillings, and fertilizer was not unknown.

Mass Rape: Frequent. The Romans celebrated "The Rape of the Sabine Women" and centuries of educated European gentlemen considered this an especially thrilling detail of their education in the liberal arts.

Drugs: Scandanavian eaters of the mushroom *Amanita muscaria* would work themselves up into a fine warlike frenzy on its "poisons."

Gluttony: Certain African queens stuff themselves to monstrous proportions to elevate the morale of their subjects.

Murder: Macbeth attempted to conceal his crime, but the chief murderer of Czar Nicholas and his family had a city named for him by the Bolsheviks.

Starvation: Practically every war. During the American Civil War this "weapon" was used in the siege of Vicksburg, Mississippi. (How many millions of American schoolchildren thrilled to the story of the population having to eat rats?)

Betrayal of People: Brutus, "greatest patriot of them all," stabbed Caesar, his foster father. In the apocryphal Old Testament Book of Judith, the heroine seduces the enemy king, Halofernes, and then beheads him to bring her tribe evidence to strengthen their morale.

I hope that this glorious recital of the history of vicious discrimination (and vicious preference) has not calloused the reader against sensitivity to discrimination in America or to the often vicious practices of Americans abroad, in war and peace. For the United States, by far the wealthiest, most prosperous . . . and all of that . . . country in the world, is finding the job of erasing vicious discrimination impossible to handle.

We had better put the Policy against discrimination on the record right away, even before going into the details of the American case.

POLICY V

Provide equal opportunities
to all persons in a group
to achieve the group's values
and correct those groups
whose intended or invariable effect
is to monopolize or curtail opportunities.

Now hear this: if your group is a UNION, BUSINESS, FAMILY, CHURCH, LODGE, CLUB, PARTY, ARMY, or GOVERNMENT—

This means you!

A Note About Ethnic Discrimination in America

The bar chart below gives a general idea of social discrimination in American history. The markings and shadings come only from my recollections. I do not know of a systematic study, full of evidence and charts, nor of any practical way of making such a study. You cannot interview dead people; you cannot find documents that never existed; the dates for the beginning and end of discrimination are not usually celebrated by holidays (except that we know a few dates such as when the first slaves were landed here and when most slaves were emancipated). So, if historians were interested in the problem, they would have to use their ordinary method of picking up scraps of information wherever they could find them: in ships' lists; in incidents involving foreigners; in name-calling and ethnic jokes in newspapers; in debates over who should vote, whether long residence should be required for the vote, and such matters; in the letters and diaries of immigrants, travelers, and others; and, here and there, an essay on social conditions or working conditions.

In fact, few historians have concerned themselves with this major feature of the American social landscape. They are more interested in the top dogs than in the underdogs, more interested in justifying American history from the point of view of the well born and affluent. So, to a tough research job is added a bias, and no wonder that one has to guess, if interested in the matter.

And, as to why one should be interested, this history, vague and hidden as it is, tells us what to look out for; it tells of the frauds and mental lapses in the writing of history; it explains why many Americans are superpatriots (to show how thoroughly American they have become, and to quiet their own doubts); it tells us why American culture has not afforded a happy home to countless millions of Americans and why we should look to the future, a changed future, as the *object* of history.

Social (Including Legal) Disqualifications in America of Average Persons from Various Groupings, 1600–1971

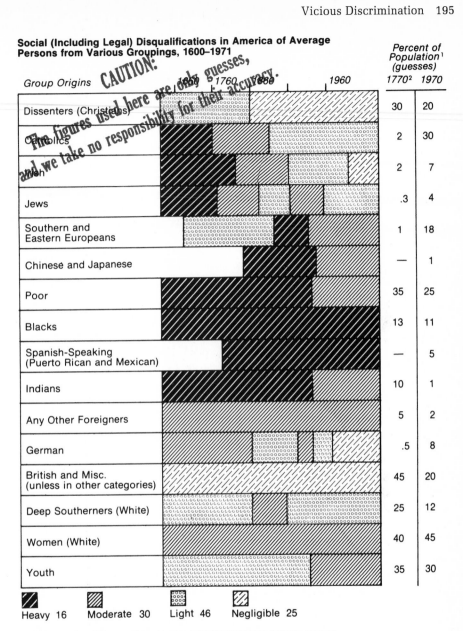

Group Origins	1660	1760	1860	1960	Percent of Population[1] (guesses) 1770[2]	1970
Dissenters (Christians)					30	20
Catholics					2	30
Irish					2	7
Jews					.3	4
Southern and Eastern Europeans					1	18
Chinese and Japanese					—	1
Poor					35	25
Blacks					13	11
Spanish-Speaking (Puerto Rican and Mexican)					—	5
Indians					10	1
Any Other Foreigners					5	2
German					.5	8
British and Misc. (unless in other categories)					45	20
Deep Southerners (White)					25	12
Women (White)					40	45
Youth					35	30

CAUTION: The figures used here are only guesses, and we take no responsibility for their accuracy.

Heavy 16   Moderate 30   Light 46   Negligible 25

1. Adds up to over 100 percent because many persons were in more than one category.
2. Includes the thirteen colonies only (therefore, not French Louisiana, etc.)

Note: The reason I have recorded the Irish, Jews, poor, and Asiatics as having recently made gains against disqualification is that their organizations and/or their presence in numerous key positions has given them much new legal and political protection. Also, bear in mind that there are many exceptions in every case. There are still, for example, many Americans of German origin, who feel that they are not getting a "square deal" as Americans. Also, the bar graph does not give a continuous picture of the proportion of the people who came from each grouping at different times. This one must know to understand why, for example, the Jews suffered less discrimination in the middle of the nineteenth century than in the later periods. The earlier Jewish immigrants were few in number and more educated and affluent. The later immigrants came by the hundreds of thousands, driven by hunger and persecution. Similar conditions affected the Italians, here grouped with southern and eastern Europeans.

This guessing is put into statistical form to extract some pattern and logic out of the whole process. It suggests, for example, a worldwide feature of vicious discrimination—that a grouping, whether it is organized as a group or exists as a social class, can compose a minority of the population and yet, by dominating the minds of the whole people and permitting them to discriminate against each other, can remain comfortably on top of the heap. Every single discriminated-against ethnic grouping has participated in discriminatory behavior against other discriminated groupings. Poor Anglo-Saxons (a term used to refer to English origin, with some Scotch, Northern Irish, Welsh, and sundry admixtures from northwest Europe) participated heartily in burning out Chinese immigrants to California, and rioted against the Irish Catholic immigrants in the early 1900s in New England. They did not need the exhortation of the rich and educated New England families, who by this time were above such tactics and who needed Irish servants and workers. The New England elite had their turn to discriminate later when enough Irish had achieved a modest position in society to begin to form a threat to their political power.

French-Canadians advanced down through New England in the twentieth century and encountered vicious discrimination from poor Anglo-Saxons ("swamp Yankees") and to a degree from Irish and Italians, who themselves were discriminated against and in turn discriminated against each other. The total history, yet to be written, is highly complex.

It is well to bear in mind that the *myth* or *illusion* of equality was transmitted by generations of schoolteachers from New England and the Middle Atlantic coastal states to new generations of teachers and pupils from Maine to California, leaving out most of the South. And these schoolteachers themselves believed that the myth was a fact and that their unruly little charges from all parts of the world had an equal chance in life if only they would behave themselves.

Furthermore, many exceptional individuals in all of these ethnic groups, whether or not discriminated against, rose above the nasty free-for-all conflict. To them, to many schoolteachers, to some writers—yes, even the much maligned Horatio Alger, and the abolitionist, Harriet Beecher Stowe—is owed some significant part of the generally fluid American social structure. Their teachings and the veritable mad movement and dissolution of American life prevented the permanent division of the country into ethnic ghettos. From a humanistic point of view, you can rightly call the history of ethnic and race relations in America disgraceful; from another point of view, you can take consolation from the fact that it might have been even worse.[5] Vicious discrimination has been driven underground. It erupts openly here and there from time to time from various executive suites, labor union headquarters, construction projects, genteel ghettos, a few schools, a

ONLY NON-HANGABLE WASP SERVANTS WANTED

[Statutes at Large of South Carolina, 2, 646–49] [June 30, 1716]*

AN ACT TO ENCOURAGE THE IMPORTATION OF WHITE SERVANTS INTO THIS PROVINCE.

[Act offered a bounty of 25 pounds per servant]

And whereas there hath been imported into this Province several native Irish servants that are Papists, and persons taken from Newgate and other prisons, convicted of capital crimes, to the great prejudice and detriment of this Province, Be it therefore enacted . . .

That no person by this act required to purchase white servants shall be obliged to purchase any Irish servants or persons convicted in England or elsewhere of capital crimes . . .

And in order to prevent the imposing upon this Province persons of lewd and profligate lives, Be it further enacted

That all merchants or masters of vessels or others shall upon their oaths declare that to the best of their knowledge none of the servants by them imported be either what is commonly called native Irish, or persons of known scandalous character, or Roman Catholics. And if any merchant . . . shall ship any servants to this Province, he shall be obliged to send a certificate . . . that such persons or servants are Protestants . . . and with such a certificate, Irish servants, being Protestants, may be lawfully imported here . . .

*Reprinted in Francis X. Curran, Catholics in Colonial Law (Chicago: Loyola University Press, 1963, 91.)

small crazy press, etc. However, by no means has equality of opportunity for wealth and respect been achieved for most of the population in relation to all of the population. The currents of discrimination may be underground, but they still flow and make people anxious and hostile, and prevent personal fulfillment on the part of many millions of Americans.

5. Despite the tremendous assemblage of ethnic and racial groupings in America (and in part because of it), outright massacre and extermination of groups has been rare and limited. The American Indian has suffered most; Negro slavery, because its very nature was totalitarian suppression for profit, did not extend to genocide. The Turkish massacre of Armenians; the German genocide of Jews, Gypsies, Russians, and Poles; the Russian massacres of Jews, Cossacks, and Poles; the Hindu-Moslem mutual massacres in India; the Indonesian massacre of Chinese; the Hausa Nigerian massacre of Nigerian Ibos; the Pakistani murder of a million Bengalis; and hundreds of other historical cases are more illuminating of humanity's capacities in this regard than the American experience.

Women

Like other groupings that are discriminated against, some women tend to praise the system and discriminate against each other in favor of the ruling formula. Many, perhaps most, women prefer a position of vicious discrimination because they get certain payoffs. Many women say, in effect, "I'm just a poor little helpless woman; what can you expect?"

Meanwhile, just as slaves used to figure out ways of beating the game, many women use their wiles to make decisions and take responsibilities that males cannot or dare not take. In practically every culture that is called patriarchal, women make a great many important decisions, and can make life miserable or beautiful for husbands, lovers, sons, and daughters, at the very least.

Women often win over men, but it's too often the wrong kind of victory. Again, as the saying goes, "this is a hell of a way to run a railroad." Many women don't like such pretended subservience and underground warfare. Many would prefer a general equality and freedom of opportunity, and would prefer to let individual differences, not sexual ones, between men and women take care of individual cases of subservience and responsibility. ME TOO!

In no case where equality between groups is sought is there an easy solution. The participants in the struggle see it differently. "Equality" can always be resisted because those who seek it are usually confused and are, in any event, a minority of their own group.

A woman who seeks liberation will *not* win complete victory by reducing every man and woman to exact equal replicas and likenesses, like mosquitoes from the same batch of eggs. She will win when any woman has as much chance as any man of fulfilling her personal needs from the available stock of social resources. And if she is to be prevented from doing something, the probable reason will be, not that she is a woman, but that she is incapable as a person of doing it, and that such incapability *does not* come directly or indirectly out of sexist discrimination.

A recent study of American workers shows–

94 PERCENT OF WOMEN ARE UNDERPAID!

"To measure sex discrimination . . . [a] study selected six legitimate criteria on which income distributions could be based—occupational prestige, amount of supervisory responsibility, tenure with present employer, tenure on present job with employer, number of hours worked per week, and education. From these the study team has predicted what a person's income should be and then subtracted the actual income. The results show that 94 percent of the women are below what their income should be on the basis of the predictors. The discrepancy between what women should be paid and what they are paid amounts to $3,458 per woman."[6]

(Based on a national representative sample of 1533 workers in late 1969.)

If the case is indirectly caused by unthinking sexist discrimination (like the absence of shop tools that a woman's smaller hands can grasp, because "this is a man's job"), then several responses should follow:

1. The proof of unnecessary historical discrimination.

2. The attempt by the responsible *de facto* discriminator to change the situation (e.g., regarding tools) to permit the "equal" employment of women. This attempt, if not voluntary, can be imposed by an arbitrator.

3. If the responsibility is too diffused (among employers, distributors, toolmakers, male-dominated unions, etc.), then this determination has to be made by a "fact finder" or "hearing officer," and the responsible parties would be compelled to produce an effective solution to the problem in the shortest possible time.

4. The parties involved in this procedure would have, among other rights, the right to appeal that they cannot support the heavy changeover costs. In this case, the appropriate legislature should be in a position to extend enough financial aid by long-term loans or subsidy to bring the costs down to a bearable level.

6. *Newsletter,* Institute for Social Research (Ann Arbor, Mich.: University of Michigan, Autumn 1971), p. 5.

5. In this whole process, a vigorous pressure group (an organized lobby) should be maintained by women. A league against sexism is needed to uncover cases and get prompt action on them. It has to follow up and spur on the participants.

Three objections to this system of advancing women's rights can be made.

One is its cost, not alone the costs of controversy but also the costs of changing machines and systems. To this objection one can reply that the costs of sexist discrimination (like all other forms of discrimination) are enormous. Ask any executive about the difference in costs and benefits among a *well-trained* secretary, a *poor* secretary, and *any* secretary in a place like Venezuela or Greece, and he (or she?) will roar like a wounded tiger and give all sorts of proof, unconsciously perhaps, that trained humanpower is America's richest source of capital. Furthermore, the cost of developing human power must be considered high priority spending, since it affects the satisfaction of many millions of citizens. How many persons get satisfactions from armaments, highways, ship subsidies, crop payments, or more of the same old schooling, by comparison? It would be much more valuable to society to cut out the second year of high school and to use the billions of dollars saved to reduce sexist discrimination.

A second objection is lack of personnel to administer and police such a system. We mention this subject again later when we come to treat justice and law. Professional schools should be set up immediately to educate the thousands of "hearing officers," arbitrators, and judges for this kind of case. A year's training, done part-time and full-time, is adequate and will provide far better personnel than the average of justices of the peace around the country. This can be part-time work and the volunteers for it, we can be sure, will be exceedingly numerous.

A third objection is directed at extreme cases, but we shall address it anyhow. "Neither men nor women would want to fly with a woman pilot." One, the statement is exaggerated; I would not mind, would you? Two, the public "confidence gap" would be reduced by experience and habit. (After all, for quite a while most people didn't want to ride airplanes at all even after they were reasonably safe.) Three, the central problem (getting to be a pilot) can be approached by making women navigators, traffic controllers, charter pilots, then pilots of civil nonscheduled aircraft, government aircraft, armed forces airplanes, etc.; the final change would go almost unnoticed. But again, extreme cases, involving perhaps one out of a thousand positions, are being used to justify all other exclusions.

Another case of history going unwritten and unread is the thousand-year experience of female monastic orders. Nuns have done practically every kind of job known to humanity, including effective defensive warfare.

Question: Why Is Vicious Discrimination Like Pollution?

Behavior of the Discriminator =	Behavior of the Pollutor =	Behavior of the Equalizer =	Behavior of the Beneficial Ecologist =
* * *	* * *	* * *	* * *
1. "We have heavy tools that women can't manage."	1. "We have a lot of mercurized muck that has to be dumped to get a clean product."	1. "Machine design was done by men for men."	1. "Harmful by-products are results of chemical and industrial inventions that assumed nature was full of harmless dumping grounds."
2. "Hire men only."	2. "Dump it in the river."	2. "Redesign tools for humans."	2. "Redesign processes to protect nature."
3. "Women have to compete for fewer jobs at lower pay."	3. "People can go elsewhere for their fish, swims, and drinking water."	3. "Women and men can perform closely similar tasks."	3. "People can enjoy and live from their river."
4. "My costs are kept down. No new tools. No problems."	4. "My costs are kept down. No expensive deep wells or chemical screens."	4. "Total social costs are lowered. Ultimately enterprise costs are lowered."	4. "Total social costs are lowered. Ultimately enterprise costs are lowered."

Answer:

Vicious discrimination is like pollution because both penalize the innocent for quick and exclusive profit. Equality of opportunity (to experience) for people and beneficial ecological policies for nature both reduce psychological and material costs in the long run and promote a justifiable kind of profit.

Social Class

Social class is essentially the opposite of freedom of opportunity or equal chances in life. A social class is a grouping of people who have similar chances at achieving values, who have more or fewer chances than other such groupings in a population, and who have some chance as individuals to move in or out of those groupings. Thus, in nineteenth-century England a poor child, like practically all other poor children elsewhere, had very little chance of going to high school, entering a profession, owning a factory, holding public office, or mingling with and marrying into families that did have such chances. The English and most other western European systems have loosened a good deal since then, owing to "poor white power," and closely resemble the American system. The English monarchy is a feudal survival, where now in fact only the monarch herself—or himself—is held to the *caste*[7] system by law.

7. You can define a "caste system" as the frozen extreme of a "class system."

Since social class is the obverse of freedom of opportunity and a large part of this book deals with opportunities and life chances, you are learning the essentials of social class, perhaps without even realizing it. If I were a Marxist, then I should feel obliged to rewrite this whole book from the point of view of *social class*. That is one of the several earmarks of the Marxist theorist. I would begin with the idea of social class and develop a table of contents around it.

POLITICS AND SOCIAL CLASS

An Introduction to Political Science

I. Economic Determinism and the Theory of Socialism
    1. Development of Class Theory before Karl Marx
    2. Marx and Engels: *The Communist Manifesto* (1848)
    3. Later Marxists: Lenin, Bernstein, Kautsky, Luxemburg, Trotsky, Gramsci, Togliatti
    4. Critiques of Marxism: Pareto, Sorel, von Mises
II. Class as a Historical Phenomenon
    1. Origins of the State and Social Class in Conquest in Primitive Society
    2. Class in Ancient Athens and Rome
    3. Rise of Proletarian Movements
    4. The Russian Revolution and Communism
III. The Relationship of Social Class to the Means of Production
    1. Characteristics of the Bourgeoisie
    2. Monopolies and Economic Power
    3. Control of the State by the Owning Classes
    4. Violence and Class Warfare
IV. Crisis of the Capitalist State
    1. Imperialism as the Foreign Policy of Capitalism
    2. The Economic Causes of War
    3. Wars of Liberation and Civil Wars
    4. The Welfare State and Fabian Socialism
V. The Struggle for Socialist Leadership
    1. Stalinism
    2. Maoism
    3. The Reconsideration of Marxism within the European Socialist and Communist Ranks
    4. The Future of Marxism

No doubt, by using the table of contents above I would be able to say many of the same things I'm saying here, but the net result would be vastly different. So I proceeded with my personal approach which is individualist and pragmatic.

The Vicious[8] Cycle of Class Position

Jim is born of poor, uneducated, country parents. He knows of no other life but theirs. His speech and manners are theirs and their friends'. His ambitions are usually the same kind as theirs. He doesn't think much of schooling and does not push the question. He drinks his 7-Up and beer, bowls, watches football and westerns on TV, marries young, holds several jobs at different times in a food processing plant. His own family takes on his characteristics.

This is the cycle that Jim and most people are part of. Each element causes the next, and each new generation has traits similar to and resulting from the preceding one.

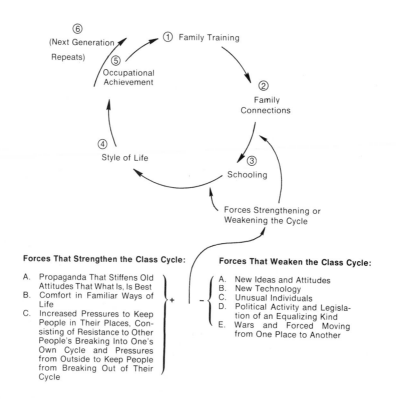

8. I call the cycle "vicious" because most people would like to, or should, break their cycle at some point to achieve values higher than those provided them by its habits. I refer not only to a poor person but to a rich man whose cycle can be strangling in its own way; for example, a rich person may be starved for affection.

Remember Al? His life could have been like Jim's. He was riding the same circle; some would call it "the lower middle class." But then he went into politics where various new friends, ideas, ambitions, and ways of life began to work on him. It is quite likely that he will end up involved in a distinctly different set of activities that will be carried over to his children's way of life. Since World War II the *cycle breakers* in America have been so strong that there may become one gigantic middle class—heavily dependent upon government to guarantee its rights, support its income level, and keep up its style of life—plus one extremely wealthy group of about 1 percent of the population, and one extremely poor group of about 10 percent.

That is, the social class structure of the people of the United States and a few other countries may become like this:

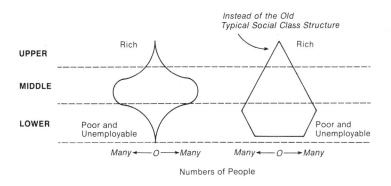

*   *   *   *   *

Q. "Where is a recession always a depression?"
A. "Among the poor, of course!"

Scene: The corner of a packing room in a toy factory

The Dialogue	Willie's Thoughts
Mr. J. "I think you ought to know, Willie, that there's not going to be any more work after Friday.	"Oh, oh, here it comes; just when I bought that refrigerator."
Mr. B. "What's that, Mr. Jason?"	
Mr. J. "We have to lay off some people, Willie."	"Why do you always call me Willie and I call you Mr. Jason?"

The Dialogue, cont'd   Willie's Thoughts, cont'd

Mr. B. "That's me, huh?"
Mr. J. "Yeah, and a couple of other   "That's three blacks to go."
fellows."
Mr. B. "I've been here a year, Mr.   "And I have a wife and baby and a
Jason."   high-school diploma, and I worked
                                               pretty hard."
Mr. J. "The others have been here   "How do you get to be anywhere
longer."   longer when you get fired so
Mr. B. "What about the union I   often?"
belong to?"
Mr. J. "That's their rule, Willie."   "Their rule and my dues. They made
                                               out it was a big thing taking me in."

Mr. B. "Maybe I can take some sick
leave to begin with."
Mr. J. "You already used it up."   "That's right. Taking care of the
                                               baby while Annabelle took care of
                                               her father down home when he fell."

Mr. B. "Was anything wrong with my   "I never took anything except a
work, Mr. Jason?"   broken toy."
Mr. J. "No, no. It's business.   "Now he's getting mad at me be-
Business is bad! Nothing to do with   cause he doesn't like what he's do-
you personally."   ing. Nothing to do with me per-
                                               sonally! I'll make him feel a little
                                               worse."
Mr. B. "But I have to have work."   "After three weeks. That's a long
Mr. J. "You've got some unemploy-   time without any money."
ment compensation coming."
Mr. B. "It won't last long and it's not   "Can't live on that. He knows it."
much."
Mr. J. "Well, you've only been here   "Maybe I should go to Pittsburgh,
a year."   and Annabelle can tell the Welfare I
                                               disappeared."

Mr. B. "Look, Mr. Jason, I didn't
complain any about overtime or
working nights, did I?"
Mr. J. "It's not up to me, Willie.   "There it goes. Nobody's fault."
When the books don't show a profit,
the word comes down to cut back."
Mr. B. "I don't mean it's you, Mr.   "Why don't you knock off for a
Jason."   while and see how it is?"

The Dialogue, cont'd

Mr. J. "Why don't you get some more schooling, Willie?"

Mr. B. "I've got enough education for the jobs I get."
Mr. J. "You never have enough education. Look at Bill Cosby."

Mr. B. "Yeah, I know. I don't think you have any right to fire me."
Mr. J. "You're fired all right. Don't take advantage of my good nature. This is St. Louis, you know, not Chicago. The other bosses around here think I'm too soft."
Mr. B. "You're wrong. I'm going up to the front office and protest."
Mr. J. "Don't make trouble for yourself. It'll be days before you get your final paycheck if you bother them."
Mr. B. "Well, why don't you fire a white man for a change?"
Mr. J. "There's no discrimination here. We're just following the rules. They're the same for everybody."

Mr. B. "OK, OK. I quit right now."

Mr. J. "You don't have to quit till Friday."
Mr. B. "I don't care. I quit now. What's the use?"
Mr. J. "I thought you needed the money so bad."
Mr. B. "Shit, I don't need your money."

Willie's Thoughts, cont'd

"What? How? When? What for? Where? Who's going to pay the bills?"

"What's this 'Bill Cosby'? Why not Henry Ford? Next thing he'll ask me is why not retire to my country estate in Africa."
"Now watch when I try my 'bad nigger' act."
"Well, what's wrong with being soft? Everybody likes to think they're hard, especially when poor blacks are concerned."

"I wonder if that would change things any. Trouble is, I'm scared."
"The S.O.B. is right. They hold all the high cards in their hand."

"There, I said it. It always comes down to that."
"Yeah. You make new rules as you go along. You could do it if you wanted to, but the other whites would kick up a fuss."
"I can't help it. I'm getting mad."

"I have to do something to get back at them."

"There I go. 'Foolish pride,' Mamma calls it. Now he's telling himself why does he have to hire such irresponsible Negroes."

The Dialogue, cont'd.   Willie's Thoughts, cont'd

Mr. J. "You're getting damned uppi-   "A little threatening makes me feel
ty, aren't you? Well, suit yourself."   better."
Mr. B. "I sure will, now, soon as I get
my stuff. And you better have that
check ready."

*   *   *   *   *

   In the United States "black" is more than a color and more than a signal
for racial prejudice to begin its destructive work. It is a sign of poverty, and
the problems of being black and fighting off poverty usually go together.
"Black" is a sign of a culture whose products range from "soul food" to the
tremendous thrust of modern jazz. "Black" conjures up many white and
black attitudes that keep expressing themselves for better or worse so long
as there is no wholehearted consensus in a nation that racial discrimination
MUST GO!
   No matter how many Black Panthers are agitating and disturbing the
"peace," the color problem is mainly a "white problem." It is a failure of
white ideals; it is a failure of *white* policies. For example, take three
"solutions" to the race problem that arouse the anger of many whites and
make them resentful of what they believe to be black aggressiveness:
busing, open admissions, and attacks upon police in black neighborhoods.

Busing

"Busing" means driving white and black children around town to different
schools so that, although the neighborhoods are segregated, the schools
are not. This is a "white" problem because the blacks have been compressed into a black area with bad schools by white forces. If the new white
leaders are following their own ideals, they are compelled either to build
good integrated neighborhoods with good schools all over town, or else
bus children around the place. Lacking the determination to do the former,
they do the latter which makes everybody, including many blacks, angry and
doesn't do much for city improvement or schooling.

Open Admissions

"Open admissions" means admitting to a college anybody who applies to
enter. This policy, which at first seems insane, begins to make sense when

you realize that the whites are trying to solve their own problems. Conditions of poverty and bad early schooling, nearly everywhere, cut down the chances of any poor student and especially any poor black student to compete successfully for a limited number of college places. Yet college education is not only a good in itself, it is a way to general advancement in life. Why should public funds be used to pay for the higher education of those who already have advantages, excluding precisely those people who could best use new advantages? True, this would turn many colleges upside down, and professors, like policemen and schoolteachers, are not mentally equipped to deal with their new clients; they have been used to quite different teaching problems.

The real question again is: Should the higher priority be given to raising the opportunities of poor (and often black) students to get ahead in America, or to raising the opportunities of the overwhelmingly white, middle-class students to get *farther* ahead? Many black and some white leaders believe that the first is more important than the second. Again, this is a great inconvenience to the white establishment (parents, professors, and educators) because they have to turn their heads inside out; they never had realized that they believed in equality but were practicing inequality. They resent the issue being put to them so sharply, so they talk about the True Functions of colleges as if these were written in the sky by God.

Attacks upon Police

Now the same process occurs when the police are attacked in black neighborhoods. (Police have always been unpopular in poor neighborhoods everywhere in the world because the poor have a great many problems and few resources to solve them, and they have little protection from exploitation by relatively affluent and corrupt policemen.) The police generally, for all the tough knowledge they have of the ghettos, are products of a different culture—unless they are black themselves—and cannot grasp readily what is going on in the minds of blacks. The police feel threatened. Now, as black power has increased, and white jurists have begun to demand some of the same rights for the poor that the affluent have enjoyed, the police have had to reeducate themselves as thoroughly as professors and politicians have had to. Often, unwilling to do so, and incapable of such a turnabout of attitudes, many policemen have decided that *they*, not the blacks, were the victims, and they could turn to the racist whites of their home neighborhoods for consolation and support.

Reluctantly, many police officers around the country have become more cautious in respect to the civil rights of blacks. A few years ago, cruelty against blacks was common police practice; this history was rarely recorded but is undeniable, and it should be taken from the lips of old policemen before that generation dies. Today, the cruelty has lessened. The sporadic rioting and burning in ghettos during the 1960s first began to introduce caution, fear, and respect to police forces; if cause and effect were ever to be traced, it could probably be proven that the deaths of the rioting days (most of them blacks) saved ten times that number of deaths of arrested blacks in other circumstances around the country. The fear of reprisals affects policemen just as it does other human beings.

Youth

A revolution of youth has been going on for about twenty years. It has been more inventive and destructive than the revolutions of race and sex, less grandiose, but as effective as the revolutions of nationalism around the world, and indeed has played a large part in all of these revolutions. It is significant that the youth revolution reached its peak in America, where it now stands waiting to decide how to proceed. For in America "Youth" was given its first isolated social aggregation, its first collectivism, its first prolongation, its first permissiveness and egocentrism; there, Youth was given enough of a Frankenstein type of artificial being to feel the possibilities of control.

As with the feminist revolution, the youth revolution as an idea seems strange and unbelievable. "Our own sons and daughters?" Like "Our own wives and daughters?" Or like Ol' Massa used to say, "Our own happy loyal niggahs?" Impossible.

Impossible, is it? Nothing is impossible. After all, motion is matter and matter motion: what is more unlikely?

But the youth is growing old? So what? Do you think that the soldiers who ended the Hundred Years' War between England and France began it?

I could write an introduction to political science based around the idea of "Youth" just like the one on social class on page 203.

Why is that so? It is so because when any *large social aggregate* turns over in great turmoil, its waves affect all aspects of society. Therefore, a great social convulsion of youth can revolutionize the family, the schools, the universities, music, dress, tastes, segments of business and industry, elements of the press, radio, TV, and movies, and the sports world—and, from all these, flood over into industry, churches, and world and domestic politics.

If this possibility, which is in some respects actuality, is understood, then one can also understand that, at bottom, there are problems of vicious discrimination and unfulfilled longings.

Youth is impotent. Take the main indices of social resources and power—youth has less wealth, respect, skill, and power itself than age has. If all were treated as youth is, we would all be in a police state! Until the age of full occupation at jobs—which may mean any time from sixteen to twenty-eight years in the advanced technical societies—there are numerous disabilities. These include infancy under the law; lack of due process of law; compulsory diurnal school and nocturnal habitation; compulsory military service; special legal restrictions such as curfew, high insurance rates, deprivation of the vote, prohibition of alcohol, etc. Furthermore, higher standards of respect are required of the young, while less respect is given to them. Their affectional life is tampered with, arranged, and restrained. They are, above all, the victims of systematic fraud and deception in practically every area of life, both as to facts and as to values. (In any society, one can compile an encyclopedia of "material fit for young minds.") As employment opportunities diminish in advanced technologies, youth is forced to prolong education on a level of minimum subsistence and reduced rights.

In some ages and some places, these holy lies can be propagated without exciting complaint, but, once the veil is torn away from them, they become exasperating mockeries. In a republic wherein all citizens ideally have equal rights, the obvious idea that presents itself to every discriminated grouping presents itself also to youth: *change the system!* So the principle and the policy must apply to youth: "Society should eliminate discrimination against the full social participation of youth," and "provide youth with equal opportunities to achieve the values of their society; further, correct those groups whose intended or invariable effect is to monopolize or curtail opportunities."

Final Obnoxious Advice

Try to look at matters this way: you can be sure that whoever you are, your turn will come to viciously discriminate in one or more of your groups or settings. It won't be worth it. So DON'T DO IT! You'll get little of lasting value out of it and simply get yourself embroiled in the degeneration of American society. No matter if the person or group being discriminated against bothers you by going against your pappy's traditions, looks, habits, ideas, or whatever; it is far better to pass your feeling over in favor of nondiscrimination. If you can't shake the feeling, live with it or join a sensitivity group.

Chapter 6

Society and Government

One morning in 480 B.C., scouts of Xerxes, king of the Persians, assured His Majesty that his tremendous army would have little trouble in taking a narrow strip of land between the mountain and sea at Thermopylae, on the road to Athens. They reported a small force, mainly of Spartans, in opposition; these people seemed more occupied with combing and arranging their long hair than with planning a battle.

Some hours later, a great many of Xerxes' best soldiers lay dead and the distraught emperor could be consoled only by the knowledge that a traitorous Greek had shown him another path through the mountains that would let more Persians come up behind the Greeks. Letting the rest of the Greek army retreat, three hundred Spartans remained behind with their king, Leonidas; they fought to the last man to protect the others and wreak more damage upon the Persians. The Persians moved on to more frustrations and ultimate evacuation from Greece.

*   *   *   *   *

A couple of hundred years before Thermopylae, the inhabitants of the area known as Laconia, in the midst of which is Sparta, were "the very worst governed people in Greece,"[1] but in other matters they were in the

---

1. *The History of Herodotus*, trans. George Rawlinson, ed. Manuel Komroff (New York: Tudor Publishing Company, 1947), 23.

mainstream of Greek culture, contributing poets, inventing Greek music, and, of course, squabbling among themselves. They began to develop a tight status system. There were three classes of people—the *Spartans*, or "Equals"; a more numerous *helot* population consisting of hereditary serfs, nearly slaves, who were assigned to individual Spartans and confined to work the land and tend the flocks, giving over half the produce to their masters; and *subject-allies*, who were free individuals living in their own communities, but bound to Spartan military rule and foreign policy. A succession of revolts by helots and subject-allies were suppressed, each one convincing the Spartans that they should be even more severe with themselves and their subjects.

The Spartans developed a military state that circumscribed their life-style to an awesome extent.

Their lives were, in principle, wholly moulded by, and wholly dedicated to, the state. Even the decision whether or not a male infant should be allowed to survive was taken away from the parents and handed over to public officials. This was one of many devices which served, both symbolically and in practice, to minimize the bonds of kinship and thereby to reduce a major source of conflicting loyalties. At seven a boy was turned over to the state for his education, with its concentration on physical hardihood, military skills, and the virtues of obedience. In childhood and adolescence he progressed through a series of intimate age-class groupings; as an adult his main association was with his military regiment and his mess hall. Various rituals reinforced the system at fixed stages in a man's growth.[2]

The Spartan warriors were released from economic concerns and activities, while their wives lived in comfort and frequently accumulated property. The helots and subject-allies provided food, trade, and armaments. The soldiers engaged in strenuous, controlled competition from childhood on; honor and shame, rather than fun or money or being "good losers," were stressed as reward and punishment. The Spartans were famous among Greeks and later students for *eunomia*, "unquestioning obedience to the laws."

The governmental structure consisted of two hereditary *kings*, a *council*, an *assembly of citizens*, and five *ephors* (general managers). The kings had priestly duties and had more power as army commanders than as domestic policy makers. The council, which consisted of thirty elders including the kings, presented proposals to the assembly of citizens. There the proposals were voted on and the ephors—who sometimes exercised more power than the kings—were elected.

2. M. I. Finley, *Early Greece: The Bronze and Archaic Ages* (New York: W. W. Norton & Company, Inc., 1970), 114.

The Spartans produced unparalleled athletes and soldiers, and great Olympic games. They built no wonderful city, but lived in a collection of villages. They established only one colony while numerous other Greek city-states founded many. Sparta was economically and culturally isolated.

Sparta's domestic and foreign policies alike might be predicted from its social order. They were generally negative, repressive, cautious, and defensive; the Spartans made narrow agreements, were opportunistic toward outsiders (unconcerned with principle), had to be talked out of crystalized positions, and went to extremes to maintain their system—as is evident in instances such as the following:

1. The decision to stand and die in a battle.

2. The decision, in a long war, when the women never saw the men, to send home a contingent of young men to have sexual intercourse and provide new cadres for the future.[3]

3. The massacres of helots whenever a revolt occurred (also annual executions of those reported by the secret service as rebellious).

The Spartan government and social order endured about twice as long as the United States has lasted, and with far less internal change.

However, the point to make here is:

PROPOSITION VI

A government of a certain kind coincides with a social order of the same kind.

For example, the helots not only had few *economic* and *social* rights, but they lacked *political* rights and, of course, *political power*. Only the citizen-soldiers, a minority, were armed. To achieve the summit of militarism, the Spartans bred militarism in all institutions—the family, religion, recreation, and the organization of the state on the basis of warriors. They did their best to exclude all other influences. For example, they did not coin money, even though other states did. Money is defined as a medium of exchange; the Spartans wanted no "corrupting" exchange. Thus the government and the social order[4] were consistent; each supported the other.

3. There was trouble, later, and the procreating group went off to found Sparta's solitary colony. This is not proven. A second version is that some Spartans did not go to the war, but provided numerous children; these draft-dodgers and their offspring were discriminated against afterwards, and therefore went off to found the colony.

4. The social *order* could also be called the *culture* or the social *system*. I do not make a distinction in this book.

Alice and Belinda Consult the Oracle at Delphi

A Second Case: Athens

Time, Place, and Duration: Similar to Sparta, about 650 to 250 B.C.

During this period, Athens had a succession of different political arrangements:

1. Hereditary aristocracy with nonslave, wholly Athenian (Attic), rural population.

2. Power shared by four-class system according to farm wealth *produced.*

3. Tyranny (dictatorship)—urbanization.

4. Democracy—all citizens equal rights; slavery (of foreigners); wide commerce; flourishing of arts and sciences.

5. Pure democracy and political bosses (demagogues)—metropolis, imperialism, academies.

These changing governments differed greatly from Sparta's. So did the changing social order of Athens. In its later periods:

1. Public affairs in Athens were run by citizen-amateurs. Every citizen had a civic role as soldier, legislator, administrator, and judge. Neither the military nor the government were professionalized, for the Athenians distrusted professionals and considered it part of the purpose of life to participate in individual and collective self-rule. It was possible in Athens, also, to free the slaves and for resident aliens to become citizens.

2. Far from a static or self-contained agricultural economy, Athens developed a pluralist economy which included encouragement of certain agricultural specialities, arts and manufactures, and an enterprising commerce to trade her products for those needed from abroad. With such development went a diffusion of skills, a high literacy rate, the coinage of metal, and the accumulation of great wealth which was liberally expended on all sorts of projects. An influx of scholars, educators, artists, and scientists from everywhere contributed to the city's atmosphere of intellectual curiosity and artistic achievement.

3. Within the city-state, Athenians experimented with the many kinds of social legislation in such areas as land distribution and taxation; their international policies were outgoing and expansionist. Where Sparta, fearing helot rebellion, kept its army at home in splendid isolation, Athens took the lead in organizing other city-states into the Delian League as a defensive alliance against the Persian threat, eventually converting the league into an empire. Athens experienced both more military victories and more military defeats than Sparta.

* * * * *

We conclude: Proposition VI holds for Athens; the governmental order (mixed, changing, loose, pluralistic) coincides with the social order. And, as an aside, Athens is preferred over Sparta because we see in it possibilities for all individuals' polyvalent and benevolent development far exceeding Spartan possibilities. Sparta was the heaven of our rigid, procrustean type. Actually it would even be difficult to say that in war the Spartan capacity to mobilize and expend effective military resources on a *per capita* basis, was equal to the Athenian ability, when judged over the total period of four centuries.

An Interview by Several College Journalists with Senator G. Macabee (R., Vt.)

Mr. George Stylos: Senator, don't you feel that college students have as much right to govern the university as the trustees and president?

Sen. M.: Yes, indeed, although . . .

Mr. Fritz Screiber: I feel that a sixteen-year-old youth knows as much about politics and society and all that as a seventy-year-old person. Shouldn't young people have the same rights as old people?

Sen. M.: The youth of this country are . . . Yes. Surely. They should have, though, of course . . .

Ms. Tillie Penn: Senator, I'm interested in being a pastor although I'm a woman, but my church won't let me. Don't you think that a law should be passed against discrimination against women in the clergy?

Sen. M.: I'm afraid that the Constitution separates state and church . . .

Ms. Penn: But it also gives equal rights to all citizens. The Supreme Court says . . .

Sen. M.: Right, the Supreme Court. I think they can handle the problem.

Ms. Hera Quink: Senator, Congress is voting on a bill to stop federal aid to dependent children whose mothers are unmarried, after three children. Why punish the children? In fact, why punish the mother? Isn't motherhood a right?

Sen. M.: A father and a mother are a wonderful thing, generally speaking, . . . and a good democratic family, absolutely.

Mr. Stylos: Isn't the government responsible for seeing that unions have fair elections? To most workers, democracy is a farce.

Sen. M.: Absolutely, the laws must

have teeth. It's a problem for the agencies. Congress has to give them more authority.

Mr. Allen Revue: Statistics show that one third of the assets of the country are owned by 1 percent of the families, while only 2 percent of the poorest third of the population go to college. What do you think of that?

Sen. M.: Yes, that's a serious problem. No doubt, something must be done.

(Senate page enters.)

Page: Senator, they are debating SR340 on the floor.

Sen. M.: Yes. Yes. As I was saying, democracy means just that. Thank you.

Spokesman for journalists: No one can have his own private government. Thank you, Senator.

(Exit Senator.)

Mr. Screiber: That guy's great. I like his opinions.

Ms. Quink: He seems to have trouble completing his sentences.

Mr. Revue: He doesn't talk a leg and an arm off of you. A genuine democratic guy.

Ms. Quink: Hey, what's that SR340 anyway?

Mr. Stylos: *(reading from a booklet)* It says here that it's a bill to restore pension rights to disabled veterans who have otherwise forfeited their rights through dishonorable discharges.

TO REPEAT: A government of a certain kind coincides with a social order of the same kind.

But—rarely do all social and political institutions match; for instance, it is a mystery why the twin kings of Sparta remained hereditary, since they were treated very much as equals by the Spartans. Rarely, too, does every smaller order mirror the nature of its larger order. For instance, the governments of many businesses (the Ford Motor Company under Henry Ford I) or labor unions (the Teamsters Union under James Hoffa) in America have been virtual dictatorships, but they are pressured to move toward more similarity to the larger society.

The pressure to eliminate contradictions between the social and political orders can be seen on the giant screen of American history.

The U.S. Constitution originally implied that the social and political order of the country could, by a form of segregation of interests called "Federalism," accommodate very different social forms, such as slavery and free labor, a landed aristocracy and an industrial system, an Anglican church and a Puritan church, etc. Therefore, the Constitution and the national social order authorized

The Plantation Order
ca. 1607–1865

A. *Who?*

A small elite of large-scale farmers, conservative Protestant in religion, highly competent in government, politics, and war, with worldwide contacts; they are decentralized territorially by states but connected by race, sometimes by family, and often by a philosophy of limited representative government.

B. *Works through what social institutions?*

These elite work through local political and social groups that are tied together in a network culminating in a national bloc represented in the U.S. Congress. They employ numerous attorneys, overseers, and distributers. They own a large slave population, deprived of

The Puritan Order
ca. 1620–1870

A large elite of mercantile and manufacturing businessmen, radical Protestant in religion, attuned to modern science, and experienced in world commerce; they lead a free population, though they prefer to manage nonpolitical institutions. The nonelite members of the order are largely free farmers and semifree workers.

These elite are somewhat stratified by family wealth; they discriminate against a sizeable foreign-born and Catholic minority. They hold an intensely individualistic philosophy; this philosophy spins off independent and agitational political and scientific movements such as almost all civil rights. Books, churches, family, law, governmental institutions, police, and federal and state constitutions support their position with full legality.

abolitionism and Christian Science. A larger percentage of the population is civically active than in the South.

C. With what effects?

Great tracts of weakly occupied territory attract the aggressive planters and their activists; they expand continuously westward. The free population does not increase greatly; applied science is neglected though the fine arts and household architecture flourishes. Personal qualities are preferred over organizational abilities. The large slave black and growing poor white population lack education, civil rights, material comforts, and opportunities to escape from or climb within the system.

Great tracts of weakly occupied territory attract the free workers and farmers. Wherever they go, they settle in large numbers, let many foreigners join their society, and introduce more real popular participation in all social and governmental institutions. Science flourishes and is applied to every aspect of life. The mass of people come to feel a stake in the society. The elite become less religious and more money-minded and businesslike.

Now, then—
The national social order was changing!
The governmental order was moving in the old directions
so either the social or the governmental order
had to be reversed, or both!

National Trends:

1. Great movement to the West, both Northwest and Southwest.
2. Northern population increases greatly in comparison with southern.
3. Diversity and abundance of industry in the North.
4. The North is full of new religious, scientific, and political movements.
5. "Open society" doctrines spread everywhere. The northern elite is used to them; the southern elite is alarmed and repressive.

Governmental Trends:

1. In the North, governments become more active; "welfare state" ideas and "collectivism" or "nationalism" are generated.

2. There also, governmental and religious institutions begin to open up to new classes of voters; laws against the poor are moderated (laws against debtors, for example).

3. The federal government is pressured by the North and West to do more and more to help free farmers, help with canals and railroads, and give aid to education.

4. The southern elite resists and angers the northern interests, both business elite and public, in their attempts to activate the national government. They want low tariffs so they can sell cotton and buy machines abroad. The North wants to help American industry by keeping tariffs high.

5. The national government becomes involved naturally with disputes between free settlers and slave owners in the western areas being newly settled.

Struggle Against the Trends or How a New Order Was Resisted:

STOP: The Puritan elite were now too small a part of the northern elite to control or manage them. The radical northern Puritan elite became abolitionists, socialists, teachers, transcendentalists, utopians, poets, and scientists, fairly attuned to the new age. The business elite hid behind laws guaranteeing the sanctity of property; they fought welfare legislation and isolated themselves from their own people, socially and politically. They turned to finance and conserved and expanded their capital. The southern elite used every means to block federal government activity. They asked for equal treatment of the slave interest with the free interest.

SEGREGATE: The South became *more* southern; more suspicious of the outside world; more hostile to the North; more repressive about initiative and opportunity for slaves and populist white movements. The frontier between North and South began to grow into an international frontier, with armed police and guards to prevent passage of slaves and agitators. The debate over the right of a state to secede from the union waxed furious.

WAR: Desperation and exasperation became common among southern and northern leadership. Both the blocking and segregating tactics lent force to the growing belief that "this nation cannot exist half slave and half free." Translated into our terms, this meant that "a new nation (as opposed to a confederation or weak federation) has grown up as a social order. The immense social forces of this order command large adjustments in the institutions of government. If the government cannot make these adjustments because the conciliatory or dominant leadership is weak, in numbers and/or ability at finding imaginative and effective solutions, then the momentum of the changing social order will force the change somehow." Thereupon the nation slid into open conflict by arms, which, until the war ended and for years afterward, meant a more intense segregation of the conflicting parties and more extreme measures. Given the segregated and hostile conditions under which they were taken, these measures of war and "reconstruction" were by no means as rational and farsighted as they could otherwise have been.

FINALLY THE SYSTEM CRACKED UP: The northern, national social order prevailed. But it was neither Plantation nor Puritan. It meant:

1. An active federal (national) government.

2. Full political and civil rights to all male Americans in national and most state constitutions (but a southern counterrevolution restored from 1875 to 1955 the subjection of blacks, allowing them only the right of escape, the right not to work if not starving, and a slowly growing contact with the world outside the South).

3. A nation dedicated to business, commerce, and industry, to applied science, to universal (mostly white male) education.

4. Increased economic, social, and political opportunity and mobility everywhere.

In brief, consistency between the political and social order in the direction of an open society. (Meanwhile the post-Reconstruction South formed its new backwater consistency between its social order and political order.)[5]

Remnants of the Plantation and Puritan Suborders

"The old order passeth" but it usually takes a long time and then colors the new social order and in some ways lingers on. There are still specific and general traits of the old Plantation and Puritan orders in the South and New England. There are general traits of both in the total nation.

The losers have largely disappeared as a solid, definite type, but so have the winners. In both areas you will find many masqueraders who dress and act "old South" and "old New England" out of romantic conceit. Much dreaming and nostalgia persist among the losers. The intense self-righteousness of the Puritan mind has found its way into science and education—the "disciplines"—and remains in finance. But generally the Southerner has become western and midwestern while the New Englanders have become more gregarious (not without some hypocrisy) and central eastern. The southern elite are strong in national politics (reversing the

5. For descriptions of this new backwaters order, you might well read many of the tales of William Faulkner.

pre–Civil War pattern) because that is where power and money concentrate. Each elite, reduced in size and importance by national trends, has also been further compressed by rising social classes around them. In the South a new industrial class has grown up.

Florida, Texas, and other border states are heavily influenced by new immigration from the North. In New England, the "old Yankee" population has moved from the rural areas; factories have moved south; education has become a heavy industry; the descendants of Irish, Jewish, French, Italian, and other nineteenth- and twentieth-century immigrant groups have occupied many elite positions once held by descendants of English Puritans.

For most practical purposes, the old Plantation and Puritan suborders are dead. (They live on, however, in the minds of people more than fifty years old—and to the extent that they dominate the minds of youth they are not quite dead among the young.)

A Stable Political Order

**A society whose people's dominant perspectives
(views and values) are part of the workings of all
its social institutions tends to be stable.**

What other people have called stable is not what we call stable. To them—
   Stability = Law and order. Obedience. Nonchange.
            or
   Stability = Lasts a "long time."
            or
   Stability = Everything works just fine and everybody is happy.

The first we find too narrow and possibly evil.
The second doesn't tell us anything new.
The third is just a synonym for "I like it."

**High stability to us, then, is a high consistency
between a people's social behavior and political behavior.**

TWO TYPES OF STABILITY. Just as there is an open type of personality, there is an open type of society. Its institutions are capable of engaging the outer environment and moving through it and with it. It is stable but in motion, like a well-balanced airplane or moonship.

Closed	Open
Perspectives limited and exclusive. Hostility to outer environment. Reliance on force and nonreasoning agreement.	Perspectives unlimited and inclusive. Receptive to and assimilates outer environment.

Examples of *closed* stable societies: Sparta; Japan before the American visit-in-force (Commodore Perry) or before 1945 (second American visit-in-force); Nazi Germany; Fascist Italy; Franco Spain 1938 till about 1955.

Examples of *open* stable societies: Athens; Japan after 1945; Germany after 1946; Italy after 1944.

What destabilizes a political and social order?

1. A change in the social order that the political order cannot handle. *(For example, owing to the immense growth of the free agrarian West and of free industry in the northern states just before the Civil War the balance planned between the North and South by the Constitution could not be maintained.)*

2. An attack from the outside. *(A few Spanish conquistadors subjugated the vast and stable closed society of the Incas in a few years, though it had lasted for centuries and was not internally destabilized.)*

3. A change in the political order that the social order cannot handle. *(The victory of Fidel Castro in the Cuban Revolution was originally thought to signal a political order that would coincide better with the Cuban social order than the Batista regime did. Instead, leftist and Communist elements prevailed in Castro's elite, and the government soon instituted measures that cracked up the old social order—expropriations of property, denunciations and arrests of opposition elements, nationalization of land and industry, elevation of workers to many high posts, breaking of ties with the United States and making of new ties with the Soviet Union, restructuring of the army, etc. In consequence, the former ruling class—and the whole social order of which it was a part—collapsed, as signified by the flight of five hundred thousand people from the country whose total population was only 7 million. A new stable order emerged, at a lower technical, economic, and cultural level, but with a higher level of enthusiasm among the promoted masses.)*

And, of course, combinations of all three. Take Russia in 1917–1918.

A. Rapid industrialization and spread of Western ideas of democracy and socialism would not suffice to bring down the Czarist regime if

B. Russia had not suffered tremendous defeats on the battlefield against Germany and Austria-Hungary, and if

C. A series of revolutionary groups had not undermined the Czarist regime and capitalized on popular distress and mutinous troops, until finally the Bolshevist faction of the Communists, under Lenin and Trotsky, emerged on top from a succession of revolutionary *coups d'état.*

Is America Destabilizing?

Remember: America is generally one of the more open societies of the world. Therefore it follows a course of development that seems *unstable* even when "normal." For example, the United States, although believed by the Nazis to be quite unstable, mobilized its population and resources during World War II even more thoroughly than did Nazi Germany.

Nevertheless, America can destabilize *if:*

1. Representative government in social institutions and increased respect and real income for discriminated groupings are blocked on grounds of "law and order."

2. The participation of America in world affairs as a nonimperialistic and constructive partner is blocked by nationalistic isolation, and a military-war industry complex.

3. The widespread disenchantment of youth (and soon the population as a whole) with authority and bureaucracy is not accompanied by new forms of belief and organization.

Question: "But can't 'law and order,' 'a strong defense establishment,' 'staying out of foreign involvements,' and 'restoring respect for the authorities' ensure stabilization?"

Answer: No. If you believe that a ship running in a storm can work best on a locked rudder, then you can believe that that formula will work for the United States. That formula will destabilize America and the rest of the world, which reacts to American political and social change.

Actually it is time for a Principle and its Policy application.

PRINCIPLE VI

Good government should extend to embrace the social order.

Good government is, of course, a government by men of good will and competence, under the control of a similar public and operating through governmental machinery. It facilitates policies in line with the qualities of the public and its leadership.

The important reasons for extending the concerns of politics to the social order are:

1. The social order is a massive housing for practically everybody practically all of the time, and

2. As has been shown, it is unlikely that you can have a political order that is good alongside a social order that is bad.

Accordingly, then, we have:

POLICY VI

Apply the same guidelines used to keep political institutions under control to every situation that potentiates and converts power.

Here is a checklist of most of the social institutions of a modern society.

Families	Fraternal associations	Book publishers
Elementary schools	Professional associations	Political parties
High schools	Scientific associations	Corporations of all
Universities	Newspapers and	sizes
Religious groups	magazines	Government agencies
Labor unions	Television	Courts
Veterans'	Motion pictures	Legislatures
organizations		

Not all of these potentiate and convert *much* power. So naturally we are interested in those that do, or those that make such a profound impression on people (like the family) that they in effect do so. The guidelines to be applied to these institutions are the same 3-P's we are applying to government. In other words, in all these social institutions we should act to favor benevolent and polyvalent personalities, increase participation, encourage a leadership which will control power, influence public opinion to take a longer and more rational view of politics, restrict hostility and vicious discrimination, and more—as we shall see in the following chapters.

This stresses the point: *you cannot have a good government without a good social order.* A good social order includes all major features of a good government.

Let us try to imagine exceptions.

Possible Exception A. A church. This church, which we might call "The

Holy Soul Shelter" has 4 percent of the population as its parishioners.[6] Its pastors are co-opted by its high priests, who are elected by its pastors. It enjoys many mysterious ceremonies. Its lay members behave and are saved, but they do not participate in selection of their church rulers. Its doctrine is strictly "nonpolitical"; members are warned never to use their church membership as a resource for obtaining political power or influence. Its members are poorer than the average of the population; 80 percent are indifferent politically.

How would Policy VI apply?

There are several features about this church that we do not like. Its members do not control the leadership. Its mysterious ceremonies suggest that one can arrive at truth through ritual. We cannot say that there is only one way to truth, but we hope that no one tries to arrive at political truths through ritual.

The fact that the church insists upon excluding governmental politics comforts us somewhat. Maybe the flow of incompatible mental operations and attitudes is blocked off from politics. The fact, too, that the membership is largely apathetic politically means that there is not much transmission of their beliefs into politics. Furthermore, only 4 percent of the population are involved in this inconsistent order. If it were 8 or 15 percent one might well expect larger repercussions upon the political order and social order generally.

But then: Are we our brothers' keepers? Is it disturbing that so many people do not share within that important aspect of their life—the religious—the kinds of open and critical ways that we believe to be essentially humane?

This is indeed a difficult case. Intervention in a voluntary association is in itself evil. The application of force of law is more evil. Besides, intervention may only stir up bitter and rigid resistance. Furthermore, no one is being directly injured; and the threat by the group to the political order is remote. Too, a member of the group may quit it.

I would conclude that this church group should be left free. But if it is adversely criticized, I should support the critics. And I should certainly discriminate between this kind of church and other kinds of churches or religious attitudes; I would not lump all churches and creeds together, either praising them all or condemning them all.

---

6. We note the passing of the old metaphor "flock." Any "shepherd" who calls his parishioners his "flock" nowadays will end up on Skid Row, whatever Jesus may have said. One more little instance of the governmental/social order changing in tandem.

The Salvation Army Means "Army"

The *Times* of London on September 18, 1970, contained a story that we here shorten and quote:

"By our Religious Affairs Correspondent:

"The rigid authoritarianism which the Salvation Army imposes on its officers, even extending censorship to the airing of personal views on any subject in a letter to the press, came under attack yesterday.

"The man who voiced the protest was Major Fred Brown, aged 47, a former professional footballer who for five years was in charge of Regent Hall, the Army's main London centre in Oxford Street. He worked with young drifters, drug abusers and hippies, but now, suspended from duty by the Salvation Army hierarchy, he lives in Cornwall, his future in doubt.

"Major Brown's offence was refusal to accept censorship of his book **Secular Evangelism,** which S.C.M. Press are publishing next Tuesday.

"'This censorship procedure' to quote the Major 'is bad and it is tainting the Salvation Army. There is a tremendous fervour in the army but there is also bewilderment. The protest I am making is long overdue, but it is supported by a growing number of Salvation Army officers. . . . '

"He supposed that if the differences were not resolved he would get another job. The army's regulations made it difficult for it to be true to itself, and were a complete denial of Salvation Army compasion.

"He believed that in the end there would be a change. When authoritarianism began to manipulate, coerce, and insist on the toeing of the party line, people who tried to come to terms, finally lost their sense of freedom."

Possible Exception B. A shoe factory of 200 workers is owned and managed by a family that resides in the city where the factory is located. The workers have very little to say about the way the factory is run. Wages, hours, work loads, supervisors, sanitation, quality of production, processing of the products, firings, hirings, layoffs—all of these are reacted to by personal or passive group methods. Morale goes down or up; more people apply for jobs here or more people quit to work elsewhere. There is no provision for workers entering into the total work process as responsible human beings. On the other hand, the owners are subject to a certain atmosphere of opinion in the town and this makes them somewhat aware of how their workers feel.

Again, the situation does not rate approval by Policy VI. This factory's little social order does not conform to the norm of the larger social order or of the political order. Ownership should be shared with the workers, and workers should participate in many of the decisions that affect them. A true representative government of the factory is one solution; a union that wrests a certain amount of power from the owners and constitutes a counterbalance to the power of ownership is another. The first mode of organization is definitely superior, even though still rare in all societies. Yet, to the extent that it is realized, the social and political orders are brought into consistency and mutually support each other.

How can this be done? We know how unions do it, and the government helps them organize the workers under certain laws. To achieve the more complete goal requires a revolution in the behavior of ownership and workers. Some producers' cooperatives and consumers' cooperatives have formed in this way. The political and social order of the town would unquestionably benefit if the shoe factory were to be reorganized. Can a law do it? Or would there be disastrous troubles again? Yes, the law can do this task, provided it follows careful procedures.

Objection A: "Just try to get away with it."

Every leadership of a traditional institution is shocked by proposals for reform. The best time to make strong proposals is in the beginning; then, when the moment for application comes, the leadership and institution will be softened by long discussion.

Objection B: "You are a totalitarian dictator."

Don't use the word "totalitarian" for every bit of power you don't like. Admittedly, this idea of passing all institutions through a screen of structural compatability extends the conceivable scope of the public greatly, so far as many people are concerned. They conveniently forget that these debates (about churches and shoe factories) are hundreds of years old. However, as outlined above, only the more serious cases should be actually within the scope of law, while alert and enlightened opinion and criticism can govern the rest.

Objection C: "Can't you make an exception in my case?"

No, but you probably can, because nothing in politics (or any other sphere of life) works so well on the visible level as does selfishness adulterated by talk of the public good, sanctity of the home, and other rationalizations in the hands of the representatives of selfishness.

Chapter 7
Government Activities

"It's public, ain't it?" said Bill angrily, as he was being evicted from a beach.

*   *   *   *   *

I suppose he meant that everyone had the right to be on the beach.

Or maybe that it was owned by the government.

Or perhaps that many people used it.

Or perhaps that, though it was in the hands of a beach club, no one could be discriminated against in using its facilities.

Or, perhaps, that no one could be charged a dollar for what used to be free.

Or perhaps he was just parroting what he had heard someone say in such incidents elsewhere.

Whatever he meant, he had the feeling that some quality of the place entitled people like him to use it.

Bill asked his friend, Al, about it—Al being a petty politician studying law at night. Al didn't know the answer, of course, because there is no unique definition of *public,* but only thousands of laws calling things "public" and thousands of activities in the name of the "public." Whatever the government (that is, those operating under a title or on a salary given by others like them) says is "public," is *public.* So Al would have to find out whether some government officials had defined the beach rights by a law and then, if he were looking for trouble, whether *these* officials in turn had some authorization from some other governmental body, or a constitution, or a court decision interpreting the action or constitution.

Meanwhile, "public" means:

1. An interest that many people feel in a thing or activity, and

Like: the price of peanuts to peanut farmers and peanut munchers.

2. An interest that the government claims in a thing or activity.

Like: Cheap peanuts cause vicious competition among candy makers, and government does not like bars full of peanuts fraudulently advertised as "chocolate bars," and causes the number of peanuts in a bar of candy to be labeled.

Would it help to say what is "private"?

Private is whatever is not public. This implies then the two preceding definitions of public. Whatever *few* people are interested in and the government ignores is "private."

"Private" means an interest that only one or two (three, five, a thousand, a million?) people feel in an activity.

Like: Nobody grows peanut bushes in Alaska except in window boxes to hide the cannabis plants.

"Private" means a lack of claim of interest by the government in a thing or activity.

Like: Government leaders know their families are growing cannabis in the shadow of peanut plants, so they keep quiet.

But now the time has come for one of those dreaded complications:

3. "Public" also means what any number of people *believe should be* of sufficient interest to others, as well as to themselves, to develop common standards about it.

Like: Many people believe that "the drug scene" should be a public concern, and therefore *it is*!

4. "Public" means what any number of government officials *believe to be* of sufficient interest to any number of people to justify their acting in the name of the whole people in reference to it.

Like: Many politicians also believe "the drug scene" is properly their concern, and so it is!

The additional ingredient is *what people believe.* As Pirandello called one of his epochal plays, "Right You Are, If You Think You Are."

Now imagine how bad the situation has become! If anybody or any official believes that any interest he has should be a public interest, well, then it *is* a public interest.

From this, we deduce that:

1. In order to be of public interest, a thing or an activity has to have activists, and the more activists, the more public; and, furthermore,

2. The more influence resources a "public" has, the more "public" it can make itself. Here the advantage lies with the heaviest authoritative power holders; they can declare something that interests them to be public and it becomes public. ("Damn," said the king, and a million loyal subjects went to hell.)

PROPOSITION VII

Every kind of activity has
at some time been done through government;
every kind of activity has also
at some time been done outside of government.

Meanings:

Activity: everything people think about or do. An activity has to have dimensions if you are to be clear about it; it is doing something at a given time, in a given place, in respect to given things or people.

Done: somebody from the government, or paid by the government, does it. In a certain sense, since the maintenance of peace on the streets affects almost all human activities, one would have an easy time proving that government helps perform every activity. We shall not slip out of the statement by using this indirect connection. Again, the government once paid off war veterans with homesteads after the Civil War. The effect of that activity persists, but we do not count it today. Also, governments interest themselves in an activity by very mild legislation or customary law of low intensity (as when a very minor tax increase is imposed, or leaders make statements about "keeping prices down," hoping to influence the rate of inflation). These activities scarcely warrant the name of activity. Thus there is no trick to the Proposition.

Government: officials acting in the name of a people and possessed of power (the right to impose severe penalties in some areas of life to back up their decisions).

What's Public If Not the Police?

Thomas Mackel is a big-city district attorney. In a typical working day as district attorney of Queens County he can call on the armed might of New York City's thirty-thousand-man police force to help him bust rackets or fight crime.

At night, his home and those of his neighbors in Douglas Manor get their protection from a patrol car and guards hired through a local company that protects people for a profit.

It's not just an isolated trend. The security industry itself claims that two out of every three law enforcement officers in the nation are actually on private payrolls. Of the eight hundred thousand private officers, about five hundred thousand are uniformed. On top of this are untold thousands of corporate employees who have been hired as full-time fire chiefs within industrial plants or who have been trained as either full-time or part-time fire wardens within both industrial and commercial buildings.

Management experts looking into the little-studied, highly fractionated field of protection believe that some $1.6 billion was spent by the private sector [in 1969] . . . with another $400 million going for protective fire and criminal alarms. Outside security services—trained for criminal, fire, and now riot duty—are appearing at normally unguarded premises and, in many cities, are actually walking a beat like a patrolman.

On a typical block of big corporate headquarters buildings in Manhattan, for instance, it's possible that perhaps twenty different private police forces are working at any one time.

And not just in New York. In California the official who licenses private investigators for the state confesses: "Regular police would have to curtail their normal activities too much to meet the demands of business enterprise." There are now 375 private companies in the field—in California alone.[1]

1. "Creeping Capitalism," *Forbes*, September 1, 1970, pp. 22–23.

Proof

Absolute proof of the Proposition is afforded by taking every conceivable activity and finding a time and place where the government performed it. We should like to publish this list here because we could then sell the book for a slightly higher price, but professional pride suggests that there is no possibility of your reading it all. We could also "prove" the proposition by extreme examples, as we did in the case of vicious discrimination. Imagine any "weird" activity and locate it in time and space: requiring every man to store guns in his house, selling dry goods, exterminating harmless buffalo, prescribing haircuts and the length of dresses, operating brothels, hiring assassins, killing weaker infants, destroying idols and images, and so on.

But I think that here we might merely offer as an example a fairly typical activity from each of the six general areas of valuing we have used in this book, as follows:

Government and Nongovernment Activities: Examples

Value and Sub-Value Area	Government Activity	Nongovernment Activity
WEALTH: Ownership	Abolition of private ownership of means of production	All industry in private hands with little regulation except protection (laissez-faire)
HEALTH: Diet	Prohibition of alcohol	Dietary fads or habits ("He's strictly a meat-and-potatoes man.")
RESPECT: How to worship	Obligatory church attendance (colonial Massachusetts)	"The family that prays together stays together."
AFFECTION: Sex	Laws against adultery and deviance	Adultery and deviance
KNOWLEDGE: Schools	Public schools and state colleges	Independent schools and private colleges
POWER: Military service	Compulsory or voluntary armies	Private police

So you think that there is nothing duller than a catalog put out by the central purchasing office of a large organization? You are correct. But here's one page from that thriller, the *Stock Catalog* of the U.S. General Services Administration.[2]

2. *GSA Stock Catalog* (Washington, D.C.: General Services Administration, October 1969), Part II, 73.

CASH BOX

Steel cash boxes. Compartmented cantilever tray. Handle on cover. With lock and key. Gray finish. $7^{1}/_{4} \times 11 \times 4^{1}/_{4}"$. Fed. Spec. RR–C–140.
7520–281–5931 .... EA $2.25

CENSORSHIP KIT

15-component censorship kit. 3" magnifying reading glass, 2-oz. stamp pad ink, 2-qts. shellac, size 1 stamp pad, 6 erasers, alcohol, sponge, 2 steel scratch knives, 9" paper cutting shears, 2 water color brushes, ten 72-yd. rolls of 1" wide cellulose transparent tape, fixed and removable rubber stamp lettered "CENSOR", sponge cup, 2-lb. lampblack, 8-oz. wide mouth bakelite jar.
7520–285–2517 .... EA $21.60

CHEST, FIELD, PRINTED FORM

18-compartment chest for blank forms. $34^{1}/_{2} \times 22^{1}/_{4} \times 15"$ deep. MC Dwg. 1121Cle.
7520–300–5296 .... EA $13.90

CIRCULAR SLIDE RULE, see Slide rule, p. 79.

CLAMP, PENCIL SHARPENER

[10] C-clamp with 2" opening. For fastening pencil sharpeners to table, desk, or shelf. Thumb screw holds sharpener in place. *Std. pack: 12*. Fed. Spec. GG–S–236.
7520–024–7305 .... EA 20¢

CUTTERS, PENCIL SHARPENER

For regular pencil sharpeners. Specially tempered; well-hardened twin-milling cutters; precisely cut and fitted. Sharpen pencils to a fine or medium fine point. Easily installed. Individually-boxed. For Pencil sharpener *see* p. 79. *Std. pack: 12*. Fed. Spec. GG–S–236.
7520–274–6261 .... Boston KS ... SE 62¢
7520–213–9251 .... Giant .... SE 76¢
7520–213–9250 .... .Chicago ..... SE 65¢

DISPENSER, GUMMED TAPE

Metal tape dispenser. Brush type moistening mechanism. Rubber feet or base. For shipping room use. *Std. pack: 12*. Int. Fed. Spec. GG–D–00450.
7520–205–2691 .... EA $51.00

It's a little gruesome. I wonder whether there was a catalog for items in the Nazi concentration camps. Then there are military catalogs and police supply catalogs (you know—"guaranteed to make everyone within a radius of 50 ft. vomit profusely" or "Dog, 100 + pounds, 3.2 in. canine teeth . . .").

Inventory of Activities

The possible examples number many thousands. Merely think of some activity, and a well-read person will be able to find an example of its being done by a government and by a private group.

Remember the dimensions of activity and power? (How many people, in what respect, with what pressure, for how long?)

We said earlier that power has never been so measured for any group.

We can say also that no one has ever made an inventory of governmental activities, providing for their domain, scope, intensity, and duration.

Such an inventory is needed and may be achieved in the next generation as a practical improvement in knowing what is going on in government and controlling it.

The question is: **Who does what to whom by what means with what effects?**

For inventory purposes, this question must have a unit—a thing, an activity—to talk about. *What* is to be inventoried.

Therefore we should break down all the programs of government into molecular bits. This is the unit of **activity.**

We give it a general definition: "An activity is a unit of operations as restricted in goal (scope), means of execution, and leadership as can be discovered." An example would be a fire control crew in a section of a national forest.

Now, spelling this out, we want to know about each unit of activity:

1. Its *authority: Who* gave *whom* the right or command to do what they are doing. Legal theory requires that every operation of a government employee be traceable to an authorization, no matter how remote from the scene of action the original authority may be. Congress, the Presidency, and the Courts are principally engaged in extending, proving, approving, and supervising the authoritative connection between the single operation and the total constitutional system. The Constitution is the point of focus for all parties.

The millions of everyday operations obviously cannot be perfectly coordinated with the Constitution. Nonetheless the belief that they should coordinate is extremely important and generally accepted as the basis of legality in the United States. Even the Congress' delegation of authority to fashion laws, rules, and orders to other branches of the government as well as the assumption of final authority (sovereignty) by state, cities, and people must fit into the plan of the Constitution, legally speaking; and whatever the proportion of deviations from the scheme may be on any day of the year, these deviations are regarded as exceptional and challengeable.

For example, if rangers assigned to a certain sector of national forest use their fire-fighting equipment to protect adjoining areas from conflagration, along with the description and rational justification of this operation must go an authorization. Who said that they may do so—their crew chief, forest headquarters, bureau chief, agency head, local congressman, congressional committee, legislation, court, President? And in relation to what proposed legitimating rationale? Ordinarily, the operations can be carried back to a statute or to a delegated power of an office of the agency.

Another common example is a search warrant. Even when it is inconvenient and hampers them, police are expected to possess a court warrant in order to enter a person's home to seek evidence of a crime.

2. The *accountability* of the operation. Who are the persons who are directed to perform the activity and who may be penalized if the authorities do not like the way it is being done?

3. The *personnel* involved. How many are there? How much are they paid? How are they appointed?

4. The financial and other nonpersonnel *resources* fed into the activity. These should include the money and time spent by those affected by the activity.

5. The *goals* of the operation. There are authorized goals and nonauthorized goals. (No colonel will admit that the goal of his regiment is to make him a general, but this is sometimes the case.)

6. *Effects* or results of an activity are difficult to measure, but if you do not try to measure results, you might as well give up all activities as a farce. There are both intended and unintended effects.

For example, the "New Deal" in the 1930s set up the Agricultural Adjustment Administration as a program that would raise the level of farmers' income by paying growers of certain crops to reduce their acreage under cultivation. One program governed cotton production. Statistical indicators in the years following showed continuous improvement of farm income and price stability. They did *not* exhibit awareness, much less a measure, of evictions of farm workers and farm tenants on a scale comparable to the ill-famed English enclosure movement. They did not show the families uprooted, the people starved, the rights violated, the miserable sufferings and grinding down of the poor southern Negroes and whites during this period of "progressive," "liberal" New Deal glory. Nor to this day do many of the writers of history books and textbooks of government refer to these covert, unintended, nondirect effects.[3]

7. The *instruments* of influencing the behavior and resources of the people who are being affected. Generally these divide into economizing, informing, and directing—and these can be broken down as shown:

Economizing	**Informing**	**Directing**
Possessing, maintaining, managing material assets	Informing, educating	Promulgating rules
Buying	Studying, research, planning, prototype development	Giving orders to individuals, groups, and companies
Subsidizing and granting free welfare		Hearing and sanctioning
Contracting	Inspecting and investigating	Coercing, guarding, compelling, restraining
Directly producing goods and services	Consulting and negotiating	Licensing, patenting, copyrighting
Lending		Managing
Paying		Taxing
Selling		
Borrowing		

Even these instruments can, of course, be subdivided further. Contracting has several important forms, such as contracts on a cost-plus-fee basis or on a fixed-cost open-bidding basis, etc. The types of education and information are many, too.

Here are a few activities turned up from a sampling of about 2 percent of all federal activities, displayed in three of the areas: contracting; informing and educating; and hearing and sanctioning.

CONTRACTING . . . contracts for hiring of passenger motor vehicles and for uniforms as authorized . . . contracting for research information from the Agricultural Research Service and the Cooperative State Research Service . . . payments by contract or fee to agricultural stabilization and conservation county committees . . . involves construction, installation, and equipment of temporary and permanent public works facilities for activities and agencies of the Department of Defense . . . acts in construction of dam projects . . . commission contracts consultants for research . . . commission contracts consulting groups for research . . . program gives equipment orders to military branches to be filled . . . contracting for equipment . . . contracts for construction of facilities.

INFORMING . . . provides information to public . . . conducts training program for own personnel . . . communicates bulletins to states on programs . . . trains own specialist researchers . . . informs and meets with groups to exchange information and views . . . informs federal agencies of work . . . flight training for own personnel . . . sends bulletins to small businesses . . . issues information bulletins to universities . . . issues information bulletins to industries.

HEARING AND SANCTIONING . . . administrates and adjudicates claims . . . reviews requests for pardons, actions of board of parole and actions of board of immigration appeals . . .

*   *   *   *   *

On October 9, 1970, *The Chicago Tribune* carried this report from Washington:

The Federal Trade Commission proposed new rules today that would protect customers from unfair charges and require many creditors to give more leeway and information to customers in monthly billings.

---

3. An exception is Arthur M. Schlesinger, Jr. On page 376 of *The Age of Roosevelt: The Coming of the New Deal*, he states, "For half a century the sharecropper situation had been a local scandal. Now AAA made it the nation's business. The plow-up and the acreage reduction uprooted cropper families and cast them onto the roads, the rivers, and the swamps." See also pages 77–83; and Volume 2 (1960), pages 431–33.

Major requirements of the creditor are that he:

1. Defer billing on disputed charges until he has made a full investigation of the matter.

2. Credit all finance or other charges on disputed billings to a customer's account if the customer wins the dispute.

3. Give full information on all charges.

4. Give notification to a customer before any adverse credit information is turned over to any third party, such as national credit rating bureaus. Millions of consumers would be affected.

The new rules would apply to bank and other credit card issuers, department stores, gasoline companies, travel and entertainment credit card establishments, and others.

Other major provisions of the proposal would make these requirements of a creditor issuing monthly billing statements:

1. The statement must be mailed at least twenty-one days before the date it will impose finance or late charges for nonpayment.

2. Included on the bill must be the name, address, and telephone number of a person authorized to handle complaints.

3. Customer payments must be posted to their accounts on the day of actual receipt.

4. Overpayments by customers must be refunded, unless the statement spells out that the excess payments may be refunded or credited to their accounts at their option.

This is an enormous stretch of government power over a clientele of many thousands who are creditors, and over practically everyone else in the country, since most of us are debtors (including most creditors, who are in other respects debtors). Though the domain is vast, the scope is limited to the single relationship of lenders and borrowers and to several procedures, but one must marvel at how intensive, how penetrating is the intervention of government. It is about to tell a vast industry how to carry out the smallest billing, under pain of fine or jail or disruption of business.

Yet who can argue against the procedures? What they do is to put the government on the side of the debtor who is usually weaker than the creditor in these regards. They will also increase the costs of the creditor's doing business. They will then probably increase what the creditor will charge the debtor for borrowing, and prevent many "poor risks" from getting credit from the creditor, who is now faced with higher costs. Finally, note that an appointive agency, not elected officials, are making this important rule.

Agencies of this type were once called the "irresponsible headless fourth branch of government" by experts on administration, who wanted the President, an elective official, to be able to hire and fire them. Weaker voices called for tighter rule by Congress over such agencies. Actually these agencies would not behave very differently in either event. Probably they should be made more representative in both these respects, plus having representative juries and councils attached to them. As matters stand, they do hold hearings and pass through review by the courts, an occasional and costly and complicated and slow process.

8. "Who gave *whom* the right or command . . . ?" our first question asked, and *whom* means the clientele of persons directly affected by an activity. How many are they? Where are they? For example, the U.S. Department of Agriculture signs agreements with the American Sheep Producers Council, Inc., and gives it money to engage in promotional advertising and market development. Here is a clientele of a pressure group, and *its* clientele, the sheep farmers. What would happen, we wonder, if the federal government financed all people's market development to keep them in business?

Or the Office of Economic Opportunity, organized to end poverty in America, worked through cities and special councils to get the poor organized to consult with the authorities on their problems. The clientele was some of the poor who wished to be represented, but included all the intermediaries as well.

*   *   *   *   *

All of this effort to produce a properly organized inventory of government activity would be worthwhile, but it has not yet been done. I attempted a small assault upon the total problem of knowing what one government, the federal, was doing. A pilot study was made to answer the original question tentatively concerning a sample of 283 activities out of an estimated 7000 that conformed to our definition above.

To do so, the required information was culled, as best it could be, from existing information published by the government. These data were put into a standardized form,[4] and then the data were punched onto cards in code and transferred electrically to a computer tape. A second tape was prepared, containing a program of questions that could be asked of the data type, such as, "Would you list for me all activities that deal with children?"

Using the information made available by these operations, a congressman or reporter or executive could call for an immediate list to learn how many and what agencies are working in the same field; one who wished to compare costs, find duplications of effort, reorganize agencies, or help decide where to put a proposed activity concerning children would find the information useful.

---

4. In studies and fields where the cases handled are numerous, the cases can be better managed and analyzed by reducing and reporting them in a similar way as far as possible. This is *standardization*.

The sample of 283 activities revealed some matters of interest. It showed the types of *clienteles* listed in the chart below.

Who Are Serviced or Dealt With by a Sample of Federal Activity Units?

44	Other parts of their own division or bureau or department
24	Other agencies of the federal government
21	State governments
13	Local governments
10	Foreign governments
75	Corporations and firms
27	Nonprofit groups
69	Individuals
283	Total activities

In other words, about a quarter of the activity units were engaged with other parts of the federal bureaucracy. Another quarter dealt with business companies; another fourth dealt with individuals.

As we might expect, every human value appears to be a concern of or affected by the federal government. A simple activity could affect more than one value such as power or health, but if the *main* value alone is counted, we get the following results with the same 283 activities:

What Values Do Government Activities Involve?

Health	35
Knowledge	90
Affection	0
Morality	3
Power	40
Respect	1
Skill	16
Wealth	97

This reveals a vitally important fact about the "Welfare State." Whereas the "law and order" state concerned itself with *power* matters, the welfare state bears heavily upon the regulation of wealth and its redistribution, upon health, and upon education. (Again, the sample is not fully reflective of the right proportions; should a full study be carried out, the proportions would change.)

Now to the all-important question of instrumentation—the means of influencing the clienteles to do what the government wants. For these we must refer back to the box on page 240. If we were to place our 283 activities in the three major categories there, we would find 163 given over to what we call economic operations of one kind or another; 95 dealing with informing, educating, and consulting; and 26 occupied with directing, ordering, and restraining. These proportions show that the modern welfare state concerns itself not only with economic values but very largely uses economic techniques to get what it wants done.

An *authoritarian* state, for example, such as Fascist Italy, old monarchic Rumania, Kemal Pasha Ataturk's Turkey, Franco's Spain, or Saudi Arabia, tends to order things to be done and let the threat of sanctions be the means of seeing that they *are* done.

The educational emphasis is remarkable, too. The increase in attempts to carry on all kinds of educational and promotional campaigns is also characteristic of the modern welfare state that strongly values education in all of its forms. It is here, too, that a trend to increase popular civic participation is reflected.

Public Preferred to Government

Suppose that the ideal inventory were achieved. All that the government does is made known. Practically every aspect of life is actually or potentially the concern of government. What should our attitude toward the condition be? Resignation? Escape? Passive resistance? Or, possibly, joy? Contentment about socialist efficiency? Or fear and rage?

It seems that a Principle is necessary.

PRINCIPLE VII

Government activity, as distinct from
public activity, should be minimized
in scope, domain, intensity, and duration.

You can gather from this, that our slogan is "Down with the State! Up with the Public!" We do not say, "Down with the Public and State" or "Up with the State and Public." For we are all in favor of the public but want the public to be organized and operating in forms other than the usual state form as much as possible. The state and government form adds to every one of its activities three major effects.

1. *Coercion,* or the tendency thereto, is inherent in government.

Force should go against the grain of every woman and man. The giving of functions to a force institution should go against the grain as well. So medals ought to go to every inventor of means of solving problems by a method other than simply ordering people to solve them in a certain way. Coercion spreads and infects all those contaminated by it.

In any activity, if the clientele feel that they must follow a prescribed course, no matter what the means taken to conceal or avoid that ultimate coercive possibility, the clientele will be deprived of equality of will, a feeling of independence, and the search for their own solutions. The United States governments are by no means the most oppressive in the world; yet those governments in all of their ramifications commit millions of illegal and coercive actions simply because the several million people who are acting in their name are related somewhere along the line to a rule or an order or a law or a policeman that may be unleashed to the harm of the people affected. If you will consider for but a moment the condition of the lower half of the economic-educational level of the population, you will find them rather helpless to question or challenge or fight authority in its many forms. They are too poor, too ignorant, and too afraid to argue.

The more goods that the government dispenses to people, the more compulsory becomes the least coercive of the dispensing activities. If a government, for example, contracts for school supplies on a large scale, the penalties of fraud in such contracts will tend to move out and cover a great many contracts for school supplies among private parties. This may be "good" but it may also make contracting an overly threatening business and bring a plague of lawyers. If the army operates a "private mess hall" for off-duty hours, military discipline will stare out of every bowl of soup; so a company cafeteria; so a family dinner table. Those other things in life that are left without the legal intervention of the government become permeated by the perfume of coercion. People come to feel surrounded by the state; any slip they make, they feel, can be held against them and cause them trouble with the whole range of benefits they are getting from the state.

To the degree to which nongovernmental organizations share the characteristics of government, they also hold this implication of coercion over the heads of their members and those they influence. This is true of political parties, business monopolies, some churches, and practically all schools.

2. *Rigidity* or the tendency thereto also characterizes government activity.

Government tends to be rigid because of its huge size. Its activities are forced into a common mold. Change is difficult, because change usually has to be initiated where the activity began in the first place—far away in some other office or the legislature.

Compared with private activities, whether conducted for profit or not, government activity is dominated by *vested* interests as compared with *invested* interests; it is conducted by people who are not in a hurry, as against people who have to get something done or must quit; and it can afford the costs of rigidity, because its income comes usually from taxes paid by a remote public to remote officers, as compared with sales to customers who may take their trade elsewhere.

3. *Centralization* or the tendency thereto is a third trait of government activity.

Whatever is put into the political sphere tends to be pushed upward and out of reach of its clientele. This happens because the leaders at the center of politics must tend to claim credit for attending to every issue, no matter how slight, that the whole political system generates. If a child wants a playground in Tuscaloosa, the government in Washington can become excited about it, whether or not it can really do anything about the playground. This often charming spectacle of the Great reaching down to touch the lowly is irresistible to the imagination, but it also engenders activity after activity as the leaders are pressed to show results on what they are paying attention to.

The failure of local leaders to provide satisfactory, decentralized activities constitutes generally an invitation to the central leaders to step in; but the failure of the central leaders to provide satisfactory activities to the people is almost never the occasion to hand down the activity. Rather the quarrel over the activity stays on the national or highest level; there it is resolved in a fanfare of publicity, if it is ever resolved.

*   *   *   *   *

Coercion, rigidity, centralization: these traits characterize government activity.

Public activity also is activity that recognizes the need for taking account of the consequences of social behavior, and for making decisions which reflect all types of persons affected. Public activity, however, can be achieved by many different types of governmental and nongovernmental organizations (See Appendix B). Hence, to the extent that activities can be publicly conducted without being governmentally conducted, the above failings may be avoided.

Referring once more to the Principle, the words "scope, domain, intensity, and duration" are now familiar. Since a government activity or power is defined by these parameters, then *their* reduction means the reduction in the adverse general effects of governmental activity and finally an achievement of more *public* nongovernmental activity. The policy that we recommend is closely related to the Principle.

POLICY VII

Favor diversity over sameness
in the organization and determination
of public activities;
maximize cooperative and educational
means of executing government policies;
introduce radical systems
of activity devolution
from state to publics.

People are all too prone to say "there should be a law against" whatever they do not like. Legislators are remarkably naive in this same respect; they will hasten to impose simple formulas: "The department of *X* will do *Y*; anyone who interferes or does not cooperate will be fined or jailed." Instead of studying an issue patiently and scientifically, they tend to reduce every issue to a probable case at law, with two sides and a judicial decision. The court system is basically skewed to this kind of thinking. An enormous effort is needed if all the molders of thought in America are to understand that public problems can be resolved in a multitude of ways without necessarily handing them over to the nearest bureau or court. This task should have high priority among a great many teachers of the country, even though only a few thousand now have any interest in or capacity for coping with the problem.

The next point is clear and can be deduced from the preceding statements. The public has to be introduced into all of its own activities. It is both author and object of social activity. Those who make laws are generally a representation, exact or biased, of those who are affected most directly by the law. All of these should be involved more definitely in the processes of both policy making and activity execution.

Not only the groups who are the source of the issue but also those who are affected by the rules coming out of the resolution of the issues should be used to create and control a public activity. Thus, suppose a problem of safety is generated about the automobile industry. Some of its production and testing practices have come under attack. Then the auto makers and all those affected by them should be consulted by Congress in legislating (which is actually what happened). But also the task of carrying on the activity engendered to raise standards of safety ought to be moved as far outside of government as possible (which may not be very far). A safety laboratory governed by public members, a government member, and representatives of the automobile industry might be set up. This laboratory could do as efficient a job of safety design and control as a purely governmental agency could do; the typical faults of governmental activity would probably be avoided and the participants in the rule-making body would enjoy the liberty of developing and exercising their own social consciences. This last pleasure is, after all, a cardinal virtue in society.

But perhaps the most striking reform of governmental activity would occur through the invention of some new method of reducing the governmental quality of all governmental activities in a systematic and continuous way. Every study made of governmental activity shows that activities rarely are softened, reformed in the ways we have indicated, or changed into nongovernmental activities. They stagnate in their original form, rarely changing, rarely diminishing in scope, domain, size, costs, or severity, and usually enlarging. For half a century or more, this fact has been viewed as proof that governments are doing more and more for the good of the people. No one will admit that the process of general growth will go on indefinitely, for that would end up in totalitarianism. Rather welfare *state* advocates (as compared with welfare *public* advocates) postpone the issue, saying only that governments are not doing enough just yet; they imply that resistance to governments' assuming new activities is like beating animals or putting debtors in cages.

To make matters worse, those who *do* want to restrict governmental activity often really want to restrict the growth of the publics surrounding the activities of society that are causing trouble. They therefore fight their battles along lines of simple resistance to public attention to their affairs. Thus, many automobile executives behaved for a long time as if the hundreds of thousands of people annually buffeted by accidents had no business trying to become part of the public of the automobile industry. This is like saying that the soldiers who go forth in the armies of a country have no right to be citizens of the country.

The answer lies neither in wholesale approval of, nor in resistance to governmental activity, but rather in setting up a system for a critical redesign of activities. Such would be a *tribunate* that would be composed of a professional corps of civil servants working for Congress but carrying out their tasks in every office of the government. A *tribune* would be given full access to a single agency or office. The task of each tribune would be to study and criticize his or her given agency. Each year the tribunes would report on ways and means of degovernmentalizing and depoliticizing the activities assigned to them. They would act as "the devil's advocates."[5] They would argue that offices would do their work better if they used different means of influencing clientele, and/or that they were not sufficiently accountable, and/or that they were wasteful, and/or that they could be removed from the government altogether by proposed reorganization without losing their public character and without losing the benefits they were providing.

Anything like this is done only rarely. Recently the U.S. Post Office Department, the largest business-type enterprise in the world, was in such grave trouble from inefficiency, politics, and waste, that it was entrusted to a special form of organization outside of the government, a government corporation in which public members joined the board of directors. It works with the resources and revenues that the postal system enjoys, with the goal of avoiding the continual losses. The Post Office is still subject to public regulation, of course, but its true public character was supposedly enhanced by moving it outside the political pressures of heated congressional and professional politics.

Vested interests opposed the move. The most intense opposition to the proposal came from the postal workers' unions, fearful of their members' security of employment.

In any advanced technology—which is to say, any society with a rich variety of skills—there is always just as good a way to organize a public activity *outside* the government as *within* it. Our tribunes would have a field day. We can imagine Dave (he's one of the original gang that Al hung around with) testifying before a House Committee on his annual report concerning his assigned agency, the Sinkholes Agency.

*   *   *   *   *

Representative Kerplunk:
Our next witness is Mr. David X. Diablo. Glad to have you with us again, Mr. Diablo. The members of this committee have read your report with interest, and you can see by the numerous representatives of the press here, by the officers of the Sinkholes Agency present, and by the many others in this open hearing of the Agency Committee that you have caused some excitement. (*laughter*)[6] You should go into politics with your fame as a critic, Mr. Diablo.

5. The name comes from the long-enduring practice of the Roman Catholic Church of appointing a church official to seek out facts and argue the case against any historical personage who is being considered for sainthood.
6. I observed that the laughter was nervous, but the stenographer is not permitted to be *that* accurate.

Mr. Diablo:

Thank you, sir. No, sir. I am happy with my work, and, as you know, a tribune cannot seek elective office for five years after resigning from the Corps, and nobody reads five-year-old newspapers before an election.

Representative Kerplunk:

Quite right. But, would you mind now summarizing your recommendations concerning the Sinkholes Agency, that you have so well served as a tribune for five years? (*laughter*)

Mr. Diablo:

My principal recommendation is that the Agency be abolished over the next fiscal year.

Representative Kerplunk:

You mean just like that? But what of its 1672 employees and the public it serves.

Mr. Diablo:

I have presented in my report a means of reemployment for the employees in and out of government. So far as the public it serves is concerned, I have found it to be quite able to take care of itself. My examination of all of the actions of the 1672 employees indicates the following:

1. Some 243 of them are engaged in providing information to the sinkholes industry and the people served by it which is 98.9 percent unused and unwanted by both groups.

2. Some 491 of them are engaged in a pilot project to show how new methods of construction could be employed in the factories of the industry. The pilot project has been three years in getting under way. My conversations with these employees and with industry engineers lead me to the certainty that the new method will not be used, unless the government subsidizes the industry to the amount of $112 million per year. But the industry is not so vital to the economy as to warrant such priority in Treasury spending.

3. Some 109 employees are engaged in the regulation of undesirable practices in the industry, including child labor, machine safety, and pollution that no one in his right mind in the industry would ever contemplate again. It would cost the industry $320 million to junk its machinery and processes and go back to polluting the Widestink River.

4. Some 418 employees are engaged in servicing the other employees, as secretaries, budget personnel, security and maintenance personnel, drivers, personnel clerks, payroll clerks, liaison with other agencies, public relations people, and so on. Naturally, their only *raison d'être* is the existence of the Agency.

5. Some 156 employees are attached to firms in the industry to see that

the provisions of the Act of 1954 respecting the use of low-interest loans given weaker members of the industry are followed. These are book-keepers, accountants, and inspectors, for the most part. Since the loans are unjustifiable exceptions to general commercial practice regarding the rates on loans, this program should be abolished.

6. The remaining 155 employees fall into various categories . . .

Representative Kerplunk:

No, that's all right, Mr. Diablo. No need to spell out their functions. It is indeed startling to hear your recommendations. Tempting as it is to rescue $62,720,000 for the Treasury, Mr. Diablo, I wonder whether we should move so hastily. The Agency itself has, in *its* Annual Report, presented a somewhat contrasting picture. In fact, they are asking for a 1.2 percent increase in personnel and a 2.3 percent increase in their budget. A number of business people from the same industry being regulated by the Agency have, in fact, presented this Committee with statements supporting the Agency's re-quests.

Mr. Diablo:

I have not criticized the Agency, Mr. Kerplunk, for the quality of its public relations staff, its capacities for survival, and the powerful friends it has made among the businessmen and women it regulates. I have rather stressed the objectives and functions of the Agency.

Representative Kerplunk:

But have you considered the feelings of the employees who would be displaced, including some who, I believe, are here today. (*applause*) You would, I suppose, agree that there is still some possibility remaining that those antisocial practices you mentioned would return in the absence of a watchful agency?

Mr. Diablo:

No doubt. But the value . . .

Representative Kerplunk:

Yes, of course. And the Agency itself declares in its own annual report that it seeks new funds to convert the existing pilot project into a new pilot project more in keeping with the developing technology of the industry. As far as concerns the need of supplying statistical information and resources to the industry, government, and public, I am sure that you would not wish to judge them by the *quantity* of demand but by the quality. For example, the Committee has before it a letter from Professors Mixtbe and Farway of Running Water University declaring the usefulness of the statistics of the Agency in preparing their long-awaited study of "Polychromatic Noise Factors in Control Stations of Industry."

Mr. Diablo:

I took into consideration such eminent individuals, but failed to see why the government should support their research more than anyone else's research. The request of the Institutes of Health Sciences for $10 million to study rat control methods was turned down while rats eat a billion dollars of food a year—besides being unpleasant.

Representative Kerplunk:

I see. That matter, I believe, came before a different committee, did it not?

Mr. Diablo:

Yes it did. And I think that Tribune Halraser had no word of criticism for that proposal.

Representative Kerplunk:

Well, you understand. We have to hear all points of view. I thank you very much for your illuminating remarks. My own feeling, as you may have gathered, is that an agency with such a fine past record as this should not be entirely dismissed. There is much in the record to show that it is striving very hard to assert its usefulness.

Will Mr. Encomium of the Agency please come forward to testify now. Thank you, Mr. Diablo. You may step down.

*   *   *   *   *

We wonder, too, what Diablo's confederates will be saying about the Department of Defense. There is a consensus that war as a government activity should be, if not abolished, reduced in scope, domain, intensity, and duration.

Perhaps they might be reporting: "Regarding the scope of the Department of Defense, we say 'Reduce the number of war commitments. The U.S.A. is not authorized to be the police officer of the world and is not competent for the task anyway.'" With respect to domain, they might say, "Abolish compulsory military service in favor of voluntary service, and release millions of men from the feeling and actuality of loss of freedom." With respect to intensity, "extend more civil rights to soldiers; fight no nuclear wars, because they cannot be won," and, with regard to duration, "provide for getting out of a military engagement once begun."

Unfortunately, these amusing ideas would not be the stock-in-trade of the tribunes. A great many persons pretend to these heavenly goals without necessarily having an effect on the continuance and growth of war activities.

Hence we must admit that the tribunes will not help abolish or greatly deactivate Defense, or many another agency. Ultimately the highest political authorities have to be persuaded and compelled. And not only the American, but the Russian, Chinese, French, and other politicians would need to heed the tribunes. If they will not give up their wars which they understand as well or better than any tribune, they cannot listen to, or even permit, contrary proposals so close at hand.

How to Judge an Activity

Whether we speak of a real politician or of a fictional tribune, who may someday soon exist, we should like that person to know fully and to apply several criteria to determine the goodness of a given instance of governmental activity.

A
The armed forces are inherently charged with reducing citizens to unequals.

B
The unmarried or deserted mothers of dependent children may be unable to get any help outside of government.

C
The U.S. Information Agency, the U.S. Agency for International Development, the TVA, and many other agencies could be "civilianized."

D
There are more public relations officers in the Department of Defense, selling it to the public, than there are members of Congress.

E
The shipping industry receives an enormous subsidy so that it can continue to build boats in America that cost more than boats built in foreign shipyards.

F
The Penn-Central Railroad was so snarled up with the Interstate Commerce Commission rules on using its funds that it decided to go into other nonrailroad businesses and went bankrupt.

G
The program of subsidies to farmers to maintain their incomes rolled on year after year, despite some criticism of the fact that a great many well-to-do farmers were being subsidized.

H
The government engages in heavy spending and at the same time fights inflation that comes from heavy spending.

Having read these examples, you will appreciate the general criteria and questions that appear below, because these are based on many such examples. Would you mind saving the author some trouble by placing at the end of each general criterion the letter of the example that applies most closely? Thank you. Meanwhile I'll run ahead and prepare a chapter for you on *Government Structures.*

We would ask whether the governmental activity stimulates individual initiative and avoids a monopoly of concern centered in the government or in some favored group. A governmental activity, that is, can enhance desires of citizens to take up and perform certain valuable operations in society, or it can discourage them from doing so.
(See Example ____)

It should be asked whether the activity helps people whom no one can otherwise figure out how to help, granted that their need has an appropriately high priority and is not a simple want, for no government can hope to satisfy all wants.
(See Example ____)

An activity may be assessed as to whether it isolates the government from the citizenry or maintains a contact between government and citizens which is reciprocal in its power aspect. When both the citizen and the official treat one another on equal terms from a power standpoint, and there is a give-and-take in the

One may ask whether the activity of the government passes along costs as much as possible to the clientele of the operation rather than levying the costs to the general treasury without regard to the interest and needs of all or to the ability of the clientele to support and carry out the activity with their own resources.
(See Example ____)

It may be noted too whether the activity has built into its organization the possibility of a change in its extent. Frozen activities litter the whole governmental scene; they should be unfrozen by internal mechanisms rather than awaiting the distant and unpredictable day when the heated gaze of Congress or the President may focus upon the scene.
(See Example ____)

We may also inquire whether the activity is consonant with other policies of the government. Society has obviously come to the point where planning, in its simplest sense of an activity that correlates state operations, must be

relation, the activity may be preferred.
(See Example ____)

The activity should avoid stressing "the majesty of the state." Since it visibly represents the nation, the national government tends to acquire all kinds of electrical emotional charges no matter how little it does or how badly it does it. The more that governmental operations are civilized and built into the normal social structure, instead of being identified with irrelevant psychological forces operative in the notion of the state, the better. It is unnecessary, costly, and rigidifying therefore for the government to insist upon extracting its prestige increment—its exorbitant psychological profit—from every operation it performs.
(See Example ____)

employed. It is possible to have an enormous government, with thousands of activities, that is tripped up by its own inner contradictions.
(See Example ____)

Finally, it may be suggested that a good activity of the government should have means of implementation that are obvious to all concerned with the activity. That means that care should be displayed from the very beginning of an activity to expose all of its means. Very often, even in a democratic society, officials of the government are tempted to cover up methods that they use to influence the behavior of their clientele, feeling some shame and, of course, some threat if the means were to be openly displayed. To the maximum extent possible all means actually employed in the implementation of an activity should be fully evident to those who would inquire, whether they be in the executive branch, Congress, the press, the academic world, or the public.
(See Example ____)

Chapter 8
Government Structures

A structure is merely a pattern of behaviors or habits. For instance, your character is a structure. It is the pattern of your habits of eating, sleeping, loving, studying, spending, learning, responding, etc. It's a pattern in the sense that your habits are related: eating habits are connected to habits of exercise, etc.

A social structure is the pattern of habits of a group. For example, your class is a structure. If an experienced professor visited it, he or she would know what to expect. Not always, but mostly. Less now than ten years ago; why? Because "the structure of classes has broken down somewhat." Generally, the visiting professor would know what to do when someone raised a hand, would know how to answer questions, and ordinarily what questions to expect. When members of the class closed their books, he would know his claim to their attention was ending. And so forth.

A government structure is the pattern of behaviors or habits of persons holding office in the name of the constituent population.

What is the difference between a structure, an organization, and an institution?

Not much. Often they can be used interchangeably. There is a difference between "a slap," "a blow," and "a cuff," but they could be used to refer to the same unhappy event. An organization is an aimed, patterned activity. It implies less rigidity than structured behavior.

HOUSING STRUCTURES PARALLEL SOCIAL STRUCTURES

The two views from my New York study while I was writing this book, photographed with my Polaroid.

A new, beautifully designed apartment building, fully air-conditioned, standing back on its own lawns, housing many low-income people.

An old, decrepit structure, with many cubbyholes, badly ventilated, used for the mathematical and computer facilities of my university.

BIG JOKE!

This is the *computer* housing. The Queen Bee, a CDC 2400, occupies a full floor lofty apartment.

This is where the *people* live, one or two to a room.

An institution is a complex, enduring organization.

A structure can be simple and short-lived. The word is used for describing "the structure of a report" or "the structure of a state."

No human organization, institution, or structure can be as preplanned or rigid as some biological structures are, but a particular institutional structure may far outlast any particular biological structure. The Roman Catholic Church has outlived many generations of individual structures.[1]

Are structures necessary?

Yes, indeed, structures are necessary. Society and individuals would collapse in an instant without them. (It is hard to imagine a structureless society or person; it's like imagining a boneless man or a hiveless colony of bees.)

You simply cannot achieve a goal without a structure. Look at a ballplayer. He stands at bat. His whole physique is trained and postured (structured) for the instant of swinging at a ball. Everything around him— pitcher, catcher, umpire, players, even the audience, the field, the bases—is structured, including past history (the score) and future innings. ("Two out in the ninth inning with the bases loaded and the mighty Casey at bat!") What a structure! What a scene!

There must be some structure even though structures vary somewhat in relation to a goal. You need similar but not exactly like structures to fight fires. And one government is structured somewhat differently from another.

Generally a structure, when adapted to a set of goals, provides outputs that are useful. It guarantees reliability of performance; the huge main Post Office building in New York City carries the proud stone carving:

Neither rain nor snow nor gloom of night stays these couriers from the swift completion of their appointed rounds.

The structure enables the organization to get rid of trivial and routine matters with efficiency. (New employee: "Where do you dump the wastebaskets from this office?" Old employee: "You dump them in the big boxes outside and every day at ten o'clock a truck picks up the stuff.")

The structure promotes quantity production. (New employee: "Where does all this waste come from?" Old employee: "Most of it is customers' complaints. Then there are all the directives from above. You see, we have a round-the-clock operation, three shifts, and each shift handles a big load of work.")

The structure permits generalized procedures, rational recruiting, and substitution. "We need a well-trained college graduate to distribute

---

1. I confess exceptions. Those explorers who ate Siberian mammoth meat that had been frozen for thousands of years were finally breaking down some ancient cell structures.

chicken feed, and somebody should be taught to do his job when he gets sick."

Structure permits better foresight, better planning. If the same job is performed in a different way every time it is done, you cannot calculate well in advance how much it will cost, how much to put aside for it, or who will do it, or how to prepare whoever will do it for doing it, or what to do with all the other operations that are affected by the job.

In view of these observations, we offer this proposition:

PROPOSITION VIII

Social structures shape the distribution of power and other values within and among groups.

SMALL-SCALE EXAMPLE: *New employee:* "How do you get ahead in this place?" *Old employee:* "You get friendly with Joe; the boss always listens to him."

LARGE-SCALE EXAMPLE: *Congressman:* "How do we limit the President's power over foreign affairs?" *Professor of Political Science:* "You pass a bill requiring that all executive agreements that the President draws up with foreign governments must be approved by the Senate, as with treaties."

If structures shape power and other values, obviously we should see to it that they are intelligently constructed. Hence:

PRINCIPLE VIII

Authoritative structures should represent both their own purposes and the general purposive character of society.

Meanings:

Authoritative structures: structures which have authority. That is, people believe that they are set up and operated according to the correct procedures and for the correct purposes. People therefore generally cooperate with them. (If some people don't, *government* structures may use coercion—physical force—to obtain compliance, and few observers will object.)

Represent . . . their own purposes: Let's backtrack a minute. In the beginning of this book, we discovered that politics is the effort to use power to
gain one's own goals. A little later we found out that it would help Al if
he organized a club to accomplish his purposes. But we forgot to
mention that Cal, Hal, Sal, and Val were doing the same thing as Al,
namely organizing similar structures to accomplish *their* purposes.
Suppose all their purposes are different. Who wins, and how?

This is where the authoritative structures of government come in.
They provide a theater for contesting and a method of deciding which
group and purpose shall prevail. In modern states, governments
have separate structures and processes to make policy decisions (the
legislative function), to see that these are carried out (the executive or
administering function), and to settle disputes about them (the judicial
function). Suppose the majority of legislators vote for the proposals
suggested by Al's club; the executive will put them into effect and the
courts will punish offenders. Thus, the legislature, the administration,
and the judiciary should each maintain its own purpose, but each
should always keep in mind:

The general purposive character of society: the kind of society to be encouraged, which, of course, is a kalotic society. In other words, a
constitution should be proclaimed. If a society has some general shared
purposes, these purposes should be set forth and used to guide the
building of government structures.

POLICY VIII

Impose a kalotic constitution upon systems of power and influence.

The constitution would be an authoritative plan of the basic structures of
our group, declaring who should perform what functions regularly. I could
also call it an organization of the group, or an institution of the group. Now,
you can look up the U.S. Constitution, or the French or the Soviet; or you
might glance at the constitutions of trade unions, teachers' associations,
etc. The charters of corporations and universities are worth examining, since
one of our ambitions is to make these more representative. Here are the
provisions I would propose for an all-purpose kalotic constitution suitable
for any large organization but especially a country.

A Kalotic Constitution

I. The laws are valid when all persons are equally subject to them.

II. The organs of government are a principal elected Assembly, various subassemblies of localities and socioeconomic fields, an executive cabinet headed by a President, a Supreme Court, and Citizens over sixteen.

III. The constitution is supreme law. It can be interpreted or changed by a majority of any three of the above or by any two of the above acting twice in two years. The subassemblies act as a unit by majority vote for this purpose.

IV. Each three years, the Assembly seats are filled through election quotas by all persons over sixteen years.

V. The Assembly elects the President for one five-year term and the President chooses the cabinet for a like term.

VI. The Supreme Court serves for six years and is drawn by lot from names submitted by each member of the Assembly. It sets up all subordinate courts.

VII. The subassemblies are apportioned out of the leading localities and socioeconomic fields of the country by the Assembly. The representativeness of their structures is audited by the Supreme Court. They have all powers over their jurisdiction and members given to them by the Assembly.

VIII. Every large organized group is governed by a representative structure. The Supreme Court determines whether the structure is in fact representative and orders the President to take remedial action if it is not.

IX. All organs can propose laws but only the Assembly can enact laws.

X. The Citizens as a body determine any issue put to them by three out of the other four principal organs.

XI. No new power over persons and things can be voted without a decentralization or quitting of an equivalent power.

XII. All official actions that direct people how to behave are matters of public information unless three organs of government agree to make them secret.

XIII. All expression is free. To be fully free, methods of counterexpression have to be guaranteed by the Assembly.

XIV. Except when determined to be sick or defining oneself as sick, a person shall not be spatially or functionally confined for more than two periods of life: before the age of fourteen and for two single years between sixteen and sixty for purposes of universal civic service.

XV. An annual accounting of the life conditions of all elements of the population shall be published, based upon intensive interviews of a sample.

XVI. Each year the budget shall be divided by the population and each person charged with his equal part of all planned expenditures. No other tax shall be levied upon any person, group, or activity.

XVII. Every person shall receive an annual life-account credit from womb to tomb sufficient to pay for the basic necessities of life.

XVIII. A corps of tribunes shall be established by the Assembly. A tribunal shall be attached to every agency, company, and group of significance to publish each year a report criticizing its goals, operations, personnel, and social value.

*   *   *   *   *

This model constitution will set you off on your own search for constitutional ideals. It shows in a major way how to bring together Proposition VIII, Principle VIII, and Policy VIII.

Representation

The kalotic constitution obviously calls for lots of representative government. By this we mean that a person who speaks in the name of and rules over any body of people should ultimately be controlled by that body. The representative principle is one of humanity's great inventions. It essentially announces a means for collecting certain characteristics of a group and projecting them variously into the operations of the group or its officers. It implies that a number of people are in communication with each other and certain communications should be stressed inside the government or group and reflected in the external activity of the government or group.

There is no other way to manage a large and complex community beneficially. Either the largeness or the complexity or the beneficialness will otherwise have to give way. Wherever a group is sufficiently general in scope and voluminous in membership and activity, it requires specialized structures, the most typical of which are an assembly, an executive, and courts. As groups increasingly form from the increase in numbers and differing purposes, they generate subcommunities. The subcommunities should generate, on the same principles, representative government, with the three subformations just referred to. Large public groupings (industries, industrial associations, labor unions, churches, etc.) should be subjected to the same standards as the governmental order.

The Pluralist Principle

A pluralist principle is embodied in the kalotic constitutional provisions, according to which all governing units and large groups should be subdivided and representatively structured. One indication of how far this condition can go is to enumerate the associations that exist in a society where they may be freely formed; they will range from hundreds to hundreds of thousands. Among the major groups of modern society are the spiritual and benevolent, the educational, the military, the commercial, the industrial, the legal, the political, the professional, and the governmental. Of course, only the governmental organs are to exercise *physical* coercion on matters of law and order in the kalotic scheme of things.

Each type of group breaks down into subgroups of considerable diversity. Thus the spiritual and benevolent orders of a middle-sized or large nation will contain from one to a hundred or more nationwide sectarian groups, and an even greater number of charitable and fraternal groups; each of these may have functional or geographical subdivisions. We speak

already of hundreds of different organizations which should have representative government internally, representative government among the subdivisions, and representative government between, on the one side, the group and its subdivisions, and, on the other side, the government as well as other groups. In the government itself, the geographical subgovernments will typically begin with neighborhood governments and go on up to metropolitan governments and finally the national assembly.

A person should have as many voices as he has memberships. The symbol and steering effect of a voice is found in the vote, among other places. How one's vote is assembled, weighted, and ultimately cast in the collective decision is a matter for determination within each group. The basic requirement of all groups, subject to a system of review and determination by the courts, will be a reasonable set of representative practices.

Thorough consideration has to be given representative structures in the armed forces. Nor should even hospitals be excluded. We believe in "patient power" and "nurse power."

Labor Unions

Imagine, by way of contrast, a one-party, plebiscitary democracy, which is really a life-long autocracy or oligarchy, with large powers of government in its own sphere, and its only limits resting in the fear of destroying its source of income, the employers: such are many labor unions. The unions are scarcely ideal republics. They lend dignity to their member-workers, but not to work, or to managers, or to customers, or to those who would like to work. They block some distasteful and unjust management decisions. They sometimes raise wages. They give some aid, comfort, and sense of equality *en masse* to their members.

But unions usually prevent very high wages being given to especially efficient workers. They also cause unemployment by their restrictions upon membership and their support of government minimum wage laws. When they have direct, large political powers over a ruling regime or party, as in Britain, they constitute a conservative drag on the government and bureaucracy. That is, in many respects, union policies and powers are antikalotic. This comes partly from the union governing structure, which must be corrected through a valid constitution. In addition, workers should participate in the ownership of industry, as ordinary shareholders. As part of their wages, they should receive voting shares, just as the top officers of a great many companies now do. Else how can we speak of a truly representative government in industry?

Labor unions should continue to provide advice and counsel on grievances of workers. They should maintain benevolent activities. They may agitate and offer candidates for directorships of companies. But a single union should not directly cast all the workers' votes. Individual workers should vote as shareholders do for members of boards of directors, and benefit too from the proposed reform of the latter.

Political Parties

Political parties should play a role of providing a choice of office-holders and opposition to current policies as they do now; they may be internally organized on the same general principles as other groups. There will long be a need for such voluntary groups to mobilize opinion and activities for the general good. It is not to be expected or desired of them that they monopolize governmental power, or that they formulate and lead revolutionary change. They should be porous vessels, open to the ebb and flow of political tides. They are furthermore useful as organizers of internal government in the legislatures.

The larger force for social change in this and succeeding generations has to be independent of routine representative frameworks, even while permeating and influencing them. In the age that we have just passed through, and to all appearances are still in, the competitive pursuit of group "interests" is supposed to furnish guidelines for public policy and control of government. This concept which even today seems to most political observers and students to be very modern and which is not even yet accepted by all as being moral, has now to be assigned to its limited role in the conduct of business-as-usual. For government by "interests," and their bargains with each other, cannot give society its direction and goals, any more than can the authoritarian principle or legalist principle which preceded it.

On top of all these principles is the principle of a revolutionary public that is no more confined to an interest or conglomerate of interests than it is authoritarian or legalist. It is apparent that the great body of people themselves cannot formulate a revolution, nor even compel one unless educated and directed. It is also apparent that the revolutionary public must be a new main force, composed of people who are generally disgusted with everyday politics and are ready to press from all sides for fundamental changes.

Inventions in Structure

Political science in the last generation underwent a revolution. It was a revolution of methodology, in favor of empiricism. That is, a number of mathematical and statistical techniques were devised to gather and analyze facts in a scientific manner. This has been called the *behavioral approach.*

The behavioral approach is now passé. Its level of methodological sophistication exceeds the importance of the problems it is called upon to answer. Who needs a better sample of the American population than is now available? Who needs a more complicated correlation of variables whose character as data is hopelessly unstable? Required now are methods of reorganizing society so as to accommodate all elements of the population in decisions on public policy, methods of cracking bureaucracy, methods of decentralization, methods of exposing the acknowledged injustices of society in so unbearable a way that reforms must come rapidly.

Although the behavioral approach is passé, those who are skilled in it are in a much better position to devise the needed new methods than any literary figures and "legal eagles" who remain from the past history of the field or who are seeking a way out of their depression by tailing the New Left. The behavioralists can at least proceed systematically, given a problem to solve. Like the Scarecrow in the Wizard of Oz, all they lack is a heart. They should acknowledge that they can be relevant and useful without being less scientists for all of that.

Let us show what we mean. It is a problem for political scientists and their students. It is especially suited to them, because psychologists who are every bit as good as political scientists on conventional studies of public opinion, are almost totally unequipped in matters of structure.

The Legend of Wicked County

In New Jersey there is a wicked county. In this county there is a wicked Democratic party machine. This machine has for a hundred years devastated the county morally, physically, culturally, and economically. The county is magnificently situated, but its cities are shambles and its rural areas are slums. The politically active part of the population is probably in the normal range (i.e., 2 to 3 percent of the adult population), but the greater part of it are dependents of the machine.

The county has a planning board. This board has many members and a hundred employees. It also hires consultants to help in its work. With few exceptions, the whole lot of them are incompetent and uninterested in improving the county's physical condition and social facilities. It is the proverbial pork barrel and gravy train. The Democratic boss names many of the employees and lets his cronies name the rest.

In theory, the county has representative government. The Planning Board is elected by the elected County Board of Freeholders. It is therefore in theory representative of the county since its sponsors are elective. But this age-old theory of representation through indirect election is untenable today, if it was ever tenable.

There are not enough politists to go around. The active independent public is not large enough, nor can it possibly be large enough for all that it has to do.

Look at the chart on the next page. You see, there are more people *potentially* watching the elective officials, but less people *potentially* watching the appointed officials, such as the County Planning Board and its employees.

This situation is typical of all sectors of government (and industry, unions, churches, welfare associations, etc.) Public surveillance of officials is less possible as population grows and activities of government increase, when merely the traditional means of representative government are pursued.

But let us assume the following:

1. A population is made up of a certain proportion of different kinds of people—fifty-five-year-olds; women; Catholics; metal workers; etc.

Political Distribution in the County

	200 *Years Ago*	*Today*
Number of people in the county	10,000	1,000,000
Number of politists in the county (using our 3 percent of the population figure)	300	30,000
Number of representatives elected to the County Board	10	20
Number of people per representative	1,000	50,000
Number of politists per representative	30	1,500
Number of appointed public officials in the county	20	5,000
Number of politists per appointed public official	15	6

2. If you paired off all the people of all these different traits, and took every other one of each kind, then one could go on a political vacation while the other watched politics, without a loss of representativeness of the whole.

or

A scientific sample could be drawn of 50 percent of the population and these could go on political vacation, without any loss of general representative quality, since the remaining half would in its voting behavior act the same way and be adequate to watch generally what was going on.

3. Actually, a smaller sample would give representation to all of the elements in this sense.

4. Suppose now that we have a hundred boards and commissions and agencies in this government, be it the federal government, a state, a county, or a city.

5. Under existing theory of representative government, we find here a situation where one or two organs are elected and watched, while the other ninety-eight or ninety-nine are supposed to be representative by downwards osmosis. The huge mass of voters piles on the one or two organs. The others are ignored.

6. But consider this possibility:

A. We sample 10 percent of the electorate to elect the one or two primary organs (such as a Mayor and Council). They become the representative constituency of these organs.

B. Then we draw a scientific representative sample of something less than 1 percent of the population for the County Planning Board, 1 percent for the Park Board, 1 percent for the Highways Board, 1 percent for the Board of Health, 1 percent for the Division of Safety, 1 percent for the Sheriff's Office, and so on until every agency, board, or other organ is given a publicly representative constituency of 1 percent of the population. Thus the County Planning Board that we referred to above would have a nearly perfect microcosm of the total electorate amounting to perhaps 7000 persons who would be "forgiven" their other civic responsibilities and asked only to approve the naming of the heads of *their* agency and to watch, criticize, and from time to time approve measures passed by such a Board.

My guess is that the representativeness, the honesty, the activity, the quality of personnel, and the devotion to duty of each Board would mount quickly to the average for the central elective Council. But, further,

(1) Since all its subdivisions are watched, the Council's behavior would be improved.

(2) Since they would feel more honored and effective, the citizens of the constituencies would tend to become politists in greater numbers, that is, to execute their duties as citizens.

All of this, I submit, would amount to an enormous improvement throughout all levels of American government. And to do it, one wouldn't need undemocratic efficiency experts, men on horseback, circus clowns, etc.

Can We Go Further?

The devices of representative government are complicated. Therefore, the next century of kalotics will present groups with simpler and superior techniques for achieving the same intrinsic goals.

A future representative system will include these elements:

1. An original constituting authority.

2. Random (equal-probability) selection from the constituency of persons to recruit high-test personnel for representative roles in the organs of the system.

3. A battery of tests of all candidates for representative on these parameters:

A. Ability to sense all groupings of the constituency.

B. Motivation with regard to kalos and its elements.

C. Characterological freedom from obsession and destructiveness.

D. Judgmental training.

E. Characterological ability to make decisions in concrete cases.

F. Technical training: applying information; methodological ability.

Future applications of this method may be distant, but an early task for political scientists is to invent such tests and to begin to apply them. It may be that there is a simpler effective and responsive representative structure to be invented and developed at the end of the search. If so, it would be as important as the cure for cancer.

Chapter 9
Wealth and Life Style

How politics should control wealth is the subject of this chapter. Lest you imagine otherwise, let me say straightaway that I am not interested in small game—like how to collect and spend money in an election, or how to keep sticky fingers out of the public treasury. I am after bigger game—how to manage the world's wealth so as to create a kalotic life style for humankind.

Wealth—in bits or in great accumulations—is deeply involved in politics. This you know already; wealth is one of our original six values. Political transactions usually have a financial element imbedded in them. For this reason, economics is too important a matter to be left to economists.

I am concerned with an adequate and balanced security and freedom for everyone. This is the basic policy problem in an age when governments of the left and of the right take turns stomping upon their peoples. To solve it I propose throughout this book drastic cutbacks of governing power and yet also some new heavy injections of the same.

What I want to do in this chapter is implied in

PRINCIPLE IX

The aim of political organization should be to realize every person's credit.

By *realize,* I mean to discover, develop, and make sufficient.

By *credit,* I mean the potential capacity of every person to give something of value to others and to receive compensation adequate to achieve satisfying levels of the various goods of life.

Is there any objection to this principle?

273

"YES, WHAT BUSINESS IS IT OF YOURS?"

Here we go again. The aim of groups should be to make the people in them happier than they would be otherwise. I am building up a set of ideas about how governments of groups might best work with people. Two things they *should* do are to help people achieve their values without being coerced and without damaging others. For this, a system of exchanging goods is needed.

"WHAT MAKES YOU THINK YOU CAN DO THIS?"

Every economic system pretends and tries to do this better than other competing systems. It rarely covers a tenth of the route. I believe that it can be done better by some innovations and inventions that I shall propose in this chapter. That is, I believe that we can discover and use the potential capacity of every person.

The faults of existing systems are implied in

PROPOSITION IX

The crediting of values and the provision of means for their exchange are generally illogical and nonkalotic.

Comment: You may theoretically exchange everything you have, whether it is material or psychic, with somebody else. Perhaps it's a book, an idea, or any other particular value that comes out of the six-value system that we long ago set up in this book.

By the "crediting of values" is meant assigning a worth to something, or the setting of a market price (what the person can get if he finds a buyer), or the setting of a price by an authority of some kind, usually the government—these are ways of assigning a value.

The "means of their exchange" stands for the medium of exchange, whether it be dollar bills, or pebbles, or a set of account books, or a system of work assignments in a commune where equal work effort of different types is set up to give people equal rights to citizenship and whatever the commune produces.

By "illogical" we mean "not thought through," or "not figured out," and by "nonkalotic" we mean "not fully considered in view of our aim of a better society." The crediting of values and the means of exchange have to be put into practice—that is, translated into reality and made into social institutions.

From the proposition and the principle, and from kalotic philosophy in general, we hope to find answers to the questions: What values should be given priority? How should these values be realized?

"The Ghostly Medium of Exchange,"
A Game between Eddie and His Guru

Eddie: If you insist, I'll play your game but it had better be more fun than the last one.

Guru: What was that?

Eddie: Sleeping on carpet tacks.

Guru: Oh, well, that had its points. . . Anyhow, you are a polyvalent type, right?

Eddie: Right. I like everything—money, prestige, women, food, books, music, sports, and especially having my own way.

Guru: Good. But do you *have* everything?

Eddie: Some of everything. Yes.

Guru: Are you happy then?

Eddie: No. Sometimes when I'm with a woman, I want money, because I'm afraid she'll leave me since I don't have it, but then if I work to earn money, I can't enjoy her affections.

Guru: OK. Point 1: You like affection more than money. Point 2: Your woman friend likes money more than she likes you. Why don't you sell her for money and buy a woman who loves you for yourself?

Eddie: Man, you're way out! This is Amerika! You don't sell women. They sell themselves.

Guru: Then, why not sell *your* love for her to someone who will love you back?

Eddie: But then I won't have any affection for her, and you yourself said that I value affection more than money!

Guru: Yes. So I did. I'm stumped. Maybe we should consult an economist.

Eddie: You mean we can't find out by eating some more of those delicious mushrooms?

Guru: Ah, here he come now! Dr. Forsythe Ecotelis. Good morning, suh.

Dr. E.:   What's good about it? My shares of Computer Futures just dropped 3 points!

Guru: Peace! How do you convert everything into money and money into everything?

Dr. E.:   You don't.

Guru: But the Vedas say, "All is in everything and everything is in all."

Dr. E.:   They didn't use money in those days.

Eddie: You see!

Dr. E.:   Shut up, layman, in the presence of specialists! I suggest, Guru, that we invent a set of accounts for everyone.

List all he or she has of everything.

Put *his or her* value on each thing in exchange for every other thing.

Thus we have a complex matrix in which we know the price at which the individual will exchange everything for everything else. That will give us about 99 trillion.

Guru: 98 trillion.

Dr. E.:   Sorry; 98. . . . Now, all we need to do is to provide him with a medium of exchange.

Eddie: Money, you mean.

Dr. E.:   Well, yes. Dollar bills, or pebbles, or buttons, or chips, or clay bricks, or kisses, or handshakes, or red cloth; it doesn't really matter, so long as we all agree what it is and will accept it.

Guru: How about gold?

Dr. E.:   You fakirs are really behind the times. There isn't enough of it. Of course, you can *claim* that part of the paper or bricks or cloth *stands for* gold that is kept somewhere, and as long as people don't ask to see it, then you can get by with the myth. No, gold is a precious commodity, like titanium. Best to leave it that way.

Personally, I think *paper* is the best; and then get a good police force that compels everyone to accept the paper, in any exchange of things where a medium for exchange is necessary, or where you want to carry out different transactions at the same time and can't drag your cows, dancing girls, copper pans, diplomas, and houses to the marketplace.

Eddie: I know! Paper money!

Guru: Please! Stay out of this consultation. It's costing you plenty! "Time is money," say the Ancient Books.

Eddie: But I told you I have no money.

Dr. E.:   Perhaps you can introduce me to that chick I saw you with.

Eddie: Elena? You're crazy. She's my girl.

Guru: That's it, Eddie, you see? You can't have everything. The experts agree.

Eddie: Oh, कऋुफ नऌ ?

Guru: I am proud of your grasp of essences, young master.

Author's Comment: As usual, everyone is right!

1. You can't have everything. (We said that!)

2. Everything you have—tangible or intangible—might conceivably be bought and sold.[1] (We said that, too!)

3. Your subjective price is important. But other people's subjective price is important, too.

4. A medium of exchange is needed to make a complicated system of exchanges and transactions possible.

5. The medium of exchange could be any common material that the government can require people to accept. Or any set of account books in which both the amount of credit a person has to begin with, and what is to be accepted for entry into the books as a new credit, are agreed to by most people and enforced as legitimate entries by the government. NOW LOOK! WE HAVE COME TO THE POINT OF SAYING, "HALLELUJAH! WE CAN ORGANIZE THE WORLD ECONOMY AND NATIONAL ECONOMIES FOR OUR OWN PURPOSES!"

"But," say Mr. Timidity and Mrs. Clutch, "that's what I've got. Don't we have a God-given or natural or some dammed kind of System that does it now?" Hah! Fat chance!

Five Bugaboos

Certainly not the present systems. In the U.S.A. and the world in general, wealth is power, poverty is not dying out; the production of wealth is mismanaged; and the government inflicts oppressive tax burdens upon its people. So, here and now we are going to examine these bugaboos: the Power of Wealth; the Losing War Against Poverty; the Standard of Living Illusion; Promiscuous Economic Growth; and the Tax Muddle. They add up to a gloomy future. Only my incorrigible optimism lets me claim that reforms of the economic system are possible.

The Power of Wealth

Our institutions have had some effect—but not much—on changing our share of the goods of life. Anyone who says that the United States has changed the causes of wealth and poverty by giving the goods to people of merit should be condemned to listen to Fourth of July speeches every day in a broiling sun.

---

1. After all, Faust sold his soul, and if you can sell something *that* intangible, you can sell anything.

But wait a moment!

When you are talking about percentages you are not talking about *absolute amounts,* are you?

No. Breathe easier. The American value pie[2] is bigger than many another that has been baked by history. It is only that the social means of sharing it out have changed little.

*   *   *   *   *

The rich in America, and in many another place, do not become poorer, neither absolutely nor relatively.

Half the families of the U.S.A. control neither the wealth nor the policies of the country. More importantly, they cannot fight a medical disaster, a law suit, or a heavy claim. They cannot argue with officials, business leaders, police, or politicians on any question in which they must go out of their way for the shortest time, or pay any expenses. They have truly only a pauper's voice.

But wealth protects itself well. Numerous tax-avoidance opportunities occur to defeat the progressive income tax. For example, oil depletion allowances, and quick depreciation of oil drilling costs, reduce treasury receipts by $2 billion each year.

Two-thirds of tax-exempt income on state and local bonds goes to the richest 1 percent of all taxpayers. Property passed at death is undervalued to an extent that costs the federal treasury $3 billion per year in uncollected taxes.

One percent of the population owned 25 percent of the nation's *assets* a generation ago. They own the same proportion today. Each dollar of assets that they own controls at least another dollar. A dollar, looked upon as an instrument of control, commands some incremental resource, even if it may earn only 5 percent per annum in a savings account. But, as the number of dollars a person owns increases, he enjoys *a more than proportionate increase* in the incremental resource-control of his dollars. Controlled wealth is an increasing multiple of owned wealth. Thus, a man with $100.00 can earn 5 percent on his assets, more or less. If he has $100,000 he can expect to govern $200,000. If he owns $1 million he can control a $10-million business. And *that* business can proceed to control other businesses through cash and credit.

One percent of the population, then, controls almost half the assets of the country, directly or indirectly, in specific or in generally significant ways. The assumption is that assets are used to control assets, which is true in most cases. Moreover, we know that wealth is convertible into political influence and power.

2. Usually called the Gross National Product. See p. 284 for a definition.

The Rich Get Richer, etc.

By TOM WICKER

George McGovern's plan for a $1,000 income grant per American citizen suffers from sloppy arithmetic, grandiose goals and overstatement, but it nevertheless takes aim at the right target—the gross maldistribution of income and wealth that may well be the fundamental American social problem.

Fortuitously, just as Senator McGovern's specific program is at its lowest repute, a strong statistical underpinning for the general idea of redistributing income and wealth has appeared. This is a study by Letitia Upton and Nancy Lyons of the Cambridge Institute, the flavor of which is imparted by its opening sentence: "There is a startling and continuing inequality in the distribution of income in the United States, and the over-all pattern has remained virtually unchanged since World War II."

In other words, the rich are staying rich and the poor are staying poor, despite rare and highly publicized exceptions. Moreover, the poor are paying relatively more in taxes, while the effective tax rate on the affluent has been declining since World War II.

The Upton-Lyons study makes the following points, among others:

¶In the postwar era, the income of the richest fifth of American families has been more than all the income received by the bottom three-fifths, since approximate income ranges have been as follows—the poorest fifth, under $5,000; second fifth, $5,000 to $8,000; middle fifth, $8,000 to $11,000; fourth fifth, $11,000 to $14,000; richest fifth, $14,000 and over, with the top 5 per cent receiving $24,000 and over.

¶The 10.4 million families in the poorest fifth receive less than 6 per cent of total national money income, or an average of $3,054 annually; while the 10.4 million families in the richest fifth take over 40 per cent of income, or an average of $23,100; if all money income had been divided equally among all families, the average would have been just over $11,000 in 1970.

¶Capital gains, percentage depletion, depreciation and interest-exclusion provisions make Federal income tax rates less progressive than they appear, so that the effective rate of tax on the top 1 per cent of income-earners in 1967 was only 26 per cent; and in 1962, the income share of the top fifth declined only from 45.5 per cent before to 43.7 per cent after taxes, while the bottom three-fifths increased their income share only from 31.8 per cent before to 33.2 per cent after taxes.

¶Percentages aside, the general rise in money income and living standards in the United States has only broadened the absolute dollar gap between rich and poor families; calculated in 1970 dollars, the lowest fifth of families gained income from $1,956 in 1958 to $3,085 in 1968, while the highest fifth gained from $15,685 in 1958 to $21,973 in 1968 (thus, the gap between them rose from $13,729 to $18,888, as the rich got absolutely and relatively richer).

Income is who *gets* what; wealth is who *has* what; and the wealth picture is even more inequitable than the income picture. The Upton-Lyons study shows, for example:

¶The top fifth of Americans, ranked by wealth, owned 77 per cent of personal wealth in 1962—three times more than the entire wealth of the bottom 80 per cent.

¶The top 1 per cent of families and individuals receives only 9 per cent of personal income but the top 1 per cent of personal wealth-holders owns between 20 and 30 per cent of all personally held wealth, and has done so for decades.

¶The number of individual stock investors increased from 9 million in 1956 to 31 million in 1970; but the proportion of corporate stock owned by the wealthiest 1 per cent of the population increased from 69.5 per cent in 1953 to 71.6 per cent in 1962.

Herbert Gans of Columbia University has argued plausibly that such economic "inequality is a major source of social instability and unrest and is even a cause of the rising rates of crime, delinquency and social pathology—alcoholism, drug addiction and mental illness, for example . . . Inequality gives rise to feelings of inferiority, which in turn generate inadequacy and self-hate or anger . . . anger results in crime, delinquency, senseless violence—and, of course, in political protest as well."

If that is so, redistributing income and wealth would not merely "soak the rich"; it might also reduce those social tensions that make American life more difficult even for the rich.

Who Are the Poor Today?

The poor are not diminishing in number, even in the richest countries. They are merely changing in kind. It has become difficult, to the surprise of many who feel that somehow the poor should be obvious, to define who is poor. Many components of poverty today would never have been included in the definition historically. Recreational possibilities and a variety of dietary, medical, mental health, job counseling, dental, sanitary, and "fringe" services are needed to keep many people from a poverty largely unknown or unrecognized as poverty before.

Many youths, it should be added, suffer from the "schooling illusion." The "schooling illusion" makes students completely unaware that *their* poverty is poverty.

There is a second kind of natural illusion that fools the poor and average classes and represses the realization of deprivation. This is the *escalator illusion.* It is easily understandable but nonetheless important: a youth moving toward maturity earns more money. He believes "things are getting better," as he is lofted up the income scale by aging. He does not realize that he is consuming his life capital too, nor that the *average* of people of his class remains stationary. In inflationary times he is likely to say, if between 30 and 45 years of age, "Things cost more, but fortunately my wages have been going up."

Another kind of poverty comes from high-intensity and nerve-straining labor; the discomfort and delays of getting to and from work; the separation from one's loved ones because the division of labor segregates people; the deterioration of the *quality* of air, water, and food, as contrasted with its quantity; the crowding of facilities of all kinds; the enforcement of social and physical restraints such as parking restrictions or times of arrival and departure of public vehicles; and the complexity of consumption procedures, ranging from bottle-openers and packaging, to posting mail and filling out questionnaires.

Inflation and Material Progress

Let us choose a recent 20-year period and find out how much the "U.S.A. Standard of Living" has gone up. Total personal income in the U.S.A. from 1947 to 1966 *more* than doubled! The population, however, increased in the same period. Therefore, "average income per person" doubled![3]

But the "living costs" of the middle-income population were raised in price by a cheapening of the dollar. If your hourly pay doubles, but the price of your hamburger doubles and all other things you customarily buy double in price, then you are no better off than before.

Also, taxes increased. Most revenues came from taxes; some came from charges for services the government performed, like the post office. Some of the taxes were supplements to money income in the form of government services directly supplied, but most of these income-raising taxes (for defense, education, roads, sewers, water, fire, and police) were already being supplied in the earlier period. It would be most difficult to say that we were getting superior service in *any one* of these regards! Hence, real money income was diminished by tax increases.

The average time a worker took to get to work and back home increased from 1947 to 1966 by 40 unpleasant minutes. Transportation conditions

---

3. The quotation marks say: Watch out for these terms.

worsened in large cities; towns grew into cities; and a great many more farmers became workers over the period.

Yet another concealed event of great economic importance is that more women worked in 1966 than in 1947. But the loss of the *domestic* services of a wife has detracted from real family and *per capita* earnings. No one has yet shown how much, if any, the personal product of the average woman has increased when employed, as opposed to working for the home, supposedly "without compensation."

In addition, nonmonetary and nonrecorded income from farming, gardening, hunting, and fishing declined. That is, a real decline per capita has occurred in this area.

Another kind of cost is the *need* for medical aid as compared with the *purchase* of medical and health aids; purchases have gone up, but the unhealthy conditions of life today have increased much faster, and these are not accounted for.

Furthermore, the nuisances of noise, pollution, and the inability to find uncrowded recreation facilities within easy distances are not given a cost basis in judging the improvement of living standards. Some part of this should be counted. For instance, clothes and cars have to be cleaned much more often (and wear out sooner) because of air pollution.

Nearly 3 million units of housing became available in the U.S.A. in 1966 through construction or death. But a million units were destroyed or merged, and more than 2 million new households were created. Despite the huge volume of housing loans, the housing situation by at least this important criterion was deteriorating.

In one year, March 1966 to March 1967, nearly one in five American families moved; *neighborhoods,* as contrasted to *units of housing,* are disappearing. This is a human disaster of immense proportions. Yet I shall not count it; I don't want to make the idea of material progress too ridiculous.

So, a number of new social costs paid by us all have not been translated into dollar equivalents.

Purchase-Credit: The Big Gain

A huge onetime pay increase has been given many persons through the consumer credit system and the home mortgage system, both of which expanded enormously between 1947 and 1966. Money which is borrowed against the future and spent now *does* to a considerable degree constitute income. The use of appliances and houses that are not fully paid for in

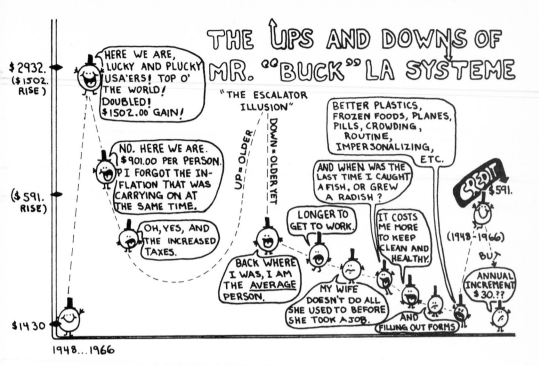

dollars is indeed real income.

Many economists will question this procedure, but we are trying, in the face of the insuperable statistical odds of a ridiculous social accounting system, *to get to the essence of the economy, the quality of life afforded by it.*

The limits of this influx of income have been approached; the average person cannot borrow much more and pay it back from his slowly increasing annual wage. Only a jump in wages of unheard-of proportions could enlarge greatly the credited increase in purchasing power. Or a jump in credit!

Note further that the credit influx has almost all been concentrated on automobiles, furniture, refrigerators, television sets, homes, and other material objects. You can get a job and a huge credit to buy a house, but you cannot get much credit to finance a college education and must depend on family and state subsidies. The government guarantees the house mortgage and helps the banks take it away if you cannot pay the mortgage each month.

* * * * *

We have arrived as far as wished to go, now, in respect to real income. In 20 years, the average American soul's income rose by one third. Spectacular innovations in credit systems helped achieve over half of this. But against this raise must be set a considerable deterioration of the environment.

That, alas, would be my conclusion. Nor did the years 1967 to 1972 change the developing picture. The hullabaloo of the politicians, press, advertisers, and producers of phony statistics is celebrating a grand illusion. Considering what man has learned and man's potential, the true record of the past generation has proven a failure of the American plutocracy and welfare state.

*   *   *   *   *

Can this treadmill be stopped? Can we get off it and onto a vehicle heading toward a society of higher quality and equal opportunity?

Yes we can. We take up the means under Policy IX below. But we have still to deal with another bugaboo.

This is the Growth Fetish, which is mirrored in the term "Gross National Product," an idea gone crazy.

The Growth Fetish

The Gross National Product. The GNP, as it is usually called, is one of the great fetishes of the twentieth century. Politicians and economists carry it in their pockets like a rabbit's foot.

> GNP is defined as the total dollar value of all goods and services delivered to their final markets from all sectors of the economy. Or you could think of it as the total value that labor, capital, and profit put into the economy in a given year.

This amounts to about a trillion dollars in the United States, and the GNP of the rest of the world amounts to somewhat more. According to our present-day witchcraft, the larger the growth in the GNP, the more jobs and profits there are to go around, and by implication, the more goods and services to be enjoyed by everyone.

For instance, if the auto industry produces 10 million cars at $4000 each one year and 12 million cars at $4000 each the next, it has increased the GNP by 0.008 percent. For this, Henry Ford II gets a glow of pride and an honorary degree from some college, in addition to more cars, labor, and profit. (All this assumes, of course, that he is a GNP fan, that the cars won't fall apart right away, that he doesn't mind making the population more sedentary, that he is not denuding the land for iron ore, that his labor costs have not risen, that polluting factory and auto exhausts have not measurably increased, and that his profit margin remains the same—to mention a few side effects.)

The GNP is actually the symbol of the Growth Fetish. I mentioned in an earlier chapter how Spain was ruined by the "Gold Fetish" of the sixteenth century. The whole world, and especially the United States, is liable to be ruined by the Growth Fetish of the twentieth century, for the GNP is a measure in which everything bought and sold is ethically equal to everything else bought and sold; the measure does not reflect any reasonable system of priorities.

Every traffic jam increases the GNP.

Every lump of scarce metal that is removed from the ground never to be replaced gives its selling price to the glory of the GNP.

Every additional bomb dropped on Vietnam adds its price to the American GNP.

If every American over 15 years of age were to be irresistibly seized by an impulse to buy this book, the GNP of the U.S.A. would rise about 0.0001 percent. But in taking time to read the book, everyone would reduce spending for other things. Since book-reading is one of the cheapest forms of consuming per hour of time, the GNP would probably decline by 0.0003 percent.

It is much better for the GNP, therefore, to get people busy flying back and forth to Florida for warmth and fun, buying drinks instead of reading en route; and Florida residents should be persuaded to ski in Vermont.

Prostitution should be encouraged:

> Girls or boys who do it for free
> Are unfaithful to the GNP!

Growthmanship has become folly. The Growthist is like a surgeon who cannot tell the difference between normal cell division and a malignant tumor.

The Japanese have made the most remarkable economic comeback in history, rising out of the ashes to achieve a gross national product that today ranks behind only that of the United States and the Soviet Union. But the price they have paid . . . has been such extensive damage to their environment that life in the most heavily populated parts of these islands threatens to become unlivable. . . . The ancient Imperial city of Kyoto, treasure house of Japanese art and architecture, is almost lost in a sea of smog as it sits astride its noisome river and beneath its scarified hills. . . .

John B. Oakes in the *New York Times*, Nov. 30, 1970.

The Soviet Union's pollution problem is as all-pervasive and destructive as that of the U.S. . . . it may be worse because it is sponsored by the Kremlin, which will brook no interference from environmentalists. . . . Lake Baikal is more than a mile deep, 20 million years old, and the possessor of more than 1,200 fish species, some of which are found only in its waters. . . . Environmentalists are trying to prevent sewage from being pumped into the lake from lumber and pulp mills which began lining the lakeshore in 1966. Some Russian environmentalists say the lake may be ruined permanently already.

Don Kirkman, quoting Professor Marshall I. Goldman, in the *Washington Daily News*, Oct. 12, 1970.

The Nixon administration has announced plans to boost farm subsidies by $600 million to $800 million next year. Virtually all of it will go to pay growers of corn and other livestock feed grains to slash production from this year's whopping surplus levels, altho wheat growers also will get a modest increase. This means that total cash subsidies for agriculture in 1972 could reach or exceed $4 billion, a record high. . . . Farmers may find themselves depending on the government for close to 25 per cent of net income.

Editorial, *Chicago Tribune*, Oct. 29, 1971.

The world's resources are rapidly being used up by expanding world industry; the environment is being polluted and degraded rapidly; population is increasing; and the whole mix of these ingredients is in any event hopelessly irrational even now, with the 5 percent of the world's people who are Americans consuming as much as the 95 percent who are not, and the ambition of the 95 percent being to Americanize their consumption habits as fast as they can.

There are many problems of applied political science, and the solutions to all of them are difficult. The solution to the problem of world production is the worst of all. But now we have to chase after another bugaboo, the Tax Muddle.

* * * * *

The U.S.A. Tax System

We have said before and can say again: "Just try to put together a sentence about government except of the dullest descriptive kind without getting involved in another social science like sociology or economics." It is not easy. You can say: "Congress has two Houses." Why? In part because the Senate was originally conceived of as a protection of the well-to-do from the excessive tax propensities of the popularly elected House of Representatives! Because of its meddling in all sciences, political science has been called the "Queen of Sciences." (It can also be called the "Scavenger of Sciences".)

In political history, the preferred method of getting booty has always been to climb over the mountain and wrest it from the tribe on the other side. When that was impossible, governments took it from their own people. To this day, taxation and war are the quintessence of government.

A tax is a compulsory governmental charge levied on people, things, or transactions. This is the broadest meaning. Actually, words like "licenses," "duties," "tariffs," etc., often come close to meaning "taxes." Also, governmental "fees," "tolls," "charges," "tribute," "fines," "subsidies" (reverse "taxes"), "court costs," "loans" (often forced), and even "prices" are often closely related to taxes.

A *tax* should obtain money in a way that conforms most generally and simply to the philosophy of the social order. A *fine* should punish malpractices. A *subsidy* should be a money grant to help whatever person or activity cannot otherwise be helped. An *income* comes from the sale of a credit to a person, company, or government. A *fee* (or charge) is payment for a specific service performed for you by the government. A *license* should be a free permit to perform a limited activity.

The United States system of taxing and revenue-raising is not markedly different from that of most other countries. For instance, the U.S. corporation tax on the profits of business is similar to the Soviet levy on the surplus of government-owned "socialist" enterprises. Generally, the richer countries collect in taxes from 25 percent to 35 percent of every dollar of their Gross National Product.

The U.S.A. has a great many different taxing jurisdictions, each entitled to get its bite—the federal government, state governments, city governments, county governments, and boards of education in local school districts.

"There is an increasing tendency to view tax policy as a welfare measure because of its redistribution potential."[4] True, but don't be fooled by the word "welfare." Just as Napoleon Bonaparte was advised by Talleyrand that "you can do anything with bayonets except sit on them," there is an increasing tendency to use taxes for every conceivable purpose beyond simply raising the money needed for government operations.

Taxes are levied to prevent harm to the environment, such as taxes on the felling of trees.

Taxes are levied on the use of facilities (rather close to tolls and fees), such as road-use taxes on trucks, and taxes on phone calls.

Taxes are levied to identify people, such as the tax on gambling that was used to spot gamblers in order to convict them of violating state and local antigambling laws (Catch 22).

Taxes are levied to reduce demand for products considered harmful, such as a tax on leaded gasoline to reduce pollution. Heavy taxes are laid on liquor because maybe people will not consume so much as a result. If this reasoning were not hypocritical, it might be anti-GNP, but in fact such taxes are cherished by governments because people will drink anyway, but won't complain very much. (Just wait until you see the tax that will be imposed on marijuana, if it is legalized.) In addition, you can find such fingernail-chewing levies as the New York City sales tax on cigarettes that makes minute adjustments from one brand to another according to the amount of tar and nicotine they contain.

Taxes are levied to lessen or eliminate competition. The dairy farmers and milk processors used to have a friendly tax that made oleomargarine cost about what butter cost, just because oleo was much cheaper to produce.

Taxes are exempted to promote the interests of special groups, such as business, labor, and religion. Church income and property are relieved from taxes, thus raising the taxes of nonsectarians. Machinery is taxed so that businessmen will hire people instead, but businessmen are then allowed to deduct some of their payments for that machinery from their

4. Gerald M. Holden, "The Nation's Income Maintenance Policies," 15 *Amer. Behav. Scientist* (May 1972), 665, p. 679.

taxable income. If you have a slick business lobby and a clever labor lobby going at the same time, your legislature can please both groups, cancel both effects, and muddle the tax system, all at the same time.

Taxes are levied to relieve unemployment, which is really a form of insurance or forced savings. Since it is involuntary, everyone in large categories of the population has to pay it and regards it as a tax. If laid off work, they get in effect a refund to carry them along for a time. It is also a form of welfare for the periodically unemployed such as actors and the chronically unemployed such as unskilled minority-group labor.

A tough question:

"Don't we *need* a tax for many of these regulatory purposes? For example, if you tax a company heavily for the pollutants it dumps in a river, won't it stop its dumping?"

This is really a *fine,* not a tax, because its purpose is really *not* to *collect* money. The policy fails if the tax brings in very much money.

The Untold Costs of Tax Compliance

No one knows the full costs of collecting taxes or has described systematically the constraints imposed upon the society in the course of their collection. To the direct governmental cost of revenue collection must be added the cost to the public of compliance with revenue laws. There are dozens of taxes, and each tax has a great number of calculations involved in its determination, most of which are paid for by the taxpayer. A single taxpayer will spend many hours in the course of a year in compliance behavior. A corporation will spend vastly more. Tax avoidance (not to mention illegal tax evasion) is a large industry, a ghost industry, since its machinations are scattered throughout the economy. In the case of such systems as social security, very small amounts in separate transactions by the millions must be assessed, recorded, adjusted, received, and paid.

Probably for every man-year of government employment given over to revenue work, several man-years of nongovernmental compliance time are expended. Abundant machinery, office equipment, and secretarial services are added to professional and taxpayer compliance time. Rarely is a business decision made without a significant proportion of the time going into costly, prolonged consideration of its tax implications. All of this activity probably costs in the area of $30 billion, or 10 percent of the total amount collected. It is also one of the most sterile and exasperating forms of human behavior; it diverts many of the best-trained minds from constructive labors. Still, the U.S. case is matched in complexity and cost by every other known system.

Tax Compliance in the New Testament

Jesus was born in Bethlehem because the bureaucrats running the Roman Empire were taking a census. Regardless of human cost, and with typical stupidity, they required that all people return to their place of birth to register their existence with authorities.

So poor Joseph had to put his pregnant wife Mary on a donkey and take the long journey to his home town of Bethlehem, where all the accommodations were taken up by other bureaucratic victims.

*   *   *   *   *

So much for bugaboos. Now for the reforms. We deserve a really large policy reward this time. Here it is:

POLICY IX

Set up a system to reduce social waste and valorize every person's credit

By *valorize*, I mean "give a value to" everyone's potential so that everybody everywhere can find a satisfying and respectable place in the total economy.

Major Reforms of the Economic System

Here are proposals for economic reform along the lines of our policy.
1. I venture a sweeping reform of the tax system of the U.S.A. (and other governments): a single equal head tax.
2. I propose a way to abolish poverty and give everyone lifetime material security: PESCALA.

3. I denounce extreme wealth as a threat to the political balance of the commonwealth and seek to abolish large inheritances.

4. I suggest the worldwide reformation of the GNP-growth fetish.

The Single Equal Head Tax

The reduction of a tax system to utter simplicity would be achieved by a single tax. Nothing that can be called a tax would exist outside of it. Any financial arrangements other than the tax would not bring revenues into the treasury of the government. The tax could be a single head tax. It would be imposed upon every living soul within a country.[5]

The tax would be the combined tax for all levels of government, collected by a central treasury, and allocated to the subdivisions of government on the basis of existing expenditure patterns. Funds newly appropriated by legislatures would be paid over only after they had been collected as part of the single tax.

The single tax would be calculated by dividing the whole population by the total amount of spending planned for the year. As an example, the approximately 200 million Americans must supply a total general revenue of about $300 billion. This comes to $1500 per man, woman, and child. This would be each person's tax for the year. He and she must pay it or owe it to the common treasury. There would be no deductions.

Were a head tax system to be established, practically every tax payment of the present time would be promptly and readily available for transfer to individual incomes to help people pay their head tax.

1. Of the 200 million Americans involved, 30 percent are already able to pay their $1500 because they pay it or more today.

2. Some 70 percent remain. Fifteen percent work for corporations that now are supposed to pay 48 percent of net profits (about $85 billion) in federal corporation tax. These companies could promptly raise the pay of their employees on a sliding scale that would permit them to pay some of their head tax.

3. Corporate organization could be reformed whereby employees are paid one-third of the stock as capital gain on their labor. (See Structures, page 263.) This would introduce a new income-earning factor and thereby a new tax-paying capability.

4. In addition to the above categories, which add up to 40 percent, 30 percent would have their taxes paid by husbands, by parents, or by em-

---

5. Wear your crash helmet if you argue this tax proposal with anyone. Henry George, a self-made economist, once proposed a single tax *on land* as the basis of government revenues; he was torn apart by real-estate interests and professional economists.

ployers who are not making a profit or paying a corporation tax for various reasons, but who could still afford to raise wages to pay the tax.

5. Of the remaining 20 percent, 10 percent will be studying (and poor), or sick (and poor), or jailed (and poor), or otherwise disadvantaged (and poor). These people would add a debit to their life account (see below), and repay the obligation whenever and if they can. Pressure would naturally be exerted to allow for their head-tax obligation when granting fellowships, or providing medical services, or inflicting penalties.

6. The balance is 10 percent of the population. A large number of persons would be told that they must pay the tax without a pay raise (equivalent or part) because the organization for which they work could not pay so sizable an increase. These people would often be poor workers; they would face unemployment because businesses could not economically hire them. They too would draw on their life accounts until the economy adjusts to the point where they could be rehired at higher wages. (I might remind you that the 20 percent and more persons referred to in 5 and 6 are already dependent upon governments and pay many hidden taxes.)

The persons who would have substantial temporary difficulties because of the new tax would also be compensated for by the 10 percent of all taxes now collected that are dissipated in disagreeable tax-fulfillment activities; by the more efficient operation of corporations; and by the greater initiative and productivity of those engaged in work.

PESCALA: The Personal Social Contract and Life Account

The single head tax is geared into a general plan for reorganizing the pay structure of the economy. This is called the personal social contract and life account. It is distinct from the single head-tax system, but connected with it, as a balancing mechanism.

The personal social contract is the system by which society acknowledges and affirms every person's worth. Every living person is worth the value of his existence. Each person at birth receives an account—a drawing and depository account.[6]

6. You may recognize in my model here a relative of numerous recent proposals—by Milton Friedman, Richard Nixon, George McGovern, and others—for negative income taxes, supplementary grants for all the poor, and universal minimum income maintenance. I believe that the drawing account should rise quickly

To pursue an example in the U.S.A., a person may draw $2000 per year (in 1972 dollars) whenever he or she pleases. For those under sixteen, this money has to be beneficially accounted for by a trustee, usually a parent. The account is continually debited. When the beneficiary works or receives income, he or she may make deposits to the account—at the least the amount of the head tax. If one passes a year's draw, it is not retrievable.

In a seventy-year life-span, a person may draw $140,000. During the same lifetime he or she would pay $105,000 in head taxes. The total debits to the account would therefore amount to $245,000.

We see that the person has a base annual income of $2000 for all of his or her years, even though this money is a debt owed the account. This $140,000 has to be credited to one's account.

A person may work as the average worker does now from the age of 20 to the age of 65 for forty-five years. Suppose that person averages $10,000 per year. This produces a total of $450,000. In addition, he or she receives $140,000 from PESCALA. His lifetime receipts then total $590,000. Subtract from this total lifetime social obligations of $245,000. This leaves $345,000 of income that may be disposed of flexibly. This brings about $4929 per year over the whole lifetime. Naturally, one's actual spending in any given year might be more or less than this sum, depending upon one's age, needs, desires, current earnings, and so forth. Now let us follow the example of a family of four over a shorter span of time, twenty years.

Actually, in the illustration, the family might in some years decide not to draw on their life accounts, and the income and debit items would therefore cancel each other. Note that the children's accounts are being deliberately balanced by their parents during this time. That means that the children can enter their work life free of debits, and in later life could take care of their parents. Or, the parents could save for their old age and let their children's debits mount up and be paid off by the children later on.

How would people earn, on the average, $11,000? People now "earn" close to this average. They should readily earn more if properly paid for their work.[7] The costly and inefficient tax system takes some of their money; corporations and employers hold back some for unemployment reserves and old-age payments; but even more, the surpluses created by the workers are partially misappropriated by the system of corporate ownership and consequent income distribution. Moreover, as already suggested, employers would redistribute as increased wages former corporate or profit taxes and the costs of tax compliance.

---

from $2000 to whatever a true minimum subsistence or survival income must be. If the sum is too small, many burdensome and complicated programs will have to continue and the expected improvement in morale will not be felt.

7. When the total system is shaken down, the typical American income would go up to about $30,000 per year during the high-earning decades of life.

A) For the Year 1973

	Receipts		Debits	
	Life Account	Wages	Life Account	Tax
Father	$2000	$11,000	$2000	$1500
Mother	2000	—	2000	1500
Boy	2000	—	2000	1500
Girl	2000	—	2000	1500
Totals	$8000	$11,000	$8000	$6000

Disposable funds = $19,000 − $6000 = $13,000.

Accumulated life account deficit for year = $8000 (allocated to each life account).

If family lives at $5000 spending level, then deficit = 0.

B) For the Period of 20 Years

	Receipts		Debits	
	Life Account	Wages	Life Account	Tax
Father	$ 40,000	$220,000	$ 40,000	$ 30,000
Mother	40,000	50,000 (part-time work)	40,000	30,000
Boy	40,000	3,000 (part-time work)	40,000	30,000
Girl	40,000	3,000 (part-time work)	40,000	30,000
Totals	$160,000	$276,000	$160,000	$120,000

Disposable funds = $436,000 − $120,000 = $316,000.

Disposable after repayment of life account debits = $316,000 − $160,000 = $156,000 (or $7800 per year on the average).

Why People Would Continue to Work

People would wish to balance their life accounts because the balancing is obligatory. The head-tax payment out of current assets and earnings is mandatory, like any other tax today. The balancing obligation is taught in the schools, and audited by a personally chosen "social technician" at five-year intervals during life. The social technician is a family-affairs consultant trained in home economics, psychotherapy, preventive medicine, and family law. The social technician is a professional agent, chosen voluntarily by a person, just as a lawyer, doctor, or teacher might be chosen. Many occupations and semiprofessions are veering toward this professional need already, so that the actual creation of the profession would not be difficult. The social technician would advise a person or family group, upon request, on how to balance their accounts, and would send a copy of their five-year balance-sheet report to an accounts agency.

The accounts of 200 million people could be computerized. Each year, warning signals would emerge from an automatic examination of the file, showing that various persons were venturing into excessively heavy obligations. These signal thresholds would have to be defined in general laws by a legislature before they were used by the accounts agency to ask for a special audit from the person's social technician.

The present system of allocating welfare benefits is far more complicated and unjust than what would occur naturally under the PESCALA system. Tangled and difficult formulas are used to determine who is "entitled" to services.

People would also work, as they do now, to improve their own lives and property, and to extend benefits to others. They would work to earn an expendable surplus, as they do now. They would work because they like to work; in order to be with others; because there is not much else they want to do with their lives; because their work is socially useful; and in order to avoid disrespect.

Those who challenge the proposed system, claiming that "people are irresponsible," should admit that such is precisely the case under the present economic system and it is getting worse; more and more people are becoming dependent, poor, harassed, trivialized, and impersonalized. The number of welfare cases in New York City alone is over 1.3 million, an increase of nearly 1 million in one decade. "Twelve years ago, in 1960, there were 9.7 wage and salary employees in the private sector in New York for every *one* welfare recipient. The ratio for 1971 was 2.6 private sector employees for each person on welfare."[8] Before you get angry at the "welfare mess," consider the "farm mess" and others; an estimated 25 percent of all American farmers' net income came from government subsidies.

Government budgets in the United States would have a much different form, and of course the changes that they signify would be profound. They would be part of a total societal budget, which itself would be more of a prediction than a compulsory directive. The clumsy, deceitful, and incomprehensible present government budgets would be replaced by simple plans with wide-range meaning.

8. Michael Kramer, "The City Politic," *New York*, Vol. 5, No. 24, June 12, 1972, p. 13.

The advantages of this social accounting system can be made explicit. PESCALA would permit a person to have an environment structured for maximum self-development and responsibility. People could spend more of their lives and resources on better activities. Corporations and groups would become more the property and creatures of those for whose benefit they are accorded life and rights in society. A person would know what he owes, why he owes it, what he gets, why he gets it, and be backed up by social technicians who work for him rather than for the bureaucracy.

In any event, the poor and rich alike would receive their social credit each year and could draw upon it if they wish. Those who are "unemployable" because of disability, age, or automation would receive social credit each year and could draw upon it if they wished. Our aim must be to lift by great power the real incomes of the independent poor and middle classes to a level at which whatever is given the poor is beyond envy. The productivity of the whole society must be elevated until the income of the mass of direct producers puts them well beyond the level where they might be obsessed by invidious comparisons.

The Fate of Wealth

Society, rather than the individual or government, should inherit wealth. The advantages that normally accrue to people in their lifetimes should not pass to any descendant or favored person of the next generation. Large inheritances block freedom of opportunity and cause concentrations of power. They are increasingly a curse on the happiness of those who receive them. However, it is well to permit modest family inheritances; their complete abolition would cut many pleasant sentimental bonds between the generations and make the older generation sad at not being able to take care of exceptional or handicapped descendants.

Therefore, inheritance laws should prevent large fortunes from being carried into the second generation. A person might accumulate and spend at pleasure during his lifetime, but during life and at death he must pass his accumulation only to certain categories of beneficiaries. He might, for example, be permitted to give or leave to a member of his family and other individuals no more than fifty times the sum set for the annual life accounts credit. In the U.S.A., using the PESCALA example, no person might be given, or inherit, more than $100,000. This sum would permit an heir to invest in a small new enterprise; or, if disabled, artistic, or somehow excluded from earnings, the heir would have an extra $100,000 beyond the minimal PESCALA stipend. Those who could be given or who would inherit the sum might be any surviving parents, spouse, and children of the benefactor plus two others; thus, a surviving spouse, a mother, three children, and two friends might each receive an equal inheritance.

All sums above this amount should be disbursed at death to certain eligible beneficiaries willed during life, or in the absence of a last will, to nongovernmental groups along the lines of a person's typical benefactions when alive, as administered by a permanent court-appointed board of trustees. The government is *not* to accumulate wealth by death. The eligible categories include new or old corporations as a gift to their capital, including university corporations, charitable corporations, and other groups, but not excluding gifts to ordinary corporations that a person admires but holds no stock in. I stress that the estates of the rich should not go to aggrandize government. Instead, they should continually refresh the voluntary and independent sectors of society.

Spaceship Earth

Suppose we are given a world in which the government's compulsory tax power is under control, every person has a secure subsistence, and the influence of inherited fortunes is greatly reduced. What is the greatest economic problem that politics still faces?

Earth is a self-contained spaceship in which the U.S.A. is an instrument system. Thus, the U.S.A. has to be changed into a better instrument for world leadership. To do this, Americans have to find leaders who are radical and competent. And they will have to readjust their own minds to new life attitudes and life activities.

We can only point to this grand objective here and exhort your attention. Even if we succeed with our three major reform systems, the overall world production system needs drastic change and leadership.

THE GROWTH FETISH REEXAMINED & REFASHIONED

The poor animal that the Growth Fetishists worship looks like this: because of <u>MISORIENTATION</u> (wrong and contradictory goals),

which, after correction, still leaves us with <u>MALDISTRIBUTION</u>,

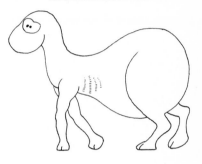

which, after correction, still leaves us with <u>MALORGANIZATION</u>,

which, after correction, still leaves us with <u>WASTE</u>, <u>FRAUD</u>, and <u>UNCONSIDERED COSTS</u>,

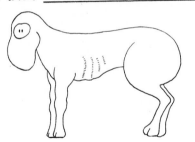

which, after correction, finally gives us this fine charging steed, <u>THE KALOTIC WORLD ECONOMY</u>.

Hence, the fourth welfare goal is to refashion the world GNP of 2+trillion dollars so that it deserves this image. That is, achieve a kalotic GNP for the upcoming world.

Chapter 10
Law and Justice

Law is what legislatures say must or must not be done.
   Like a law to prohibit speeding.
No. Law is what bureaucrats say must be done.
   Like a law to label certain bottles "poison."
No. Law is what most people obey.
   Like laws against killing people.
No. Law is what police and prosecuting attorneys say it is.
   Like, "It's OK to park there," even though it's illegal. Or like, "If you plead guilty to creating a disturbance, I won't charge you with arson."
No. Law is what judges say it is in cases coming before them.
   Like, "It's constitutional to force a man to serve in the army."
No. Law is what a person should or shouldn't do.
   Like, don't bribe building inspectors while building a hotel.
No. No. No.   Yes. Yes. Yes.
   Have it your own way. In these pages, we'll bring out all of these meanings in one way or another.

*   *   *   *   *

HISTORICAL DIVERSION: Once upon a time, people usually believed in the *law of tradition.* If it has been done this way before, it works, so that's the way it must be done now. Sometimes this was called *common law* or *tribal law.*

In addition there was the law fashioned out of naked power, "Do it and don't ask questions"; or of divinity, "God wills it; I speak for Him"; or of expediency and heroes, "Follow me and you'll go places."

Today most laws are on the books partly because they've never been taken off, but mainly because in the last century and a half the idea fixed itself on the Western world that society could be reconstructed by passing laws.

Now I believe in this principle too, so I would like to attack it only partially. The world can be reconstructed through the laws only if we know the nature of law, who obeys it, who carries it out, what its results are—and only then would we know whether *law in the solemn sense of the majesty of law* is the best way to get things done through law. In other words, this nineteenth-century notion of law was unfortunately a simplistic belief that if you declared something was law, that was what behavior would be.

Therefore, I should like to suggest Principle X.

PRINCIPLE X

Law should be whatever it takes to make future human conduct what we would like it to be.

That is, law is a directive that is designed to make the future better for people. If it doesn't, it is bad law and should be corrected as soon as possible. (At this point, all of my readers who are connoisseurs of John Dewey, Oliver Wendell Holmes, Brandeis, Cardozo, or their followers will smell some old sausages frying, and they are right; essentially what I am preaching is law as experimental or hypothetical probes into the future.) What I believe will result from this theory of law is that for once we shall have law that will help solve human problems instead of making them worse!

"What do you mean, author, making them worse? Nothing is worse than non-law."

"Nothing is worse, dear hold-on-to-your-whatever-it-is-lest-you-lose-it, I agree." But pretty close to the worse is what we have now.

The Six Dikaic Improbabilities

(or what is bad about present law, especially in the United States of America, because other countries are not modern enough to have had a chance to be "Americanized.")

By *dikaic*[1] I mean juridical in my meaning of what is good law, justice. By "improbability" I am arbitrarily asserting that in each and every case there is a likelihood of only one out of five, say, that justice is being done. Here they are:

1. Not one true offense in five against persons and groups is named a crime. For example, to be hostile or aggressive against a harmless person is a moral offense. But it is not a crime in the law. You can say, "I hate foreigners," or you can give people a shabby deal, or you can take a sadistic delight in their sufferings and no police will arrest you or prosecuting attorney indict you. You can go through life hurting thousands of people without violating any law. You can hassle your husband or wife, beat your child (up to a certain limit), play destructive games of all kinds against your fellow men, and nobody will drag you before the bar of justice. You can abandon your friends, betray your associates, be a goldbrick or a squanderer, etc., etc., and be a law-abiding citizen. In fact, you can be a disgusting scoundrel without violating a law on the statute books.

All right. We admit all this. So let us go on to the next dikaic improbability.

2. Five times more actions are labeled criminal than should be. For example, in New Jersey, you can be an excellent driver, sober, safe, considerate, but unless you are seventeen you are a criminal if you are behind the wheel and your vehicle is in motion. It scarcely matters that you are driving on an errand of mercy.

Or you can be (in the 1930s) a person who likes a scotch and soda after a hard day's work and be a criminal. Or (in 1973) you can be a person who likes to smoke a cigarette made of marijuana plant instead of tobacco plant and be a criminal.

Or you can be a builder in New York City and want approval of your plans and construction by the inspectors involved, and you can wait until shrimps whistle for your proper papers unless you pay bribes, which is a crime.

Or you can get a divorce in some places most easily by committing

1. It comes from the classical Greek *dikeos* or "just rule of law."

or confessing adultery, so you are encouraged to commit or admit to a crime in order to gain a liberty.

It is a crime to spit on the sidewalk, let your dog run without a leash, keep your lawn unmowed, or fail to mend or paint your house in many places.

In fact, given so many crimes manufactured wholesale by legislatures and executive agencies, if people stopped committing crimes the whole productive, artistic, inventive, familial, political, and other social machinery of the country would grind to a stop. (President Franklin D. Roosevelt once joked that he was breaking 299 laws a day.) Only by continuous and wholesale "criminal" activity can society live and breathe.

Most impressive of all crimes that are not crimes are actions performed by persons who did not know what they were doing, did not know how not to do what they were doing, did not know that what they were doing was criminal and anyhow were not in possession of *their* normal or *others'* normal faculties when they were doing it.

One of the worst crimes against humanity is the fiction piously announced by courts everywhere that "ignorance of the law is no excuse." If ignorance of the law were no excuse, millions of persons in the U.S.A. would be in jails that are miserable habitations for one-tenth as many. But still, ignorance of the law does cause a great many crimes that cannot be crimes except by the most "savage" theory of personal responsibility. In addition to managing to live in a very complicated society, a person is supposed to know all the laws governing his complicated existence!

3. Under such circumstances, it should be no surprise to hear it said that not one legally defined crime in five enters the judicial system. That is, actions that are called crimes by the law usually do not result in arrests. Partly, this is the result of what has already been said, namely that too many actions are crimes unknown as such to the actors. But more than that are payoffs, favoritism, class prejudices, and incompetence of the enforcement machinery. In America where the records of crimes are only beginning to improve, for every 100 reported crimes an average of 18 persons were charged.[2] This is about 1 in 5. But most crimes go unreported—vandalism, gambling, pilfering, racketeering, robberies, assaults, rapes, bribery, swindles, etc., in large numbers. So the rate of charges is much lower.

Let us not pause on incompetence. The methods of most police forces in the detection of crime and arrest of criminals are the subject of countless negative reports. Much of the criticism comes from national agencies in the U.S.A., such as the Federal Bureau of Investigation, and many Americans rightly prefer local "bad" rule to distant "good" rule.

---

2. *The New York Times*, April 6, 1970, p. 35, covering the period 1961–68 (seven years).

Police crimes are not often reported, we need scarcely add.

In an eleven-month study of the police and crime patterns in eight slum precincts in Washington, Chicago and Boston, Dr. Albert J. Reiss of the University of Michigan's Bureau of Social Research found that, "Altogether, 27 percent of all the officers were either observed in misconduct situations or admitted to observers that they had engaged in misconduct." Misconduct is a mild word for what the report elsewhere cites as "behavior that could be classified as a felony or a misdemeanor." The major classes of police misbehavior were shakedowns of traffic violators, businessmen, drunks, and deviants; thefts from burglarized establishments; acceptance of payoffs to return stolen property, to alter testimony in trial, and to protect illegal establishments. The carrying of weapons by policemen to plant on citizens as "evidence" in case a police officer injures or kills someone was also found on occasion. Shakedowns for free meals, for drinks, and other small favors were so common that they were simply excluded from the Reiss study.[3]

4. Not one arrest in five ends as an indictment that is appropriate to the crime. That is, if a person is arrested, he is supposed to be arraigned or brought before a court of law where a judge agrees or disagrees with the reasons why he has been arrested. He may be held or released on bond. (A charged person with a record often cannot afford bond unless he is protected by bigger crooks.) Then he is brought to trial later on, charged with a crime. The naive public believes that this charge has something to do with the crime. So it does, but in the same sense that a St. Bernard and a Chihuahua are both dogs.

It is common to book (i.e., place on the police record) a defendant on as many and as serious offenses as possible so that he can be pressured later on to confess to the least of the charges. Thus he will be charged with attempted homicide in order to try him later on the charge of assault and battery. This works both ways; a well-connected upstanding citizen will find himself miraculously charged with assault when he really attempted to kill somebody.

The courts are congested beyond belief, so hundreds of thousands of cases each year are kept out of court by private deals with the police, the prosecutors, the bailiffs, and the judges. The whole system is so rotten that honest men get caught up in it and make matters worse by trying to work inside of it. In this chaos there is almost nothing of rational pretrial handling of an arrest, considered in the context both of the crime and of the larger needs of the society.

RIGHTS IN COURT: We are already into the judicial, or *procedural legal rights.* A *right* is whatever you do that the government will protect you in

3. Louis A. Radelet, "Police-Community Relations," *Proceedings of the Third Annual Conference on Human Relations. March 29, 1969.* (East Lansing: Michigan State University, Office of Human Relations, Institute for Community Development and Services), p. 3.

doing. In contests at law, it is the court, of course, that gives whatever procedural rights are available.

5. Not one defendant in five gets due process of law. These procedural rights* include protection against persecution; illegal detention; coerced confession; unreasonable search and seizure; sheer confiscation of property; inadequate notice of trial; no proper hearing; denial of counsel; denial of a speedy trial; compulsory self-incrimination; trial twice for the same offense (double jeopardy); cruel and unusual punishment; trial for a criminal act that was not a crime when the act was committed (i.e., an *ex post facto* law); and laws that are so vague that no one can understand them.

Cardinal Richelieu, virtual ruler of France during one of its most glorious periods, once said with both truth and humor, "Give me any sentence a man has ever uttered, and I'll give you enough cause to hang him."

Where do we stand on such rights? We have already said it: It's highly improbable that a defendant in a criminal case (and in many cases between private parties, in civil cases, that is) will get all of them. The poor, the black, the young, the stranger, the hippie, the woman, you may be sure, get less of them. The ordinary woman or man will go broke if she or he should become embroiled in the legal process.

Gresham Sykes, the Director of Studies of the Administration of Justice at the University of Denver Law Center, has said that the legal needs of the poor are overwhelming. A study he did found an average of three legal needs per poor family.

So multiply three times twenty million families and you have sixty million matters awaiting due process of law. But, you see, the whole social,

Class Test on Civil Rights

*Let's try the hypothetical method of establishing the credibility of these statements. Ask for a personal or a familiar experience from the members of a group reading these pages. Remember that a college class is far above the law in comparison with the majority of the population:

1. Has anyone been followed or stopped or searched by the police because he's known to them and they don't like him?

2. Has anyone been held in jail beyond the reasonable time it takes to get help and bail?

3. Has anyone been frightened into a confession?

4. Has anyone been searched or had his house searched without a proper warrant? (Or do you know what a proper warrant is?)

5. Has anybody had things confiscated by police or customs officers with no real chance to pursue the return of the property?

6. Has anyone received a finely printed document that he later discovered to be a summons to a trial?

7. Has anyone been brought before a police desk sergeant and a court and heard some gibberish and then learned that he had just had a hearing?

8. Has anyone been beaten by police, wardens, teachers, etc., not in self-defense?

9. Has anyone had a delayed and slow trial?

10. Has anyone discovered that he had to confess to one offense if he wanted to avoid trial on a graver charge?

11. Has anyone suffered a trial in a state court and then another in a federal court for the same offense? (This is technically not double jeopardy.)

12. Has anyone been surprised to learn that what he had always been doing was now a crime because somebody decided to enforce some law? (This is technically not **ex post facto**.)

13. Has anyone had an indifferent or bad lawyer, who took too little time to prepare a case?

14. Did anybody ever get into trouble because of a law that was incomprehensible to him?

Some of these violations of due process of law might not be technical or legal violations. Others are. My presumption is that in a class of twenty college students speaking honestly about themselves and their families and friends, there would be several examples of each violation of due process of law. What is said in the classroom does not, unfortunately, wear the same confidential cloak that confidences to a lawyer or a doctor have, so my advice is to not confess to any offense that will cause reprisals or disciplinary (without due process of law) school action. The enemy may be listening!

political, and legal order is chaotic; it's all of one piece. You cannot hire a million lawyers for the poor and then another million for all others. There are far less than a million lawyers in the whole country, and, even if they were not misoccupied for the most part with ensnarling each other and their clients in socially unproductive ways, they could not service chaos. The whole social order suffers from a lack of love, of accommodation, of care, of organization for the essential needs of people. Ways must be found of preventive law, just like preventive medicine.

6. When a person is adjudged guilty, he or she has no better than one chance in five of receiving treatment or punishment that will cure him. Society is the other side of the coin, so, forgetting the individual for the moment, how does society fare? We must still insist that society too has no better than one chance in ten of coming out of the punishing or sanctioning process better than it went in.

The city and county jails of New York, wrote a State Senate Committee in 1969, are "more fertile breeding grounds for crime than the street." Karl Menninger, one of America's greatest psychiatrists, a doer and a thinker both, calls the system of criminal justice in America "a public ritual of theatrical character," "a social monstrosity." This is in his book, *The Crime of Punishment.*[4]

Around the country, prisoners are restless. Sometimes they riot and revolt. What do they want? A change of clothing. A right to see their families. Freedom from beatings. A little more space to stretch in. Something less than total civil death. These are what a million people a year want.

They do not want what prison reformers, a small handful of idealists, dream of—cure instead of punishment, punishment calculated to avoid the next crime, clean prisons, intelligent and trained wardens and guards, reeducation, self-government, and, yes, especially the abolition of prisons. They do not dare to want these things that they should have and would have if they could ever feel free to think about the universal concept of justice as what one would do to himself to be just and to be justly dealt with. They must think only of the barest human necessities: survival, bodily integrity, and affection from someone who may still love them.

What does society wish of them? What is the interest of society in the "guilty" (who, remember, are only an unrepresentative fraction of the millions who are guilty but not in prisons). Unconsciously, society wishes terrible things. (By society we mean most of the people some of the time, many people most of the time, and those who work in the area of crime— the punishment elite—a great deal of time, for they are *self-selected*.)

4. New York: The Viking Press, Inc., 1968.

Aggression and indeed asocial aggression dominates criminal law, including even the legislature and the criminal law philosophers; aggression controls the spirit of criminal law.

A profession related to the enforcement of criminal justice, which makes use of force to such a degree, and moreover has need of it, attracts the aggressive elements in society, for it provides an excellent opportunity for exercising aggression.

The criminal law is built around counteraggression. It conjures a war. Like other armies, if it cannot find criminals, it will try to create them.

Man is neurotically fixed on crime and the criminal . . . he places the whole force of his projection on to the asocial . . . in the same breath he fights and preserves the criminal. . . .

So speaks the Swiss criminologist Paul Reiwald.[5]

The crimes of punishment are like war crimes. They are collective acts of a society, performed in its name by officials and leaders, of which the members of the society profess ignorance. If the crimes of punishment are to be avoided, we need a new class of police leaders, prosecuting attorneys, judges, and wardens (or substitutes for them). Prison and other sanctions (fines, probation, injunctions, compulsory mental institutions) cannot be improved bit by bit. A heavy wave of reform has to batter our whole system of law and order, washing it away and setting up in its place a new system worthy of American culture and humanity.

To sum up the probability of complete justice, we could not of course assume that all of these improbabilities are operating in every instance in which an offense is allegedly committed, but we must admit that there is a staggering probability of a miscarriage of justice occurring in the history of any given instance. Whether the chance of some mishap occurring in the system is a million to one or ten to one is too complex a question for anyone but the statisticians. We must be satisfied with a more prosaic proposition.

PROPOSITION X

The present system of law and justice profusely breeds laws, law cases, failures of law, and disgust and disrespect in regards to law.

What needs to be done?

5. Paul Reiwald, *Society and Its Criminals*, trans. and ed. T. E. James (New York: International Universities Press, 1950), pp. 261, 289.

Lofty Judges and Lowly Criminals

Could it be that in the most civilized societies[6] the loftiest judges and the lowliest criminals are in the greatest accord on what the law should be like?

To operationalize this question, you'd have to do something like this:

1. Take a Supreme Court Justice who is highly regarded by the "best," "most reputable" scholars, attorneys, and judges. Add a typical affluent businessman. Choose a typical salaried worker, a skilled worker, an unskilled manual worker, and, finally, a typical delinquent.

2. Ask them the following questions:

—Are there many bad laws?

—Are there enough means for an accused person to get justice?

—Is our good old American system of law and justice the best there is anywhere?

Chances are that the judge and delinquent will say Yes, No, No; the others will say No, Yes, Yes.

Don't accept my test. You can draw up a much better one yourself.

Maybe the reason for this strange phenomenon is hidden in St. Augustine's words: "If justice be disregarded, what is a king but a mighty robber? Since what is a robber but a little king?"[7]

Suppose our typical characters 2, 3, 4, and 5 above got into trouble with the law. I suspect that they would suddenly start shouting Yes, No, No, instead of No, Yes, Yes. And they would try their best to define "the means for an accused person to get justice" in eloquent terms worthy of a high judge—and of a general delinquent. For, when it comes down to reality, justice and law in a society tend to be made and kicked about by the citizens who think that they won't get into trouble, while the high justices and the lowly delinquents know that troubles are not the causes of law but that laws often cause trouble, or, in any case, tend to aggravate it.

Hence, we say, everyone should be persuaded to think like a typical delinquent in order to be able to think about law and justice. We could say, "or like a high judge," except that it is less difficult for an ordinary person to think like a delinquent than a judge, even though he imagines himself to be a high judge.

We might even say that universal justice should be developed out of every person's capacity for self-inquisition. How do you like that for *anarchy?*

---

6. Defined as societies with the largest proportion of people who have read many good books, appreciated *good* food and fine art, are interested in the customs of other people, etc.

7. *The City of God* (413–26 A.D.), IV, 4.

You are seventeen and you are hanging out by a gas station at Kankakee, Illinois, and you watch an old car drive in and pick up a couple of gallons of gas. There's a guy hot and sweating who's driving and he gets out to put some water in the steaming radiator. The car has several people in it. They look like Mexicans or something and all the junk and people make the rear springs sag. The tires are bald and you bet they couldn't pass a safety test. And the fat lady looks like she's going to have a baby. And the skinny dark girl inside has a wild look in her eye. You figure that if they're going to Chicago they're going to have a hard time making it before dark. Then you forget it because your friend comes up and you split.

What you've seen are Troubles—six, eight, fifteen—who knows? They've been hit by the law before, and they'll be hit again. And every time they do something, some authorities will be on their backs, and each time the law will make things worse for them, not better. And if you try to think of what good is going to happen to them in the next couple of years, about all you can be sure of is that the skinny girl is going to say when the car rises on the enormous skyway to show the rearing-up mass of concrete Chicago, "Now ain't that sumpin', Mama?" And later the baby will be born, and the old lady will say, "Ain't he a cute li'l fellow? Looks like Henry used to, don't you think? 'Course he's gone now."

It's not so bad, when you remember:
**That most criminals go unpunished.
**That most people punish themselves better than the authorities anyway.
**That the job of trying people is usually bungled.
**That people everywhere in the world have a pretty good notion of what it would take to defend themselves properly (especially the best judges and the general delinquents)!

If we granted this statement that all people agree as to what justice is, we should simply impose upon the police and courts those procedures that are universally agreed to. However, we shall take a shortcut. Rather than try to teach everyone according to Socrates' principle of "know thyself," we shall go directly to a policy based upon our own notion of justice:

POLICY X

Impose upon all penalizing powers the views of a future society where conflicts and offenses are treated systematically, equitably, and benevolently.

Comment:

Who shall "impose"? The ruling public, as it is created, shall impose, through its representatives.

"Penalizing powers" include all organs of society that can force people to follow a prescribed course of action and punish them heavily if they do not. "Heavily" means that one or more of the six value positions of the penalized person is significantly affected in his or her own terms—as, for example, confinement (power), fines (wealth), bad publicity (respect), ostracism (love), therapy (health), education (knowledge), or as in the following combination:

Carl: Well, Old Al's done it again!

Frank: What now?

Carl: The Association of Judges awarded him the "Jeremy" prize for his judgment on that bank clerk who stole his own mother's savings.

Frank: What did he do?

Carl: He ordered the guy to work every weekend for six months without pay at the Latter Day Rest Home, to write about his experiences to the court psychologist and to publish an explanation of his actions and experiences in the Court Journal within a year.

Frank: What about paying back his old lady?

Carl: That too.

"Views of a future society" means that justice should look forward to the way things are becoming, not backward to what they once were.

The terms "systematically, equitably, and benevolently" are involved in the six reform proposals that will now be offered.

* * * * *

In February 1971, the day when we discussed in a class at New York University what should be done about giving a basic income outright to the poorest part of the population, a man offended the sensibilities of the class by saying that nothing could be done and each person should fend for himself.

A few days later, the same man entered the discussion of law by reciting an experience. Walking with his girlfriend, he accosted two policemen who were beating up a stranger. He tried to intercede. They beat him up as well, while a third kept his friend from interfering. Later on, he visited every apartment in the area to find witnesses to the event. Not only did he fail, but he was looked upon as a threat and a queer. (I might add that he is "masculine," pink-skinned, sturdy, well groomed, doesn't curse, and has an open, frank look.) His depressing experience probably reinforced whatever beliefs he might have that the only way to survive is "every man for himself."

When a huge society begins to decompose, a vicious cycle sets in: people withdraw from social concerns at the very moment when they should be mustering up civic courage. When others see them withdraw, these give up too. Soon the society is in full retreat. Nothing but a reactionary counterrevolution of the right or left, or a constructive revolution can stop the retreat.

Anyone who believes that the courts will or can render legal process where it is due, is without proof, is politically naive, and is bereft of any sense of urgency. One who relies solely upon commissions of inquiry and other palliatives for reform anywhere is too weakly motivated to trust; results, not reports, must be demanded. A purely formal system of law can provide exquisite protection to an affluent party in a closed society, but it is unlikely to realize itself in changing times because it lacks political dynamism. The revolution of the degraded legal systems of most countries can come about only in conjunction with general social revolution in local, national, and international spheres of human activity.

Political Orders Usually Make Justice Impossible

We have concentrated our reform proposals upon the legal system. We should remind you, however, that a political order reflects its social order and a special political order, such as the legal system, reflects the general political order and in turn the social order. A grave problem that no society has ever settled for all of its people is how to assure that the governmental order as a whole does not make it impossible for the court system to grant everyone a fair chance to resist and be heard. Since governments have a near monopoly of power, a few idealists and revolutionaries have been seeking without much success to solve this problem for thousands of years.

The best solutions that have been produced in all of this time are the following:

*Keep governments weak. If they don't do too much, they can't do as much damage. (But then gangsterism of the private kind abounds, and exploitation also, unless governments that are inactive are strong as well.)

*Keep governments corrupt: If governments can be bribed from all sides, a kind of rough justice can be preserved, a hearing can be had, etc.

*Keep them incompetent. If they cannot run anything well, they can't try to do as much. (If they can't set up a computer system, they can't check I.D. cards.)

*Let people govern themselves.

*Make the branches of government correct each other. If the legislative committee violates a person's right to be tried by fair process of law, then the courts can refuse to let that individual be sentenced. Or if the police get evidence by torture, the courts can throw out the evidence.

*And, finally, do not forget our old friend and cure-all, education.
If children are brought up to respect the rights of others, a lot of injustice can be avoided later on, especially injustices of procedure. If they are educated in details, all the better. In every child's storybook there should be a tale about each and every procedural right. Now they learn their rights as they learn their sex—in the gutter.

My belief is that a combination of education, checks and balances, and self-government are the best assurances of civil liberties. However, in all of these respects governments and societies are still retarded, unimaginative, undetermined.

Changing the Legal System

If the general political order is moving ahead kalotically, then even changes of staggering proportions in the legal system can be accomplished. These might be the following:

1. A rewriting of the law and a junking of much of the old law.

2. A reconstitution of the science of social (individual) deviance to make it more relevant to urgent social problems and their solution.

3. The reform of methods of selecting cases for presentation before the institutions of justice. Much more thoroughgoing and systematic investigation, psychological screening of contestants, mediation, arbitration, and other less formal procedures should precede and often preclude heavily formal court action.

4. A drastic revision of jurisprudence, which first merges social justice with law, and then merges psychology and sociology with legal procedures and legal sanctions.

5. A parallel reconstitution of the science of lawmaking by *legislatures* to lift from the courts their burdens in this regard. To say that the U.S.A. and its states "are governments by legislature" takes too much for granted. The legislatures, in an understandable but timid way, have shoveled off important responsibilities, originally granted to them, onto the courts—in the fields of civil rights, crime, war and peace, and economic regulation, for example. But the courts, which are constituted to work well on a case-to-case basis, cannot cope with the problems of overall policy-making without damage to their real jobs.

6. Vastly increased allocation of social resources to treat torts and crimes; the reeducation of all participants in the social control machinery; more judges; new neighborhood courts; selection of jurors through new sampling forms; a great expansion of the social counselor functions for families in trouble.

A Virtual Model of Justice

An effective technique for bringing about some of these changes would be the organization of a *virtual* judicial system. (See box.) Those who wish to revolutionize the law can write new codes of laws, set up "courts" to try cases under them, and process all who would come before them. Each case should be conceived and processed in its total context—true judicial planning, that is. Especially invited to participate should be all those caught up in the toils of the existing system. Then let the world match this model of justice with present justice.

Virtual or Shadow Rule

Virtual means "being so in effect or essence, though not in name or formally." Thus, Edmund Burke, the eighteenth-century English philosopher of traditional conservatism used the term "virtual representation" in asserting that persons who didn't have the right to vote or whose votes were not counted equally nevertheless were "virtually represented" by the members of a legislature who *had* been elected by other voters. He assumed a connection that may have been partially there, but never in the magnified way he imagined. American colonists of the time, for example, were furious at the use of this presumptuous term and raised the cry of "no taxation without representation."

But we are now reversing E. B.'s conservatism and using the term for a radical purpose, making "virtual" pertain to what is good in fact and in being, even though it is not yet the law or the government. Virtual institutions and virtual processes might be set up to compete with many government institutions, waiting for the moment to step in and become the right way *in law* as in fact. In this connection, it is well to recall, in addition to the examples cited on the next page and in the chapter on governmental activities, the thousands of independent organizations in the U.S.A.—from the Boy Scouts to Ralph Nader's "Raiders"—that perform public functions. Some of these groups should, and some need not, have "virtual governmental processes"; that is, some should, and some should not, move directly into the governmental institutions that are performing badly.

Let an accident victim, a boy accused of drug pushing, a couple wishing to separate, a student expelled from college, a manufacturer beset by the tax authorities—yes, even a murderer—try a parallel route to justice. But then also, remembering the first dikaic improbability of justice, bring persons before the bar who would not otherwise come before it as well as release those who have been failed in one or more ways by the prevailing scheme. How is the base disregard of moral, aesthetic, traffic, and structural standards in the erection of a huge building to be compared with the crime of stealing a car? How is hostile prejudice against a group to be dealt with if dropping out of school before the legal age is an "offense" that stigmatizes the poor generally and ethnic and racial groupings as well?

Then, as the new model obscures the old, it can be moved in, and the old legal system abandoned.

End of Chapter

??? End of Chapter ???

"Author, get back to work. You can't stop so abruptly! I mean, you can't expect me to go out just like that and start up a new LEGAL system!"

"Why not? The early Christians did it in their catacombs. The Jews have done it throughout history. The Puritans did it. The early Catholics in America did it. The Methodists, the Evangelicals did it. All sorts of cults, sects, hippie communes, tribes, and castes have done so in history. Even the underworld does it, and so do the prisoners in penitentiaries. Do you see? All you need is a good philosophy or morality about human relations and enough people who agree with you. You begin to practice right conduct. You try to get cases resolved in a manner appropriate to your moral system. And, voilà, you have a virtual legal system, competing with the state, minus the coercion that the state seeks to monopolize. Meanwhile you bring pressures all along the line to reform the state structure and, sooner or later, it will give up in your favor.

"In effect, a number of students, lawyers, welfare workers, governmental officers, and professors have formed kalotic gangs around America already, where they are studying and working within the system for justice. They should go one step further and treat their work and clients according to a hypothetical virtual system, even if they are not able yet to substitute the virtual system formally in place of the established systems."

"OK, but one more question? What do we do with all these courses on public law, constitutional law, and with the law schools?"

"Well, there's nothing like some of these beautiful legal opinions that judges write. Clever, hairsplitting, profound, literary, contradictory; they are lots of fun once you get into the spirit of the game. And the payoffs can be high in conventional prestige and money if you play the law game well. If you can endure the long process of legal training, you become a magpie; a search warrant would find your house full of pins, buttons, hair, and baubles. You will also have the keen eye of a magpie and can advise clients on all manner of ways to avoid and overcome legal hassles. Meanwhile, you can do a lot of good because the same social system that throws a lot of good men into the army, throws a lot of good men into the legal profession."

"You mean, become a lawyer?"

"Why not?"

End of Chapter
(and I *mean* it)

Chapter 11

Obedience and the State

MAO AND KALOS

How does the totalitarian state or for that matter any state with a positive program of intellectual and material reforms deal with free expression? The answer is inevitable: it restrains and molds it.

Letting a hundred flowers blossom and a hundred schools of thought contend is the policy for promoting the progress of the arts and the sciences and a flourishing socialist culture in our land. Different forms and styles in art should develop freely and different schools in science should contend freely. We think that it is harmful to the growth of art and science if administrative measures are used to impose one particular style of art or school of thought and to ban another. Questions of right and wrong in the arts and sciences should be settled through free discussion in artistic and scientific circles and through practical work in these fields. They should not be settled in a summary fashion. A period of trial is often needed to determine whether something is right or wrong.

Such are the words of Mao Tse-tung, leader and idol of Communist China's 750 million people. But then a few paragraphs later Chairman Mao considers what may happen and interjects one of his famous contradictions:

What then, from the point of view of the broad masses of the people, should be the criteria today for distinguishing fragrant flowers from poisonous weeds? In the political life of our people, how should right be distinguished from wrong in one's words and actions? On the basis of the principles of our Constitution, the will of the overwhelming majority of our people and the common political positions which have been proclaimed on various occasions by our political parties and groups, we consider that, broadly speaking, the criteria should be as follows:

1. Words and actions should help to unite, and not divide, the people of our various nationalities.

2. They should be beneficial, and not harmful, to socialist transformation and socialist construction.

3. They should help to consolidate, and not undermine or weaken, the people's democratic dictatorship.

4. They should help to consolidate, and not undermine or weaken, democratic centralism.

5. They should help to strengthen, and not to discard or weaken, the leadership of the Communist Party.

6. They should be beneficial, and not harmful, to international socialist unity and the unity of the peaceloving people of the world.

Of these six criteria, the most important are the socialist path and the leadership of the Party. . . . Naturally, in judging the validity of scientific theories or assessing the aesthetic value of works of art, additional pertinent criteria are needed. But these six political criteria are applicable to all activities in the arts and the sciences.[1]

What Mao is saying (and what actually happened) is that the Communist dictatorship comes before any other value. Freedom, even in science and art, cannot be let to threaten the top power elite. And, of course, the power elite defines the word "threaten."

Am I, in this book, doing the same as Chairman Mao? Yes, in a way. I agree with the proposition that art and science (the extreme bastions of freedom) cannot be free if you wish a society of a certain kind. They must be limited by various means in one type of society and different means in another type; there is a greatly significant difference between giving a few more research grants to "our kind" of art and science, and suppressing ruthlessly a competing or opposing art and science. Moreover, what holds for art and science holds for business, farming, and politics.

The three differences between my views (call them kalos) and Chairman Mao's are: (1) in the *ways of pursuing* the ultimate goals, such as the flowering of arts and sciences, food, housing, medical care; (2) in *organizing society* for work and living, especially *before* the success of the revolution; and (3) in the *form of governing* that can best cope with both the short-term and long-term problems of liberty and order. I doubt that there are serious *ultimate* differences; that is, we may want the same kind of healthy autonomous person living in an uncorrupted environment, in the final analysis. But, naturally, whoever is most correct about the means will be most likely to achieve these ends.

I doubt that Chairman Mao would follow us happily through our next set of 3-P's, but if he does: "Welcome aboard."

1. From *Four Essays on China and World Communism* by Mao Tse-tung (New York: Lancer Books, 1972), 113–20. Reprinted by permission.

PRINCIPLE XI

Obedience to authorities is recommended when the authorities are benevolent and beneficent.

The main point is that authorities have to be forgiven some errors but they should not be allowed to be typically in error or basically structured to be in error.

Pope John XXIII put it another way:

To safeguard the inviolable rights of the human person and to facilitate the fulfillment of his duties, should be the essential office of every public authority. This means that, if any government does not acknowledge the rights of man or violates them, it not only fails in its duty, but its orders completely lack juridical force.[2]

PROPOSITION XI

More crimes result from obedience than from rebellion.

True? _____
False? _____
Equal? _____
Maybe? _____

Nobody knows, because *crime* is defined by government, and obedience to government is no crime; anyhow, bear this hypothesis in mind and you will be less likely to commit crimes of obedience.

Meanwhile Let's Examine
A Study by Stanley Milgram

Stan was bothered by this problem of obedience and developed a brilliant idea, an experiment! He advertised for people around New Haven to help in a study at Yale University in psychology. Forty males then were selected (who didn't know they were to be the subjects). We shall let him explain the procedure that followed:

2. *Peace on Earth*, encyclical (New York: America Press, 1963), 60–61.

It consists of ordering a naive subject to administer electric shock to a victim. A simulated shock generator is used, with 30 clearly marked voltage levels that range from 15 to 450 volts. The instrument bears verbal designations that range from Slight Shock to Danger: Severe Shock. The responses of the victim, who is a trained confederate of the experimenter, are standardized. The orders to administer shocks are given to the naive subject in the context of a "learning experiment" ostensibly set up to study the effects of punishment on memory. As the experiment proceeds the naive subject is commanded to administer increasingly more intense shocks to the victim, even to the point of reaching the level marked Danger: Severe Shock. Internal resistances become stronger, and at a certain point the subject refuses to go on with the experiment. Behavior prior to this rupture is considered "obedience," in that the subject complies with the commands of the experimenter. The point of rupture is the act of disobedience.[3]

A "True" Experiment

There is a large literature on what a "true" experiment is. It can rarely be achieved. Some say you have to have a subject that you do something to or experiment on and a matched group that you don't touch but use to control the experiment. Then, if the experimental group does change in the way you predicted, and the control group doesn't change in that way, you can be more sure that the change was caused by the experiment.

Stanley Milgram didn't use a control group, but as you can see, he still had a powerful study.

Most "social experiments" so-called are thus not "true" experiments. People called the Tennessee Valley Authority a "great social experiment," but there was no foolproof way of telling whether the area experimented upon would have changed as much and as well **without** the TVA. No control group was possible.

Most human problems don't lend themselves to experiment although amazing advances have been made. Let us say this: Experimental method is fine when you can use it; when you can't, keep an experimental frame of mind; in any event don't let the crazies and the ignoramuses make social policy while you are waiting for the perfect experiment to prove your case!

Stan asked some Yale psychology students and psychiatrists to guess at what point the naive subjects, seeing their victim, the "learner," in pain, would stop and refuse to obey the command to go farther. They guessed

3. "Behavioral Study of Obedience," by Stanley Milgram *Journal of Abnormal and Social Psychology* 67, 1963: 371–78. Reprinted in L. S. Wrightsman, Jr., *Contemporary Issues in Social Psychology* (Belmont, Calif.: Brooks-Cole, 1968), 141–42.

that only rarely would a subject press on beyond the point of Very Strong Shock (about midway in the intensity-of-pain scale).

In fact, our fellow Americans, in 26 out of 40 cases, pressed the button up to the very end, where they believed that they were following an order to hit a person with 450 volts and the victim, who had been making agonized noises up to a certain point, was probably ceasing to react. Not one of the 14 who disobeyed did so until they had administered an Intense Shock several times.

The subjects were not inhuman robots. They suffered from their jobs.

I observed a mature and initially poised businessman enter the laboratory smiling and confident. Within 20 minutes he was reduced to a twitching, stuttering wreck, who was rapidly approaching a point of nervous collapse. He constantly pulled on his earlobe, and twisted his hands. At one point he pushed his fist into his forehead and muttered: "Oh God, let's stop it." And yet he continued to respond to every word of the experimenter, and obeyed to the end.[4]

Why? Why? How could they?

The answer is written on thousands of pages of history, if you can bear to read them. Stanley was *Dr.* Stanley Milgram, *Professor* Milgram, the Scientist, the Authority, the Boss, representing Yale, the Great University, the Establishment, in a "real scientific laboratory." He wasn't just Stanley. Indeed, they would have electrified Stan, too, if he had been only the man in the chair.

Murder in authoritative context is a public good!

So you see keenly why political scientists, sociologists, and some other people are anxious about the structure of government, the rule of law, and constitutions. Structures, constitutions, and laws may be dull subjects but they shape behavior. So does the personality structure typical of the *elite.* Unless we can figure out how to avoid in real life the situations in which Stanley Milgram placed his subjects, we shall have to be continuously fearful that *real* happenings like this will occur, and occur often, as they do now and have done throughout history.[5]

---

4. Ibid., 147.

5. Professor Milgram, by the way, came under attack for making Nazis out of his subjects for a few minutes and for causing them pain. There is every reason to be careful and considerate in experimentation. However, between the actions here and the real-life occurrences, there is an enormous difference, which only an amoral or quite naïve person can deny. Nazi, Communist, and authoritarian governments don't play around for a matter of minutes. Moreover, think for a moment just of "liberal" governments. Think how many laws knowingly and deliberately experiment with people. (For example: "Let's reduce the welfare allowance for dependent children and see if their mothers have fewer babies as a result." Or, "Let's have a 5 percent unemployment rate and see whether that will cure inflation." Or, "Let's send a battalion of our [drafted] troops into Thailand to scare China and show her we mean business.")

POLICY XI

> When authorities have to resort
> to "murder as a public good,"
> they should be justifiably desperate
> (as under direct murderous attack themselves),
> and their retaliation
> should have justifiable consequences.

Nationalism Again?

What is the cause of unthinking obedience? Possibly the churches at one time, but probably not any more. People stop obeying the church rather frequently in modern times when some disturbing action is called for, such as a religious boycott of films, or marrying always within the group, or a public denunciation of a heretic.

The state, of course, is the main proponent of blind obedience. It has always been evil in this regard. The state has for two centuries been building unthinking obedience on new skyscraper levels. "Democracy" made matters worse, because people believed they were slaughtering for their own welfare rather than the king's. So many crimes have been committed in the name of the state and nationalism that the only two positive things about them are: they can give masses of people a cheap thrill of communion, and if one nation lacks nationalistic frenzy other nations will pounce upon it.

Just how does *Der Staat* originate and infuse our vital fluids? A poem may explain. It is dedicated to the hundreds of thousands of Germans since the time of Goethe who have suffered prison or death for their opposition to the cult of chauvinism.

Der Staat

Die Logik ist schwer
>   *Eins:* What is not
>   cannot know what it is.
>   *Zwei:* It knows not itself,
>   hence cannot know others—
>   *Drei:* for nothing can know nothing.
>   *Vier:* Magnificent nothing,
>   as only can Non-being be.

Gut! Jetzt alle
  zusammen
      SEE IT!
      HIGH ABOVE ALL!
        HEIL DER STAAT!
Singe träumerisch:
      Pseudopodic protoplasm
      practically ooze
      millionfold projection
      of its creator, man.
Mehr laut:
      HEIL DER STAAT
Hier vortrag wie ein Pedägog
      The slime that fascinates
      the genius of ages,
      whose enemies are its lovers:
      Virgilius, Registrar
      of the vires of Rome;
      R. Kipling, Architect
      of imperial English facades;
      Walt Whitman,
      Grand Prurient Exalter
      of the American mass:
      dizzied protagonists
      who create what they hate,
      licensed contemptuously
      to exercise feebly
      the liberties needed
      to extend its memory.
Aber macht nichts;
  sprech mit Kraft;
      SALUTE *DER STAAT*
Und hier muss man
  die Logik unterscheiden:
      Others are different,
      being others,
      though the same.
      The good outside
      is as bad as others.
      The others die
      unheralded, unhallowed;

326 Twelve Principles, Propositions, and Policies

their past is telescopic,
their future nowhere.

Schrei rüstig!

THREE CHEERS FOR OUR ETERNITY!

Mehr Soziologie:

Its past is bloody,
its prate pacific;
hate flourishes
beneath flaunted community.
Impersonating
universal consent
where few are acting;
by its definition,
justice there is,
for it must be.

HEILIGE FAMILIE!

Und mit Enthusiasmus:

Elevated for the sightless
on the shoulders of genius,
high above all.
(See it,
for if you don't,
you are against it.)
Whip, flags, the wind.
Blare, bands.
Scorch the imbibulous
awe-numbed gullets
with pledging toasts!

Mit gründlich   Ernst, sagen:

Fire, cannon!
SALUTE *DER STAAT*

What is the poet saying?
(self-service test)

	Yes	No
1. The logic for understanding the state is difficult because we are dealing with an intangible idea, something in people's minds.	___	___
2. The state has no existence in itself and therefore cannot know anything, but that does not stop people from animating it and adoring it.	___	___

3. The imaginary traits of the state are creations of humanity's wishes for power and glory.   _____ _____

4. Even some great writers, regardless of the real interests of intellectuals in freedom and truth, have succumbed to the mystique of the state in its various forms.   _____ _____

5. The services of writers and artists are useful in glorifying the image of the state and falsifying its history.   _____ _____

6. The existence, and even the history and prospects, of other peoples are suppressed so as to magnify "our" state and justify its moments of "peace through strength."   _____ _____

7. No one can identify all those who have consented to acts committed by the state, but the state claims unanimity. It is a holy family.   _____ _____

8. Justice is defined by those who command the idol of the state.   _____ _____

9. Those who cannot "see" this nonexistent monster are punished and those who do "see" it have great fun.   _____ _____

Scoring. If you answer "Yes" to all nine statements, you not only understand chauvinism, but you also get three stars for poetry reading. * * * The tenth question that follows carries no credit.

10. The poetry of *"Der Staat"* is (check one) Bad_____ Good_____.

The First and Last Strike

Today *Der Staat* has nuclear weapons to help it be awful and destructive. When I think of the grotesque threat of nuclear bombs, I am reminded of an ad of a Parisian undertaker:

Why go on living when we can give you such a beautiful funeral for only $50?

This book could have been written on the happenings of any day in history. There are ample examples of all of its propositions and of the need for its principles and policies in every day's events. Thus as I think today of having to say something of the *continuous threat of nuclear war,* I glance into the newspapers and find:

If Talks Fail We May Face
An All-Out Nuclear Holocaust

But I don't suppose 98 percent of the readers noticed the story or headline. If they did, I doubt they read it. Why should they? This business has been going on since 1945. Many people believe the holocaust will come. *It just hasn't happened yet.*

Everyone knows THE POTENTIAL OF NUCLEAR DESTRUCTION IS TOTAL. Bernard Weinraub wrote several years ago that "nuclear stockpiles were vast enough to blast every person with the equivalent of 15 tons of TNT."[6]

But I'm sure every true American's heart beat a little faster when the yearbook of the Stockholm Peace Research Institute reported in 1970: "The United States appears to be the pacesetter in the large-scale incorporation of new technologies into its armory."

* * * * *

Can anything more be said? Can anything be done?

Not much. But enough. The *Yearbook* listed seven approaches that might be adopted by the U.S.A. and U.S.S.R.:[7]

*An exchange of views about current and future developments and about strategic concepts in the arms race, without seeking to reach agreement on any limitation.

*Agreement to limit on each side the total number of offensive delivery vehicles within some broad category.

*Abolition or limitation of antiballistic missile systems, or other defenses, in order to avoid or reduce an offense-defense race.

*Agreement not to introduce specific technical improvements. The most important immediate step would be to agree to ban MIRVs, multiple independently targeted reentry vehicles.

*Agreement not only on the number but also on the characteristics of each side's deterrent force, thus stopping technical advance by freezing designs.

*Agreement to stop tests of all nuclear warheads and of new weapons, namely MIRVs, and so cut research and development expenditures.

*Reductions of numbers of nuclear weapons. Combined with a freeze on characteristics, this would produce a minimum deterrent which might lead to the eventual abolition of nuclear weapons.

* * * * *

These are exactly the kind of disarmament proposals that filled the air between World War I and World War II: then . . . the EXPLOSION!

But where is *unilateral disarmament* in all of this?

---

6. "Stock of A-Arms Is Termed Huge," *The New York Times,* November 3, 1970, p. 13.

7. *New York Daily News,* November 3, 1970.

Every one of these plans calls for an impossible agreement between the heads of two states that together have a proven incapacity to bring peace to the world. None of them even if adopted gives assurance against nuclear war.

From an article by Bernard T. Feld, professor at Massachusetts Institute of Technology, we obtain the following:

No matter what the nature of the first strike, the victim should be able to deliver a huge retaliation—two hundred nuclear bombs . . . .

These, targeted on industrial centers in the United States or Soviet Union,

would kill at least one third of the population and destroy two thirds of the industrial capacity of either nation. These estimates are only for the immediate consequences of the nuclear explosion—blast, heat, and nuclear radiations. . . .

. . . There is no plausibly forthcoming means for eliminating any substantial fraction of the nuclear submarines by a surprise attack. . . .

. . . We have not yet mentioned the effects of radioactive fallout. . . . [It would produce countless mutations, as well as a great many deaths.]

. . . Antiballistic missile systems [ABM] will only make things worse. . . .[8]

*   *   *   *   *

So now we can say:

1. Neither the U.S.A. nor the U.S.S.R. can escape destruction by attacking the other first. (No "preventive" war will prevent self-destruction.)

2. There is scant consolation to a person in the throes of death knowing that the state's retaliation will probably soon kill his or her counterpart in the attacking state. After all, the common people over there who will die are just as innocent as you are, even if their dying words are spoken in another language.

3. Even the elaborate protective measures against initiating nuclear attack through madness or accident cannot be trusted.

4. The threat of massive retaliation does more harm through inciting a premature attack than it does "good" in restraining a deliberate attack.

5. The control of nuclear weapons puts the military at the top ranks of the American and Soviet governments and fosters the general powers of the executive chiefs of government.

6. The costs of armaments for "nuclear peace" could, if used for beneficial purposes, guarantee a birth control and minimum subsistence program for every person on earth.

8. "The Stake at Salt—Survival," *The New York Times*, December 9, 1970, p. 35.

The solution to the problems of nuclear bomb threats can be the following:

1. The U.S.A. and U.S.S.R. should exchange two million persons as students, workers, and tourists at all times. These hostages, while enjoying themselves and learning something, will personify to the missile launchers what will happen if a nuclear mistake or an attack occurs.

2. A peace movement outside of each government but inside each country and all other countries should be organized with the goal of persuading each government to adopt unilateral arms reduction, and to use the resulting savings for kalotic purposes.

3. The United States should begin to reduce its armaments without any reciprocal commitment by the Soviet Union, until it reaches a point at which, in an accidental or deliberate nuclear war, the Soviet Union will lose some substantial part of its population and industries. This "Point of Sufficient Deterrence" exists probably at one fifth of the present nuclear war capacity of the U.S.A.

Would the Russians disarm themselves unilaterally following the American example? Probably. And this would be all to the good.

What evil can happen under such circumstances?

The U.S.S.R. might "accidentally-on-purpose" strike at the U.S.A., wreaking havoc, killing most Americans, and alienating the world, but suffering crippling losses itself, let us say, at one third the extent otherwise. Would such losses be acceptable to the U.S.S.R.? No. Only a few theoreticians can play statistical games of such self-destructiveness.

If they did "win" on the first strike, would Communism establish itself on the wreckage of American society? No. If not shattered themselves, the Soviets would face a totally new psychological condition. Hated by the world, demoralized by their own damaged condition and their crimes, what new society could they take over? What expeditionary force could they send out of the country? Where would it go? How would it be treated? Who would respect the new rule? Even if there were only twenty million Americans left, the Soviets could never invade, occupy, and organize Communism in America. On the contrary, the Soviet system itself would crack up in Europe and in Asia. Indeed, the scattered remnants and allied elements of the American coalition would draw together in tight cohesion and be unconquerable by whatever force the Soviets could muster to follow up their partial nuclear victory.

In sum, what we declare is that a nuclear war cannot be won; but even if it were won as "a generals' war game" it would be lost in all other senses. Therefore,

Unilateral nuclear disarmament by America is recommended.

It is urged, regardless of Soviet behavior, knowing full well what that behavior could be, or would be. With its newly gained peaceful resources, America should launch its own peaceful revolution.

Chapter 12
History of the Future

Well over two thousand years ago, Xenophanes said:

African gods have snub noses, the Nordic gods are blond with blue eyes. If lions and oxen cd. paint . . . we shd. doubtless see them also making Gods in their image.[1]

Every society writes its own history, which means that every ruling group, when it can, writes the history of its society. When a society is transformed, its history is redone. When a revolution occurs, a society's history is rewritten fast. For many years before a revolution you begin to see history being rewritten.

"History is prologue," says an inscription on the fake classic facade of the U.S. National Archives. We agree, adding that it is *our* prologue to *our* future. Just any old history will not do. So much of it is relativistic, random and petty chatter, chauvinistic, or dedicated to opposing dogmas.

PROPOSITION XII

All social systems and
movements write their own
versions of history.

1. Ezra Pound provides the translation in *Guide to Kulchur* (New York: New Directions, 1938), p. 118.

The history of slavery in America is very different when written by racists, academicians, chauvinists, and blacks. It will be written for the future much differently than it is being written now. Blacks may think they have tapped all the positive history for their purposes, but they have hardly begun. Their historical materials were deeply buried by the white historians, of both the South and the North.

Think of other lands too. Some of Soviet history has been rewritten several times in fifty years. In their eagerness to reach the future, the Chinese communists both rewrite history and ignore it: the first batch of American journalists to visit China in 1972 were surprised to discover that fewer courses in Chinese history were being offered at all Chinese universities than at Harvard University alone. English history, especially the history of the "lower classes," has hardly begun to be rewritten, though writers like G. D. H. Cole have worked at the task.

SOVIET HISTORY OMITS BIG PURGES

Jew Volume on Party Makes Little Mention of Stalin

By THEODORE SHABAD
Special to The New York Times

MOSCOW, Jan. 8—Russians received their latest version of history on the agitated period of the Stalin purges of the nineteen-thirties this week as a long-delayed volume of a Communist party history went on sale in Moscow bookstores.

It turned out to be a bland and highly depersonalized kind of history, with bare mention of Stalin and other leaders of the Soviet state and no mention whatever of the great purges of 1936 and 1937.

With publication of the present volume, the pendulum of the rewriting of history appears to have come to rest in a neutral position somewhere between the impassioned extremes of the Stalin and Khrushchev versions.

The latest book, which is part of a six-volume history of the party, covers the period ...ng to 1937. It appears ...e compilers ...s publica-
...ile a vol-
...sequent

ar

PRINCIPLE XII

History should be continuously rewritten.

As soon as a social revolution has occurred, every "great" man needs to have his biography rewritten. The life of George Washington is treated hopelessly in terms of a new American history. The young are taught about a human machine with strange outputs that don't make sense except as a stilted formal justification of a static society. I learn more from a General George Washington who was so crazed and desperate when the Americans promptly broke and fled at the approach of the first British musketeers in the Battle of Manhattan that he charged about swearing and wildly striking at the soldiers, trying to turn them around, until his staff officers seized him and forcibly dragged him to the rear.

I learn more from a Thomas Jefferson who in his old age barely escaped being evicted from his home by a bank because he had signed on as a guarantor on the loan of a friend and the friend had not paid the loan. I learn from a Benjamin Franklin that he had a hundred talents, and his money-making, wheeling-and-dealing, his respect for science, and his imaginative experiments, not to mention his promiscuous sex adventures, were all part of a man who made a great revolutionary. And do children know how angry and busy Ben Franklin became when some whites brutally attacked an Indian settlement? I am reminded of a saying among civic leaders that might properly be in the section on political activity: "When you want to get something done, go to a busy person."

The Great Seal

Pick up a dollar bill and examine it front and back. On the front is Father George; also the signature of the token female in the federal elite, the Treasurer; too, the dismal news that this is a Federal Reserve Note and not a good old Silver or Gold Certificate that you could at one time exchange for real silver or gold. The back is mysterious; it contains the "Great Seal" of the U.S.A. Notice the designs on the two sides of the Seal.

There is the American eagle, the national totem animal, which Americans have just about managed to exterminate.[2] On the other side of the seal is a truncated pyramid, whose top wafts upwards containing a great eye; two mottos are noticeable.

The Seal did not spring virginally from the minds of the Constitution-Makers; its design was pieced together by numerous individuals and committees of Congress from 1776 to 1782, then passed along to and approved once more by the Constitutional Congress. The pyramid stands for the architectural principle that is supposed to underlie the Universe, and the All-Seeing Eye spreading its light represents the Mind that designed and oversees the Universe, an impersonal God. These symbols go back centuries and were developed by the Masonic Order, a secret society to whose hundreds of lodges over two millions belong. The Masons are loosely connected by a common philosophy, a rich symbolism, and mutual aid, as a kind of giant social club of worldwide affiliates. Like the Roman Catholic Jesuits, the Masons often turned to politics, alternately penetrating the seats of power and being evicted from them. Thousands of revolutionaries in many countries, including the U.S.A., were Masons. The Masonic mystic symbols of the Near East offered sharp competition to the Catholic Church for centuries and there is still an uneasy edge of distrust and occasional flare-ups, even in modest American communities.

Secret orders have frequently been useful to politicians with ambitions; in both despotisms and democracies, they can operate within parties and factions, organizing their friends and resources under cover. The bad and good of movements are intertwined; America has witnessed abundant discriminatory practices by Masons and, more lately, reverse discrimination by anti-Masons. I suppose that many Americans would prefer to have a sketch of the Catholic Church of St. Augustine,

2. My dear friend Benjamin Franklin, recommended the turkey over the eagle: the eagle was the Imperial Roman symbol, unsuitable for a republic, and it was a predator, while the turkey was uniquely American, useful, and pacific. Franklin was head of the Congress Committee appointed to work on the Great Seal. He asked an artist friend, Pierre du Simitière, to help. The latter introduced the All-Seeing Eye.

Florida, on the Seal. On the other hand, aren't we lucky it does not hold a drawing of the mythical happy slave ginning cotton?

The "In God We Trust" motto on the dollar, incidentally, is a bit of hypocrisy that the original Constitution and its supporters would not have tolerated (but they didn't like paper money much, either). However, beginning about the middle of the last century, the motto worked its way onto small change and the Congress of 1956, to which God will no doubt be eternally grateful, proclaimed it the official U.S. motto.

Let's include symbols (the seal) and sacred institutions too as examples of historical mythmaking. The so-called private colleges make a big point of their independence of government and how this helps to keep a free country. I believe this too, in a way. Most students of law have been taught the "Dartmouth College Case," where the state of New Hampshire wished to change the college charter and the U.S. Supreme Court said, in effect, "Oh, no. You have made a sacred contract, protected by the U.S. Constitution." Well, this is not such "good law" anymore, as the lawyers would say. What I would most object to is that my professor, while telling me the "law," neglected to tell me that "New Hampshire between 1833 and 1921 added $200,000 to the resources of Dartmouth."[3] That's what is called "talking out of both sides of the mouth."

Dartmouth *un*history is matched by Harvard *un*history.

Speaking in 1873 against the creation of a tax-supported national university, President Eliot of Harvard advanced the argument that "our ancestors well understood the principle that to make a people free and self-reliant, it is necessary to let them take care of themselves as some superior power might." Had this principle actually been well understood by Mr. Eliot's ancestors there would have been no Harvard and no presidential office there for him to use against the principle of government-financed higher education. On over one hundred occasions before 1789 the General Court (Legislature) of Massachusetts appropriated funds for Harvard College, which clearly was not capable of taking care of itself.[4]

But note: The Author does not believe in huge state subsidies to these bureaucracies. The American tradition in our rewritten educational history is "good old individualism"—meaning a personal choice of schools when and if one wishes formal education; the costs might be paid for by withdrawals from one's life account (see pp. 293–95 above).

3. Frederick Rudolph, *The American College and University* (New York: Alfred A. Knopf, 1962), p. 189.

4. *Ibid.*, p. 185.

One can take up any history anywhere and write it in revolutionary terms. For example, the world, even when hostile to the racist nationalist government of South Africa, does not have a picture of the numerous wars and rebellions conducted by different black nations against the intruding whites. Between 1657 and 1906, there were anticolonial wars of the Bushmen, Hottentots, Xhosa, Zulus, Basothos, and Babepedi, not to mention resistance struggles, and the nonviolent Hindu movement led by Mohandas Gandhi in 1913. Nor have the histories of the American Indian wars been rewritten yet. Who knows that Geronimo fought the last "campaign" of his war against five thousand cavalry of the U.S.A. with fifteen Apache warriors?

We are not asking for a false history. We have a choice of facts and theories to dig out and present in our own way. We are asking for a history in terms of the kalotic future and the problems of making the future. That means we must see men and women of the past as flesh and blood, as battered by character and society and fate; their hands clutched, their stomachs ached, their flesh crawled, their blood boiled. Unless we understand these things, we would be ashamed to seek change. We have to expect success to be barely outrunning failure. We have to show how our future is a conditioning, a clarifying, a triumphing of what is good in our past.

Probably the whole of American history will soon be rewritten preparatory to reconstituting the American MIND for the next century. Here is a synopsis of it. When this history is part of the American MIND, that mind can handle the future benevolently and beneficently.

POLICY XII

Rewrite history in accord with the visualized and desired future.

The History of the United States of America

I. The Western Hemisphere was inhabited by hundreds of Indian nations and tribes, many of them on a high level of civilization. Spaniards entered it with gun and horse as soon as Columbus showed them how to get there. They quickly subjugated the major nations and reduced their cultures. They settled the most pleasant climates. There they set up Catholic bureaucratic colonies of Spanish provincial culture which survived until the nineteenth-century revolutions. Frenchmen, who traversed most of North America, adjusted their settlements to Indian needs better than other Europeans, but their colonies ultimately fell under English dominion in Canada and under U.S. rule in the middle continent.

Meanwhile, England was bursting with social disorders. The radical Protestant revolution and the Industrial Revolution were giving it bountiful human and mechanical energy. A few minor nobility and speculators led some countrymen into the unhealthy southern areas of the present U.S.A., where they used men as slaves, at first whites of the most depressed classes, and then blacks who had been kidnaped from their homes in Africa. The northern areas were settled by radical Protestants from England and the central areas by several ethnic types, among them Dutch Protestants, English Anglicans and Quakers, Swedes, French Huguenots, and angry poor whites, mostly from Scotland and northern Ireland.

The greatest gift of this period was the freedom to flee the coast and start one's own life afresh, and many took advantage of it owing to the abundance of wilderness. It was terribly hard to do so but what else could one do? Blacks, meanwhile, were kept in savage bondage, their cultures driven underground and progressively mutilated.

II. The Revolutionary War was a rebellion against the bureaucrats, Anglicans, and arrogant commercial exploiters. It was fought by youths, supplied by aggressive farmers and small businessmen, and led, as is customary in revolutions, by educated and leisure-class men. Most of the ideas came from despised English radicals like Tom Paine. The faithful subjects of the Crown, who numbered half of the population, were driven out of the colonies, expropriated, or forced underground where they soon accepted the new allegiance. The Revolution adopted a radical popular philosophy that was well accepted in the wilder areas and affected the eastern areas as the Revolution succeeded. The revolutionaries could not have obtained freedom without help from the French monarch.

The U.S.A. thereupon began, with a Chicago-sized population. It owned a tiny educated and cultured class, a huge forest, and a restless people who had been buffeted by society before they came, suffered many hardships in America, and were ready to try anything to relieve their material needs. They treated the Indians and blacks as *they* had been treated and they treated new foreigners as *they* had been treated, and so it was ever after until the fourth American World Revolution (explained below). Each generation presumed to be better than the old, which it wasn't, and better than the next, which it was not either.

III. "The crisis of the foothold," followed by the *Revolution of the Foothold,* was succeeded then by the "crisis of slavery." A few transcendental writers beat frantically at their countrymen's consciences to no avail; but they seeded many good teachers. Then, because this social monster would not be mollified or bought off, the northern businessmen, free settlers of the West, and abolitionist idealists joined in the second Revolution, which was against slavery and the plantation aristocracy. Like practically all war victories, the *Revolution Against Slavery* did not stick with the problem that had generated it. The northerners turned to the West, accompanied by masses of immigrants from Europe, first from the north and later from the south and east. One third of Ireland, having fled to America from starvation, began a century of bitter social struggle to achieve social, religious, and economic equality. A million people moved into industries. Both ways of life were terrible: the open frontier lands could be ravaged but they reacted against their exploiters with all the forces of unfriendly nature. The factories raised the United States in forty years to equality with German, French, and English industry but at a backbreaking cost to the Yankees and foreigners who worked in them. A small group of super-rich shot up like a mutated giant flower. The South's ideas, people, and culture withered. The blacks, deprived of property, free expression, and education, originated popular musical forms that came ultimately to dominate twentieth-century music in America and western Europe. It was the age of industrial meanness masquerading behind the "free frontier"; of agricultural growth exhausting free labor to the profit of banks and brokers. Every ounce of material gain was hailed as progress, and served to spur on the north and midwest. Whiskey flowed like water. The Bible was everywhere, inspiring, terrorizing.

IV. The third revolution took over a century. It was the *Revolution of Techno-Cultural Self-Confrontation.* It began with the industrial and nationalistic triumph of the Civil War and ended with the degradation of materialism and authority. It ended with a calling of the roll to which, for the first time, every element of the population declared itself present and demanded to be taken into account. By the 1920s and 1930s most of the scientific and literary elite were denouncing American society: its economic structure, its dead universal education, its worship of material productivity, its hopeless individualism that led to alienation, impersonalism, and physical deterioration of the country. At the same time a full cosmopolitan culture began to emerge. There was a Great Economic Depression; only a mobilization for war finally brought "full employment." World War II came, and for six years the nation turned to the destruction of fascism in Europe and Japan. Again, before the victory was consolidated, the willpower of American society collapsed; the U.S.A. could have led the world into a new order of humanity, but turned away, casting some shekels to the world's needy and leaving its corporations and military bases to keep shop overseas.

Thereupon the prewar process of internal criticism resumed. Unexpectedly, in the 1950s and 1960s, as the crazy-quilt material production expanded, the social morale of large numbers of people declined; among millions of youth, it crumbled entirely. The U.S.A., as it became thoroughly "modern," grew disgusted with what it had. Hierarchy, property, and politics were increasingly rejected. Hypocrisy, self-delusion, and pretension were scorned.

The society split up into alienated and unfriendly segments even while the U.S.A. was leading the world in many fields. The banks, the great fortunes, the political parties, the corporations, and the unions stood up for a dying order. Venal writers of the mass press and television told the people countless stories of the U.S.A.'s glorious history of violence, goodness, and progress, of the respectable classes who never existed but were to be followed. So the country followed socially irresponsible businessmen, cunning, small-minded politicians, and the respectable ghosts of a society that never had been.

What could this mean to youth imprisoned in bureaucratic institutions and city pigeonholes? To white workers who exhausted themselves in work and the self-imposed struggle to maintain their small properties and cars? To those highly skilled and creative people who had built the arts and sciences, half of them Jews? To technicians offended by technocracy, renegades from Puritanism, everyday refugees from Babbittry? Or to the blacks—a third unemployable, and yet at the other end with more college graduates than all the country possessed before World War I? What did the country and its history mean to a nation over half of whose people were sick of the system to the point of neurosis, even when they could not realize what was hurting and torturing them? What could America mean as a mass of mutual hostilities instead of a country of neighbors?

It could mean only one thing. The total American social, cultural, and political order had to be reformed. Americans had the intelligence to recognize that the myths of old America would entrap them in a frantic bureaucratic system while denying them a role in the history of freedom. They had the skills to do something about it.

V. The theme of the Fourth American Revolution was the future. The past fell into its place; its preachers had had their say. The past that was the future could be used. This past contained a record of mutual, individual, and commercial exploitation. It held a dismal record of vicious discrimination and social hostilities, of erratic disregard of the world, of irresponsible innovation.

On the positive side, it had somehow maintained a back-against-the-wall Colt-45 tradition of personal worth. The ability to give and take in a deal, to figure out deals in which both sides could win: this priceless asset of the American psychology also remained. America continued to create small numbers of indignant, even maddened, idealists, brimming with the energy that was so squandered by other Americans. It had created a technical know-how both in mechanics and human relations that might happily begin to explode in the right directions. The pragmatic philosophers had blended American character, science, and institutional processes into a usable life form. This could guide *The Revolution of the Future.*

So the history of the American future could be simply formulated. Those who perceived the enormous hurting in the system would combine with those who had mastered the method of change; they would put aside neither their desperation nor their skills until the nation was translocated on simpler and more humane foundations.

The time had come to cleanse America of its original and ensuing mass anxieties. Since it was a people that had never really known itself, nor had ever had a satisfying identity, it was a people that could choose its role in the ultimate confrontation with the future world. Future Person met Future World.

Land of the foothold.
Of hostile perceptions all around.
Funland.
Land of mad production.
Of schizophrenia.
Land of lost lands.
Land of worlds gone.

Look now.
Here is your future coming.
Well-formed, full-blooded.
Smiling.
Telling of a clear course ahead.

Politics for the Better

*"Good evening, ladies and gentlemen.
This is your pilot speaking. We are
flying at an altitude of 35,000 feet.
I have two pieces of news to report
to you, one good and one bad. The bad
is that we appear to be lost. The good
news is that we are making excellent time."*
(anonymous)

We Are Making Excellent Time Towards Nowhere.

*"It is bad when some people create disturbances,
and we do not approve of it. But when disturbances
do occur, they enable us to learn lessons,
to overcome bureaucracy and to educate the
cadres and the masses. In this sense,
bad things can be turned into good things.
Disturbances thus have a dual character.
Every disturbance can be regarded in this way."*[5]
Mao Tse-tung

Many Disturbances Are Occurring and We Must Learn from Them.

5. "Contradictions Among the People," in *Four Essays on China and World Communism* (New York: Lancer Press, 1972), p. 125.

"If you're not part of the solution, you're part of the problem."
Eldridge Cleaver

What Is to Be Done?

Principles, propositions, and policies do not by themselves make a society transform itself. New attitudes and radical activities do. And good attitudes and activities make a good revolution. If you agree with what is between the covers of this book, you are receptive. If you act on what is said, you are effective. If you know what you are doing, you will be beneficial.

What Will the Future Be Like?

The principles and policies that are urged in this book cannot be achieved without pain and anguish on a large scale.

But the present ways of life cannot be continued except through *even greater* suffering. Besides, the moral and intellectual substance of the present ways is crumbling.

Therefore we return to our own principles and policies, believing that they will result in an acceptable future for us. They will bring:

> A life-style that is much less materialistic in fact and belief. The well-to-do will have fewer possessions and habits that use up natural resources and energies, but more creative possessions and pastimes.

> Greatly expanded chances to work toward improving the lives of the 95 percent of the world's people who are poor and toward adjusting both rich and poor to the great world changes.

> Much less pollution, much more conservation of resources, a stationary population.

A basic economic security for
everyone, without apology. Greater
equality of wealth within countries
and among countries.

A world government that will reduce
national prides to a safe and healthy
level, and encourage peaceful rather
than violent change.

Better human relations all around
the world, and less anxiety, disgust,
and hatred in the individual person.
More self-expression, closer and
longer-lasting circles of friends, more
private peace.

It is said that there are many rooms in the mansion of the Lord. I have tried
my hand at designing one of them for you. Now, begging your pardon for
having imposed upon your time and thoughts, I'll step aside and let you into
your real future.

Appendix A

Synopsis of Recommended Curriculum for Concentration in Political Science: Junior Year to Doctoral Preliminary Examinations[1]

Junior Year
1. Power
2. Political Anthropology
3. Political Geography
4. Political Sociology
5. Political Economy
6. Political Psychology
7. Political Historiography
8. Legal Process

Senior Year
1. Political Doctrines
2. Applications of Power
3. Political Epistemology
4. Techniques of Study in Political Behavior
5. Case Studies in American Government
6. Principles of Administration
7. Western European Government "X"
8. Poor "Third World" Government "X"

---

[1] I am opposed to rigid requirements and the everyday lecture system, hence I would like to see my ideal curriculum bubbling in our minds rather than instituted as coercive rote.

This curriculum was first published in *The Behavioral Sciences: Essays in Honor of George A. Lundberg*, Alfred de Grazia, Rollo Handy, E. C. Harwood, and Paul Kurtz, eds. (Great Barrington, Massachusetts: The Behavioral Research Council, 1968), p. 132.

Master's Year
1. Logical & Quantitative Method for Political Scientists
2. Librarianship & Information Retrieval for Political Scientists
3. Literature of Political Science
4. Scope of Political Science
5. Ideology, Political Doctrines, and Political Formulas
6. Comparative Political Systems and Cultures
7. Comparative Political Parties and Public Opinion
8. Comparative Governmental Institutions

(Thesis optional)

(Languages tailored to need)

Doctor's Year
1. Political Society I (Advanced)
2. Advanced Principles of Organization: Behavior and Applications
3. Conflict & Negotiations: Behavior and Applications
4. Participant Observation and Reporting
5. Political Society II
6. Legal Analysis and Sanctions
7. Pedagogy of Political Science
8. Research Design

(Dissertation required)

Now should you feel that at the end of all of this there will be an easy Professorship, here are some reflections of the Author, written in 1958[2], on what you might be getting into:

If a professor were permitted to be a scholar and a gentleman he might spend his time like this: He would teach six hours a week and use twelve to prepare his presentations. He would keep abreast of the tide of literature by reading five books a month; two would be new books, three would be old; if he read thirty pages an hour, he would require about eleven hours a week for the task. Then twenty-five new and five old articles would need study each month, consuming seven hours a week. The New York *Times* and two weekly magazines would take up about nine and a half hours. His creative literary work would consist of preparing syllabi and other instructional

2. From *PROD (Political Research: Organization and Design)*, Vol. II, No. 1, Sept. 1958, pp. 38–9.

352

materials (one hour a week), and writing one article (250 hours), one book review (twenty hours), and about thirty pages (thirty days) of The Book, per year. Thus far our professor has used up 52½ hours of the 168 hours in a week.

Since our professor's university is one of the best (*viz.* six hours of teaching), his additional duties are minimal. An hour a week for MA and one-half hour for PhD students, one hour for grading papers, two hours in committee work, one hour for personal typing, one hour of extra appearances before students and outside groups, three hours visiting with students, and two hours of professional correspondence and activities. Our scholar has now given up sixty-four hours.

Today field research is important. Our professor—alone, with a colleague, with his students—would be engaged yearly in at least one small field research project leading to the publication of an article. Whether it is spread out or is concentrated in the summer, an average of five hours a week per annum will go into it. Our man's week is now sixty-nine hours long.

So far no gentleman he. But then he belongs to a church (two hours), spends time with his family (fourteen hours), reads "broadening literature" such as novels (one hour), and listens to music (one hour). He has to spend two hours in commuting. Being an active citizen takes another hour.

Recreation and two weeks of vacation had best be counted as substitutes for some of the tasks of the academic year, for we are already up to ninety hours a week. Perhaps the family will not feel neglected if some eating time is counted as family time. But still at least five eating hours must be added. Seven hours are not excessive for personal care, nor two hours for housework and one for gardening. We settle at 105 hours per week, leaving sixty-three hours for sleep and many other activities.

Under the circumstances, any interest he might have in the problems of leisure in modern society is academic and altruistic. So persistent are the extra nonscholarly demands, that only the rarest scholar can live on this minimum intellectual level for more than a few years. Thus illness, romancing, raising infants, holding a government or private position, engaging in politics (including engaging in campus politics), heavier teaching loads (at eight schools out of ten), being a "pal" to the students, having an avocation or regular sport, army service, hyper-broad reading habits, and conviviality, will singly and together cancel out many years of an academic life.

Yet some minimum number of years, say ten, must go into this schedule or a better one in order to create a scholar, if he be such other than by fiat. Therefore, inevitably, only a platoon of men will be productive and informed scholars in a generation and these men must typically be so eccentric as to justify the populace's stereotype of the intellectual and scientist.

The highly touted planned society can hardly redeem the situation—as by wooing productive scholars into foundation and government jobs, or by convening endless committees to manage the planned reforms. The scholar himself can do much more, primarily by not trying to be a gentleman. He might also make himself repugnant to whoever steals his time—college committees, public officials, ladies' clubs, student social groups. (But so strong is the desire for charitable relations, that he may devote even more time to fringe groups composed of repugnant friends.) He might join a holy order, but God takes up more time than his wife would. He might form a bread-and-butter union to strike for higher pay and shorter hours, but this would be unscholarly. He might inherit or marry into a fortune; we highly recommend this step. But best of all is the policy of drift—let come what will come; a man can be decent and prosperous if his incompetency is in the order of things.

Appendix B

A List of One Hundred "Public"
Independent Organizations
(Suggested by Richard C. Cornuelle)

1. Sierra Club
2. RAND Corporation
3. National Council of Churches
4. Boy Scouts of America
5. Urban League

6. Bedford-Stuyvesant Redevelopment Corporation
7. Harvard University
8. American Civil Liberties Union
9. Nader's Raiders
10. Mayo Clinic

11. National Gallery of Art
12. Watts Writers Workshop
13. Sloan-Kettering Institute
14. Committee for Economic Development
15. Police Athletic League

16. Planned Parenthood-World Population
17. National Alliance of Businessmen
18. Rockefeller University
19. American Museum of Natural History
20. Children's Television Workshop

21. United Way of America
22. NAACP Legal Defense Fund
23. Hoover Institution on War, Revolution and Peace

24. American National Standards Institute
25. Phillips Exeter Academy

26. G. I. Forum
27. PTA
28. National Geographic Society
29. Opportunities Industrialization Centers
30. American Medical Association

31. Little Leagues of America
32. National Fire Protection Association
33. ACCION International
34. Salk Institute
35. American Humane Association

36. League of Women Voters
37. Underwriters' Laboratories
38. Synanon
39. American Red Cross
40. Phi Beta Kappa

41. Museum of Science and Industry
42. YMCA
43. Brookings Institution
44. Boy's Town
45. National Safety Council

46. Blue Cross-Blue Shield
47. Actors' Studio
48. CARE
49. AFL-CIO
50. Lincoln Center for the Performing Arts

51. American Council on Education
52. Gideon Society
53. Consumers Union
54. U.S. Chamber of Commerce
55. Center for the Study of Democratic Institutions

56. Farm Bureau Federation
57. Anti-Defamation League
58. Good Samaritan Hospital

59. American Foundation for the Blind
60. General Federation of Women's Clubs

61. Republican National Committee
62. American Association for the Advancement of Science
63. Christian Science Monitor
64. Ford Foundation
65. Alcoholics Anonymous

66. Veterans of Foreign Wars
67. American Academy of Political and Social Science
68. Scripps Institute
69. American Automobile Association
70. Audubon Society

71. National Education Association
72. Selective Service Boards
73. Civil Air Patrol
74. Salvation Army
75. American Arbitration Association

76. National Welfare Rights Organization
77. U.S. Jaycees
78. TIAA-CREF
79. Conference Board
80. Knights of Columbus

81. USO
82. United Farm Workers Organization
83. Aspen Institute
84. Educational Testing Service
85. United Student Aid Funds

86. National Council of Better Business Bureaus
87. Lions International
88. American Jewish Committee
89. American Bar Association Foundation
90. 4-H Clubs of America

91. American Iron and Steel Institute
92. American Friends Service Committee
93. Bank Street College of Education

94. Nutrition Foundation
95. Foreign Policy Association

96. American ORT Foundation
97. Institute for the Future
98. Junior Achievement
99. American Council of Learned Societies
100. American Cancer Society

Bibliography

BOOKS to READ about
things said and unsaid in *Politics*
for Better or Worse
(including suggestions about Films and Fiction)

The sculptor Michelangelo once said to a chiseler who was complaining about detail, "Details add up to perfection, and perfection is no detail." Preparing a reading list is enough to put one on the side of the chiseler. For one thing, there is almost no chance of perfection. There are now thousands of books and articles that seek admission to the list. If I knew them all, I couldn't list them, and if I listed them you couldn't read them. At the same time, I am bound to omit "that Great Book that did more for you than anything you've ever read." Or, the Great Book of your instructor; or, worse, the Great Work *by* your instructor. In the end, it takes as much guts as brains to offer a list.

Hence I shall beat a strategic retreat from the massive advancing front of political literature. I'll present a few classics (recall the citations already in Part One, Lesson 1). I'll suggest a few titles of interest in each area of politics. I'll mention a few sources where you might find what you're looking for. And I'll point out some ways of learning politics through other media.

A FEW CLASSICS

If the work of a dead author lives on, it becomes a "classic." So I begin with Aristotle and Plato, long dead but classic in every good sense. Even if you cannot take time to read them now, you might at least take them in hand and go through them like a car-parts catalogue. Gaze upon the *Politics*, *Ethics*, and *Rhetoric* of Aristotle. Examine Plato's *Republic*, than his *Laws*, and then his other dialogues. (Those who are more mystic or artistic or of sterner disposition may prefer Plato.) Then onwards to the *New Testament*; the Gospels should be read whether you are Jew or Gentile, front-pew or back-slider; don't let others tell you what the Man was like. You'll probably like St. Augustine's *Confessions* once you get into them, and will find the cerebral system of St. Thomas Aquinas of a thousand years later difficult to appreciate unless you're driven to it (collected as *The Political Ideas of St. Thomas Aquinas* [1953]). St. Thomas (nicknamed the "Dumb Ox" in school) gives you the Roman Catholic establishment view of the last seven hundred years.

Ancient currents then revived, and by the end of the 1400s, you not only could discover Christopher Columbus but also Niccolò Machiavelli. "Old Nick" shucks everyone who's gone before, and lays it on the line: if you want *power*, you have to know and follow the rules by which power is gained and lost. (A Hindu equivalent of Machiavelli is Kautilya, incidentally. And the Chinese political philosophers up to the Han Dynasty are accessible now in a reader edited by Sebastian de Grazia [1973].) A century and a half after Machiavelli, you will meet John Locke whose *Second Treatise of Government* (1690) brings you the social contract, the theory of government by consent of the governed, majority rule, a sterling defense of private property, and an individualism that diffused into most American writers and statesmen (dead politicians). (Hence see *The Federalist Papers* and *The Records of the Federal Convention of 1787* [Farrand, ed., 1937].)

Then you can see in Tom Paine's *Common Sense* (1776) or *Rights of Man* (1791–92) the radical ideas of equality and populism that had been stifled in Europe but became the leading ideas behind the French Revolution, and even behind Marxism (which in a way is the turning of democratic gunsights upon the realm of economics). That brings us to Karl Marx and his great friend and collaborator, Frederich Engels; they prepared in 1848 a *Communist Manifesto* for a shabby group of workmen on the continent who were fired up with the injustices of the feudal and factory systems and searching for a communist ideal. The socialist-communist ideal spread but so did the liberal theory of the good society, which received one of its finest expressions, because of its historic breadth, in the *Ruling Class* of Gaetano Mosca, who wrote from the 1880s on.

Despite the magnificence achieved by European culture before World War I, a great anger was in the air; it was felt throughout the world, wherever anti-imperialist movements began to stir. I think that one might read Leon Trotsky's autobiography, *My Life*, or his *History of the Russian Revolution*, to understand the chain of explosions that began to occur, and then, to understand the fascist counterrevolutions, a work such as Ignazio Silone's *School for Dictators* (1938), Herman Rauschning's *Revolution of Nihilism* (1939), or William Shirer's *The Rise and Fall of the Third Reich* (1960).

America tried to find its way without the socialism and communism and developed the New Deal of the 1930s, expressing somewhat the pragmatic or instrumentalist movement, the best expositon of which, for political purposes, came from John Dewey—in *Ethics* (1908) (with Tufts), in *Education and Society* (1922), and in *The Public and Its Problems* (1927). Pragmatism digs the good out of the social process; it soils its hands, seeks ever-expanding communication, and scoffs at hierarchy and formalism.

Here is about where we stand now: with Marxism, meaning many different things to different parties; with liberalism, ranging from acceptance of the free form that events take to vigorous efforts to achieve a greater Welfare State; with pragmatism; and with many philosophical factions (like Thoreau survivalists, Gandhi passive resisters, Garibaldi ethnic nationalists, neo-Fascist nihilists, and Edmund Burke catatonics).

INTRUDERS: SCIENCE AND PRACTICE

Now we pause because we are disturbed by two facts. Much scientific and fiction writing has gone on without a union card in political philosophy and ethics. Science, as you know, is out to discover the truth, not to tell us how to behave; it says that excessive smoking causes cancer, and leaves it up to us to regard health as a value; nevertheless, the population smokes less. We can scarcely exaggerate how scientific discoveries in fact determine our morality. Therefore, every important scientist becomes *ipso facto* an important moralist, even when he or she doesn't want to be such. Think what Darwin's theory of evolution did to old-time religion, and Freud's theory of sexual repression did to marriage counseling. Others, like Herbert Spencer, have drawn conclusions from Darwin. Freud himself has skirted politics so that his *Civilization and Its Discontents* and the *General Selections from the Works of Sigmund Freud* (John Rickman, ed., 1957) are pointed towards political understanding. In general, B. Berelson and G. A. Steiner's *Human Behavior: An Inventory of Scientific Findings* (1964) illustrates well the point of this paragraph.

Secondly, all the world's peoples have had great practitioners of politics, but all the world's people have not written much about politics. Machiavelli, in fact, was angry with the Italian statesmen of his day for neglecting his propositions, while the "barbarians" were applying them without even reading him. So, to view the marvellous practices and institutions of politics that humans have devised, you have to go, not to political philosophy alone, but to reports about these events—in other words to historical and contemporary studies. We shall turn to these now, realizing that our ethical principles will be affected by their discussions of political behavior in different settings.

PERSONALITY AND COMMUNICATIONS

Rollo May treats some acute social problems via psychology in *Power and Innocence* (1972). Erik Ericson explores the differing "me's" in *Childhood and Society* (1964) and each different "me" is a different political animal too. Sebastian de Grazia goes after the origins of *The Political Community* (1948) in the insecurities of the infant and young.

Making the quick jump from personality to communications, one finds works by Schram, Nafsiger, and others, including Marshall McLuhan (*Understanding Media* [1971]), and a collection of basic readings in B. Berelson and M. Janowitz' *Reader in Public Opinion and Communication* (1966). Moving to "primitive" peoples, we find Marc Swartz, V. Turner, and A. Tuden's *Political Anthropology* (1966). Clyde Kluckhohn and Dorothea

Leighton's study of the *Navaho* (1946) gives a closer feeling for the material. So do Margaret Mead's *Coming of Age in Samoa* (1928) and Ruth Benedict's *Patterns of Culture* (1934).

COMPARATIVE GOVERNMENT

M. Fortes and E. E. Evans-Pritchard deal technically with *African Political Systems* (1940, 1961); Time-Life offers a picture book by Basil Davidson, *African Kingdoms* (1972). Barrington Moore, Jr., discusses *The Social Origins of Dictatorship and Democracy* (1966). Lucian Pye edits *Cases in Comparative Politics* (1970) from India, China, Indonesia, Japan, and the Philippines. Myrdal's *Report from a Chinese Village* (1965) watches an ancient settlement of Confucian China catch up with the Communist revolution. See also James Townsend's *Political Participation in Communist China* (1967). For England, see Sampson; for France, see Noonan; for Italy, see La Palombara; for an integrated comparison of the U.S.A. and U.S.S.R. see Brzezinski and Huntington; and so on (the *Sources and Data Banks* section below will help). The American Institute of Management published a mindboggling efficiency study of the Vatican, the "world's oldest and most successful government" (*The Roman Catholic Church: A Management Audit* [1956]). Arpad von Lazar offers a primer on *Latin American Politics* (1971). Oscar Lewis gets down to personal Latinos cases in *La Vida* (1966) and the *Children of Sanchez* (1961). On *Social Democracy versus Communism*, see Karl Kautsky (1946). Modernization and the third world are treated from an economic standpoint in L. J. Zimmerman's *Poor Lands, Rich Lands: The Widening Gap* (1964) and given political treatment in Claude Welch's reader, *Political Modernization* (1967).

One of the greatest studies of comparative politics, unionism, bureaucracy, and leadership is Robert Michels' *Political Parties* (1912). Today, general surveys of political science are provided by Carl Friedrich in his *Constitutional Government and Democracy* (rev. ed., 1950), and Alfred de Grazia (that's me) in *Elements of Political Science* (1952). Harold Lasswell and Abraham Kaplan publish a toughie called *Power and Society* (1950) which will propel you into advanced circles or into a daze; Lasswell's *Politics: Who Gets What, When, How?* (1936, 1958) provides a happier alternative. Surveying *The Evolution of Political Thought* (1958) is C. Northcote Parkinson (whose several laws are too close to real political science laws for comfort).

AMERICAN GOVERNMENT AND ECONOMY

The best source of available titles in this prolific area would be your professor. *The Congressional Quarterly* is a news service covering the full range of issues, with material on their background. Robert Dahl presents an advanced text on *Pluralist Democracy in the United States* (1967). Wahlke, Eulau, Buchanan, and Ferguson deal comparatively with the characters and beliefs of state legislators in the *Legislative System* (1962). Dan Nimmo writes of the *Political Persuaders* (1970) and Agranoff deals with *The New Style in Election Campaigns* (1972). David Truman provides a compendium of the group process throughout American government in the *Governmental Process* (1951); Robin William's *American Society: A Sociological Interpretation* (1970) merges the political with the social order well. A caustic and witty treat is Herbert Block, *Herblock's State of the Union* (1972). Charles Clapp's book, *The Congressman: His Work As He Sees It* (1963), is a fine collective portrait based upon group interviews.

On the economy, we arrive at Philip Taft's *Movements for Economic Reform* (1950), Paul Baran and Paul Sweezy go after *Monopoly Capital* (1966). Ferdinand Lundberg attacks *The Rich and the Super-Rich* (1968). Oscar Ornati comes up from below with *Poverty Amid Affluence* (1966). Adolf Berle (*The American Economic Republic* [1963]), G. C. Means (*The Corporate Revolution in America* [1964]), and J. K. Galbraith and M. S. Randhawa (*The New Industrial State* [1967]) discourse upon the structure of the economy. William Abraham presents *National Income and Economic Accounting* (1969).

Elites and social classes in America are dealt with by W. Lloyd Warner in *Democracy in Jonesville* (1949), J. A. Kahl in *The American Class Structure* (1957) and C. W. Mills' *The Power Elite* (1956). Geraint Parry treats of *Political Elites* (1969) in general. For middle America in the twenties and again in the thirties, two favorite works are by Robert and Helen Lynd, *Middletown* (1959) and *Middletown in Transition* (1963).

On the metropolis, you might delve into the readings collected in two volumes by H. W. Eldredge and called *Taming Megalopolis* (1967); H. Gans' *Urban Villagers* (1962), E. Liebow's *Tally's Corner* (on a black small group network, 1967); Sebastian de Grazia's *Of Time, Work, and Lesiure* (1965); and William Meyer's and Park Rinard's *Making Activism Work* (1972) which should be coupled with the works cited below in "Where Did the *Good* Go?"

Crime and justice occupy Albert Reiss (*The Police and the Public* [1971]), S. Dinitz and W. Reckless (*Critical Issues in the Study of Crime* [1968]), Richard Quinney (*Crime and Justice in Society* [1969]), Carl Auerbach, et al. (The Legal Process [1961]), and the *Report of the National Advisory Commission on Civil Disorders* (Otto Kerner, Chairman [1968]). Finally, see the more philosophical Morris Ginsberg (*On Justice in Society* [1965]).

Let bureaucracy buffs consider Max Weber, at least his selections in *Basic Concepts of Sociology* (1962), Ludwig von Mises' *Bureaucracy* (1944), Peter Blau's *Bureaucracy in Modern Society* (1956), J. March and H. Simon's *Organizations* (1958), Victor Thompson's *Modern Organization* (1961); F. E. Rourke's *Bureaucracy, Politics, and Public Policy* (1969), and Louis Gawthrop, ed., *The Administrative Process and Democratic Theory* (1970). You might view scientists as a kind of bureaucracy if you read Watson's *The Double Helix* (1969) or De Grazia's (me again) *The Velikovsky Affair* (1965) (and remember, for the past, Thomas Kuhn's *The Structure of Scientific Revolutions* [1962]).

REVOLUTIONS AND WAR

Now into revolutions and war, where we suggest Crane Brinton's *Anatomy of Revolution* (1957) that makes it all matter-of-fact, or Feliks Gross' *The Seizure of Political Power* (1958). Back of it all may lie *Frustration and Agression* (John Dollard, et al., 1939); more general is the collection E. B. McNeil made on *The Nature of Human Conflict* (1965) and even more magnificent are Jay Zawodny's volumes, *Guide to the Study of International Relations* (1966). Eric Wolf goes into *Peasant Wars of the Twentieth Century* (1969). Gene Shapp offers a thousand-page study of *The Politics of Non-Violent Action* (1973) that contains every imaginable technique except dropping the huge book on their toes. Clinton Rossiter relates how several societies handle crises through *Constitutional Dictatorship* (1948, 1963).

THE WORLD AND THE FUTURE

The subject begins with *Transnational Relations and World Politics* (1972) by R. O. Keohane and U. S. Nye, and moves into *Multi-National Cooperation: Economic, Social and Scientific Development* by R. S. Jordan (1972). It must consider *Patriotism and Nationalism* psychologically (which L. Doob did in 1964). R. Vernon goes into the multinational spread of U.S. enterprise in *Sovereignty at Bay* (1971). Richard Falk describes *This Endangered Planet* (1971). W. W. Wagar tells of the story of world movements in *The City of Man* (1967), and Pickus offers *To End War: A Citizen's Guide to the Ideas, Books, Organizations and Work That Can Help* (1971).

On revolution and imperialism, there occur lately Pierre Jalee's *Imperialism in the Seventies* (1971), dealing with both the U.S.A. and the U.S.S.R.; N. Miller and R. Aya's *National Liberation: Revolution in the Third World* (1971); and R. Swearingen's *Leaders of the Communist World* (1971).

For the depressing prospects up the line, look into the Meadows, et al., report on *The Limits to Growth* (The Club of Rome Report for 1972). For a history of futuristics consult Armytage's book, *Yesterday's Tomorrows* (1968). Herman Kahn and A. Wiener's *The Year Two Thousand* (1967) is full of ingenious calculations about the new dawn acomin'.

METHOD

Every student has her or his unique method of discovery and reporting. Yet there are rules that improve the science of politics and its applications, just as there are rules that help you play cards (see *Scarne On Cards* [rev. ed., 1965]). One ignores the rules at one's peril. The less one's experience and training the more must one guide oneself consciously by them. Emile Durkheim's *Rules of Sociological Method* (1895, 1950) gives an idea of what's involved. Howard Becker and Harry Elmer Barnes are the best surveyors to date of *Social Thought from Lore to Science* (3 vols., 1966). The methodology of politics divides into several categories: conception; perception, observation, and data collection; data storage and retrieval; data analysis; and exposition and application.

Conception deals with time, space, power, family, authority, human nature, relation, causation, validity, etc. (definitions, ideologies, logic, and semantics). See John Dewey's *Logic: The Theory of Inquiry* (1938); Robert H. Thouless' *Straight and Crooked Thinking* (1932); Robert S. Lynd's *Knowledge for What?* (1939, 1969); Morris Cohen and Ernest Nagel's *Introduction to Logic and Scientific Method* (1934); and Stuart Chase's *The Proper Study of Mankind* (1956, 1962).

Perception, observation, and data gathering deal with training direct observation via the eyes and ears; self-observation including introspection; role-acting as in psychodrama, sociodrama, and sensitivity group training; self-delusion and resistances to observation; instruments of observation (film, "bugs," etc.); sample surveys and panel surveys; with setting up experiments and interviewing. See Abraham Kaplan's *The Conduct of Inquiry* (1964); James A. Davis, *Elementary Survey Analysis* (1971); R. Bauer, ed., *Social Indicators* (1967); and H. Hyman, *Interviewing in Social Research* (1954).

Data storage and retrieval deals with librarianship, with punched cards and tapes, with computer data banks, with microfilming and microfiche, with classification systems. Consult the introduction to *The Universal Reference System*, Political Science Series, for an example of computer information retrieval. In general, Kenneth Janda's *Data Processing: Applica-*

tions to *Political Research* (1969) and A. C. Foskett's *The Subject Approach to Information* (1969) are useful.

Data analysis goes back to logic and classification and adds content analysis, statistical analysis, historical analysis, and case analysis. Examples of work in this field are Louis Gottschalk, *Understanding History* (1950, 1969); Robert North, et al., *Content Analysis* (1963); E. Sheldon and W. Moore, eds., *Indicators of Social Change* (1968); and E. A. Suchman, *Evaluative Research* (1968).

Exposition and application: the U.S. Office of Education publishes materials on audio-visual education. The University of Chicago Press publishes *A Manual of Style* for authors. But these are mechanics. The deep problems give rise to some of the finest literature. Examples are Benjamin Cardozo, *The Nature of the Judicial Process* (1921, 1960); Daniel Lerner, ed., *The Human Meaning of the Social Sciences* (1959); N. Eurich, *Science in Utopia: A Mighty Design* (1967); Oliver Franks, *Central Planning and Control in War and Peace* (1947); F. Znaniecki, *Social Role of the Man of Knowledge* (1940, 1965); Barbara Wootton, *Freedom Under Planning* (1945); and R. Lippitt, et al., *Dynamics of Planned Change* (1958).

SOURCES AND DATA BANKS

If your grandma or your lottery ticket lets you outfit a bookshelf with reference materials, you might purchase *The International Encyclopedia of the Social Sciences* (17 volumes), a set of *The Cambridge Histories,* Adler's *Index to the 100 Great Books, The Statesman's Year Book* (annual), a subscription to *Facts on File* (weekly), a *Merriam-Webster Unabridged Dictionary*, Langer's *Encyclopedia of World History Chronologically Arranged,* and William Safire's *The New Language of Politics: An Anecdotal Dictionary of Catchwords, Slogans, and Political Usage* (the 1972 edition).

The New York Times will swamp you, so browse only occasionally there and in *Time, The Village Voice, The National Observer, The Washington Monthly,* and *The Public Interest.* Take an hour twice a month to walk among the shelves of the political and social science journals (like *Psychology Today*) to see what you are (or are not) missing. Then you would want to know where your reference librarian keeps *The Universal Reference System*, some 20 volumes of a computer-generated annotated catalogue and index to books and articles in political science; Clifton Brock's *Literature of Political Science* (1969); Blaustein and Flanz' *Constitutions of the Countries of the World* (1971 ongoing, with 12 volumes projected, but who knows how many new constitutions will be written?); *Black's Law Dictionary*; the *International Index to Periodical Literature*; *Public Affairs Information Service*; the *Reader's Guide to Periodical Literature*; and many other special and general listings.

THE MULTI-MEDIA SIDE TO POLITICAL STUDY

Political science departments could present many a festival program of political films. Rutgers' Eagleton Institute does so annually. The more one has read and lived politics, the more one learns from films, and often the films come crashing through in a way that books can hardly manage: *The Great Dictator*, on unlimited power and arrogance; *Twelve Angry Men*, on the jury process; *The Oxbow Incident*, on a young man caught by crowd justice; *The Manchurian Candiate*, on brainwashing in war; *2001*, on who knows what in far-out space; *Dr. Strangelove*, on blowing the world up accidentally; *M*A*S*H* on army life; *The Great McGinty*, on city politics; *The Battleship Potemkin*, on a sailor's revolt; *The Damned*, on the social order collapsing into Nazism; *Open City*, on tragic resistance to a ruthless occupation; *The Gospel According to St. Matthew* and *He Who Must Die*, on the imitation of Christ; *The Seven Samurai*, on feudal systems; *The Last Picture Show*, on a dying part of America; *The Graduate*, on the struggle of generations; *The Hospital*, on responsible administration of a complex organization; *It's All Right, Jack*, on unionism and industrial management; *No Love for Johnny*, on British politics; *The Sorrow and the Pity*, on the French under occupation and in resistance; *Dr. Zhivago*, on the Russian revolution; *Sacco-Vanzetti*, on the misguided execution of two Italian-American anarchists; *Battle of Algiers*, on a people's struggle for independence; *Z*, on extremist terrorism protected by the authorities against a liberal regime; *Carnival of Flanders*, on Spanish troops occupying a small Flemish town in the sixteenth century; *Medea*, on a priestess-ruler going berserk in a strange land; *Clockwork Orange*, on the twin evils of nihilism and automatism; and so on into a couple of hundreds.

The great political poets can be treated with the dramatists and novelists. Homer's *Iliad* is a sexist, frightening, bloody, mad episode of a series of ancient wars amidst catastrophes that the "gods" were bringing down upon man. Every culture and subculture—Asian, African, North European, etc.—has its similar sagas. Shakespeare's historical tragedies should be recalled to mind. Voltaire (especially the unmatchable *Candide*) and Ibsen also deserve perennial rediscovery. The proletarian dramas of Bertoldt Brecht are solidly in place, and, today, the theater of the absurd (e.g., Ionesco's *Rhinoceros* and Genet's *Our Lady of the Flowers*) rides the main track.

Then to the novelists and dramatist of old Russia—Dostoyevksy (*The Idiot*, *Notes from the Underground*, and many more), Gogol, Tolstoy, Gorki, and others. From Central Europe, Kafka's symbolic novels are devastating. In Western Europe, Stendhal (*The Red and the Black*), Thomas Mann (*Magic Mountain*), Malraux's *Man's Hope*, Koestler's *Darkness at Noon*, Albert Camus' *The Plague* and *The Stranger*, and Céline's *Castle to Castle*. England's Evelyn Waugh's several satires, George Orwell's *1984,* and E. M. Forster's champion tragedy of East-West misunderstanding *Passage to India*. America—well—there's Walt Whitman, a cubit above the others. A lot of junky novels on politics have been written by Americans and I don't want to let you waste time and rot your minds. But you won't miss on Edgar Lee Masters' *Spoon River Anthology*, Robert Penn Warren's *All the King's Men,* and now Allen Ginsburg (e.g., *Howl*), Kurt Vonnegut, Jr. (e.g., *The Sirens of Titan*), and Jerzy Kosinski (*Being There*).

In conclusion, I'd like to say a word about political novels; they are rarely good, but every great nonpolitical novel prepares one to understand politics (for examples, Thackeray's *Vanity Fair*, Melville's *Moby Dick*, and Thomas Wolfe's *Look Homeward, Angel*).

In graphics and plastics, the range is from *Peanuts* to R. Buckminister Fuller's geodesic domes and ideational sparks flying all over the fields of knowledge. (He speaks his best political piece in *Utopia or Oblivion* [1970].) Somehow the totality of this tidal wave is conveyed by *The Last Whole Earth Catalogue* (1971), a climactic synthesis of the *Sears, Roebuck Catalogue*, the Boy Scouts of America, and the Eternal Search.

WHERE DID THE *GOOD* GO?

You just won't believe it, but I tell you that there is little around these days on how you and I and everybody else should behave. Or, at least, little that deserves much respect. Sunday School is out. And when you find some of our brightest people saying, "You get it in hallucinogenics" or "*Revolution for the Hell of It*" (which, read), you know we're in trouble.

Try these out; I begin with the more technical affirmations; I find something in them and you may too. Robert Dahl's *After the Revolution* (1970) penetrates some problems of public opinion and leadership in America. Anchor Books puts out readings called *The Liberal Papers*, *The Conservative Papers*, and *The Radical Papers*. Wayne Leys goes after criteria for *Ethics for Policy Decisions* (1968). Schattschneider does as well as anyone in setting a role for the electorate in *The Semi-Sovereign People* (1961). T. V. Smith comes up with an ethic for *The Legislative Way of Life* (1940). A. de Grazia (ho-hum) urges on Congress in *Republic in Crisis: Congress Against the Presidency* (1965). John Dewey left us with *The Public and Its Problems* (1927) and *Freedom and Culture* (1941, 1963) as a Jeffersonian-Pragmatist heritage.

The struggle for individuality against bureaucracy is reflected in much of what's worth reading. Richard Cornuelle's *Reclaiming the American Dream* (1965) is simple, clear, and conceivable. Pope John XXIII cheers up pluralism and fights off the state in his encyclical, *Pacem in Terris.* Arnold Toynbee cuts back technology and infuses East into West in *The World and the West* (1953). F. A. Von Haybk speaks out for the old liberalism and rule of law in *Roads to Freedom* (1970). George B. de Huszar's *Practical Applications of Democracy* (1945) summarizes what the best progressives and human relations specialists believed about achieving democracy in groups before the New Left revolted. A. de Grazia (me, again) goes on interminably about the full range of reforms and revolutions that the country and world need in *Kalos: World Revolution and Order* (1973). But so do W. W. Wagar (*Building the City of Man* [1971]) and The World Law Fund which sponsors numerous proposals (Mendlovitz and Baldwin, eds.). Who has the Answer?

Politics are treated in local America. Saul Alinsky saw the politics of confrontation coming in *Reveille for Radicals* (1945, 1969), but you'd be surprised at how closely he and the whole movement were anticipated by Ms. Mary Parker Follett in *Creative Experience* (1924) and *The New State* (1918). She came close to the popes, too, and to Fascist corporatism, and yet her mentors were the pragmatists like Dewey. The theory of corporatism, by the way, is clearly argued in an encyclical of Pope Pius XI, *On Reconstructing the Social Order* (*Quadragesimo Anno* [1931]).

Abraham Maslow, on top of Dewey and G. H. Mead (*Mind, Self, and Society* [1934]) it seems to me, caught the needed psychology for self-fulfillment amidst social advance (see *Motivation and Personality* [1954]). Now Ivan Illich in education, that is, *Deschooling Society,* 1971, is superb. There are works such as C. G. Benello and D. Roussopoulos, eds., *The Case for Participatory Democracy* (1971), Milton Kotler's *Neighborhood Government* (1969), and Warren Breed's *The Self-Guiding Society* (1971) that continue to uncover the independent association's capacities for expressing and executing the public interest. I wish I could bow more deeply to Charles Reich for *The Greening of America* (1970) or to Philip Slater for *The Pursuit of Loneliness* (1970), or to John Steinbeck for his *Travels with Charley* (1962) through a land gone sour, or to Henry Miller for castigating the country after *his* travels, via *The Air-Conditioned Nightmare* (1970), or to Alvin Toffler for

Future Shock (1970), but, as you know, they catch the feelings of a lot of souls without committing themselves to *their* Future or *a* Future.

Ethicists of black power are many; some of the bitterest testimonies occur in Frantz Fanon's *Wretched of the Earth* (1965), James Baldwin's *Notes of a Native Son* (1957), and George Jackson's *Soledad Brother* (1971). *The Autobiography of Malcolm X* (1965) cannot be ignored. Betty Friedan's *The Feminine Mystique* (1963) and Kirsten Amundsen's *The Silenced Majority* (1971) open up the front against sexism. Each country has its own reformers and their number is legion: J.-J. Servan-Schreiber talks of *The Radical Alternative* (1971) for France; Theodore Roszak indicates *Where the Wasteland Ends* (1972) in America, while Jack Newfield and Jeff Greenfield heap up dozens of editorials in *A Populist Manifesto* (1972) and Herbert Marcuse tells where he's at now in *Counter-Revolution and Revolt* (1972). Robert Theobald goes after *The Guaranteed Income* (1970). Medical professor Albert Szent-Gyorgyi's *The Crazy Ape* (1971) and the aviator-explorer Antoine de Saint Exupéry's *Little Prince* (1943) are gentle little books with stout morals. Margaret Mead's *Twentieth Century Faith* (1972) is better still. Perhaps we should conclude with the hope which these afford. A list of books, no matter how lengthy, will not win us our good new world.

Index